It is high time for this gene
pastor of Kidderminster. 1
of the great Puritan pasto.

Christian scholarship. Beougher simultaneously introduces Baxter to
a new generation and sets the record straight concerning some of the
controversies that marked Baxter's ministry and enduring reputation.
The question of genuine conversion to Christ was a preoccupation
of the Puritans -- and for good reason. Our own generation of
Christians would do well to follow Baxter's example and think about
the meaning of conversion and its true signs. Professor Beougher
combines scholarship and evangelistic passion in this important
book, setting the record straight and raising all the right questions.
If we misunderstand conversion, we misunderstand the Gospel. We
are in Professor Beougher's debt for this timely book.

R. Albert Mohler, Jr.,
President, The Southern Baptist Theological Seminary Louisville, Kentucky

Richard Baxter believed that a faithful system of theology, when created
by a skillful hand, would not add to the Scriptures, but merely draw
out what is already there. *Richard Baxter and Conversion* reveals that
Timothy Beougher is just such a skillful hand with respect to Baxter's
writings. He has drawn out of this classic and controversial Puritan's
writings the theological and practical strengths and weakness that
are there, and in the process clarified the historic controversies that
have surrounded this great Puritan pastor's doctrine of conversion.

Peter A. Lillback,
President, Westminster Theological Seminary, Philadelphia, Pennsylvania

Timothy Beougher's study of Richard Baxter offers a fresh interpre-tation
of a very important early "evangelical." Baxter's advocacy of "mere
Christianity" was important in the contentious milieu of seventeenth-
century England, and as Beougher shows persuasively it remains
important in the midst of our contemporary contentions as well.

Mark A. Noll,
Francis A. McAnaney Professor of History,
University of Notre Dame, Notre Dame, Indiana

The publication of Beougher's important book confirms that Baxter
was a fresh and independent thinker who wrestled first-hand with
the scriptures. Baxter's theology was aimed at the strengthening of
the church and the conversion of the lost, and his passion for truth
reverberates throughout the work. We can be thankful for Beougher's
wonderfully clear and perceptive analysis of Baxter's theology of

conversion. Beougher dispels some misunderstandings of Baxter's theology, reminding us that the study of church history has immense practical benefits, for Baxter comments on many of the debates that we still face today. I commend this work enthusiastically.

Thomas R. Schreiner
James Buchanan Harrison Professor of New Testament Interpretation
The Southern Baptist Theological Seminary, Louisville, Kentucky

We are indebted to Timothy Beougher for providing a rich historical and theological study of Christian conversion through the lens of the great 17th century Puritan pastor and theologian, Richard Baxter. Few in the history of the church cared so much, studied so much, and wrote so much about conversion as Baxter, and Beougher offers here both a well-documented and eminently readable account of Baxter's deep and nuanced thought. I highly recommend this book, both for the fascinating discussion of theological themes of central importance to the Puritans and to all thoughtful Christians, and for the profound richness to mind and soul that comes through considering afresh the nature and process of true Christian conversion.

Bruce A. Ware,
Professor of Christian Theology,
The Southern Baptist Theological Seminary, Louisville, Kentucky

RICHARD BAXTER
AND
CONVERSION

*A Study of the Puritan concept
of becoming a Christian*

TIMOTHY K. BEOUGHER

MENTOR

Timothy K. Beougher is Billy Graham Professor of Evangelism and Church Growth at Southern Baptist Theological Seminary, Louisville, Kentucky. Prior to that he served for six years as assistant professor of evangelism at the Wheaton College Graduate School and associate director of the Institute of Evangelism at the Billy Graham Center. He has written and edited numerous materials related to evangelism, discipleship, and spiritual awakening. He has ministry experience as an evangelist, church planter, pastor, and interim pastor.

ISBN 1-84550-310-4
ISBN 978-1-84550-310-9

© Timothy K. Beougher

10 9 8 7 6 5 4 3 2 1

Published in 2007
in the
Mentor Imprint
by
Christian Focus Publications,
Geanies House, Fearn, Ross-shire,
IV20 1TW, Scotland, UK

www.christianfocus.com

Cover design by Daniel Van Straaten

Printed by CPD, Wales

CONTENTS

Dedicated to
my precious wife, Sharon,
in gratitude for her love, support, and patience
during the writing of this book.
Like Richard Baxter's Margaret, she is
'the meetest helper that I could have in the world.'

And to my children, Kristi, Jonathan, Kari and Karisa.
A dad could not be any prouder of his children
than I am of you. May your lives be characterized
by the passion for God that the Baxters displayed.

FOREWORD

BY

J. I. PACKER

Even where evangelism goes vigorously ahead (and, thank God, there are many places where it does), mental muddle about conversion is widespread, as is liberal Protestant hostility to all forms of evangelistic practice. Liberal prejudice can quickly be diagnosed as the result of equating Christianity with universal natural religion and seeing the Christian mission in terms of social uplift rather than personal change. But the evangelical muddle is not got rid of so easily.

Whence comes the muddle? It is a case of cognitive dissonance, the presence of unrecognised incompatibles side by side in the mind. In this case, the dissonance results from trying to combine evangelical theology with an evangelistic ethos of pressure tactics which for the past century and three-quarters has gripped the evangelical imagination and has not yet let go. Its sociological roots seem to be Enlightenment man-centredness, the romanticizing of evangelists as hero-figures, the development of techniques for manipulating human groups, small and large, and the modern craving for mastery in every field of endeavour. Its spiritual (or maybe I should say, unspiritual) fruits are that whenever evangelism is the agenda item, evangelicals jump to thinking in terms of special out-of-course meetings at which a hero-evangelist in the Finney-Moody-Torrey-Sunday-Graham mould "draws in the net" – that is, skilfully induces the immediate response of conversion to Jesus Christ in repentance, faith, and whole-hearted discipleship. The trappings of the close of the meetings are well known: in contrast with its bright, lively and relaxed beginning, tension is whipped up; the choir, which at first sang loudly, now sings softly; the evangelist, who earlier shouted, now purrs; counsellors stand poised to instruct and pray; persuasive pressure, playing on felt deficiencies, holding out help for the helpless, hope for the hopeless, and security for the insecure, is at its height; the insinuation of all that is being said and done is that everyone can actively, savingly, respond to Jesus Christ in this net-drawing moment, and here and now find the fulness of a totally new life. So says the evangelical imagination; but evangelical theology tells us that it's not necessarily so, for grace does not always work in this fashion; hence the dissonance and hence the muddle. The regular altar call in some churches witnesses to the same muddle.

Evangelical theology tells us that personal conversion, or God's effectual calling, as older Reformed theology labelled it, is a process whereby, under the light of constant instruction about faith, repentance and true life in Christ, new creation – regeneration, that is – takes place secretly in the human heart, and shows itself by first desiring and then seeking Jesus Christ, and continuing to reach out for him and open one's life to him and invoke his promises and adore his mercy till one knows that one has found him (or, putting it more correctly, knows that one has been found by him); after which one continues to walk with him in discipleship to him, living and obeying, loving and serving, worshipping and working in peace and in joy. Though realisation of the reality of the Saviour's nearness, and consequent change in thought and behaviour, may be sudden in the final decisive stage of conversion, as it was for Paul on the Damascus road and has been for very many since, the process as a whole takes time, and it is God, not we who labour for conversions, who will decide how quickly or slowly it will advance, and when it will come to fruition, in each particular case. Pressing on others the urgency of seeking the Lord in conversion, which we must ever do, is not to confer on them the power to instantly repent, confidently trust in Christ, and radically turn one's life around, changing everything from the inside out – only God can do that. We who evangelize must resist the temptation to put our trust in techniques for, in effect, speeding up, short-circuiting, and forcing forward the conversion process. Let God be God in evangelism, as in all else!

This is where the team of Baxter (seventeenth-century Puritan pastor-evangelist) and Beougher (twenty-first-century Southern Baptist professor, student of Baxter) can help us. Baxter holds it all together – the sovereign grace of God, the renewal of the heart, the need to teach and learn the faith with maximum seriousness and urgency because of the eternal issues at stake, and the importance of every Christian congregation being an evangelistic powerhouse. And Beougher holds Baxter together, presenting him, his wisdom and his passion, with clarity of both thinking and writing.

Anyone who observes that a third of this book is endnotes and bibliography will jump to the conclusion that it was once a doctoral thesis, and he will be right. (I can testify; I supervised it.) It seems to me an outstanding piece of work, of great pastoral relevance for our time. So do not be frightened by the apparatus of scholarship; look for the jewels of wisdom. You will find them, and you will be blessed.

J.I. Packer
Regent College, Vancouver

Introduction

It is the very drift of the gospel, the main design of the whole Word of God, to convert men from sin to God, and build them up when they are once converted.

> ... if you be not converted, you are not true Christians. You may have the name, but you have not the nature.

> It is all one to be a man, and not to be born; as to be a true Christian, and not to be new-born: for as our conception and birth is the passage into the life and world of nature, so our conversion or new birth is the passage into the life of grace.

> Conversion is the most blessed work, and the day of conversion the most blessed day, that this world is acquainted with.[1]

Puritan religious experience centered around conversion, the 'new birth' of the soul. This focal point, exemplified here by the Puritan pastor, Richard Baxter, has been called the 'essence of Puritanism'.[2] Even those who argue that the heart of Puritanism is found in other characteristics[3] cannot deny that the Puritans regarded conversion as extremely significant. One cannot read far into the Puritans' works without encountering this emphasis time and time again. Preachers preached on it, books were written to explain it, and the saints painstakingly examined themselves as to its progress in their own lives.

This study seeks to answer the question, 'What understanding of conversion [the process of becoming a "true Christian"] did the Puritan pastor Richard Baxter have?' This analysis is called for because few of the earlier treatments of Puritan conversion have dealt with Baxter,[4] while those works which have focused exclusively on Baxter have usually examined other areas of his life and thought.[5]

Why should we study Baxter's views to help us in our understanding of Puritan conversion? First, he wrote a great deal on the subject. Baxter devoted four of his major works exclusively to conversion,[6] and the theme occurs regularly throughout the remainder of his writings.[7] His methodical treatment of the subject provides ample material for an equitable examination of his views.

Second, Baxter's writings enjoyed widespread dissemination, both in England and abroad.[8] Others eagerly read and applied what he taught concerning conversion.[9] Baxter himself gives some indication of the influence of his *Call to the Unconverted*:

> God hath blessed [it] with unexpected success beyond all the rest that I have written (except *The Saints Rest*). In a little more than a year there were about twenty thousand of them printed by my own consent, and about ten thousand since, besides many thousands by stolen impressions....
>
> Through God's mercy I have had information of almost whole households converted by this small book.... God ... hath sent it over on his message to many beyond the seas.[10]

Orme suggests that the overall effects of this book in the conversion of people 'have been greater probably than have arisen from any other mere human performance', and that its influence is 'beyond all calculation'.[11]

Third, Baxter, arguably the greatest of the Puritan pastors,[12] provides an excellent example of a theologian/pastor who not only wrote a great deal about conversion but also put it into practice in a parish ministry.[13] The often quoted passage from his autobiography demonstrates his tremendous effectiveness:

> The congregation was usually full, so that we were fain to build five galleries after my coming thither.... Our private meetings also were full. On the Lord's Days there was no disorder to be seen in the streets, but you might hear an hundred families singing Psalms and repeating sermons as you passed through the streets. In a word, when I came thither first, there was about one family in a street that worshipped God and called on his name, and when I came away there were some streets where there was not passed one family in the side of a street that did not so; and that did not by professing serious godliness, give us hopes of their sincerity.[14]

Baxter's ministry resulted in large numbers of people becoming 'true Christians'. What did he teach concerning conversion? How did he put that teaching into practice? To provide a context for our study, we next will undertake a brief review of the existing literature on Puritan conversion.

Review of the Literature
The interest in Puritan studies cultivated by scholars such as Haller, Knappen, Miller, and Woodhouse has blossomed into a prodigious literary output which shows no signs of slowing. Books and articles treating different aspects of the Puritan phenomenon continue to emerge from the presses on a regular basis. While several of these essays perpetuate the unceasing debate over definition,[15] others highlight areas such as the Puritan view of work, family, education, ecclesiology, and bibliology, to name only a few.[16] The study of Puritan conversion has received a great deal of attention in recent years. The purpose of this review of the literature is not to give an exhaustive list of the works on Puritan conversion, nor to evaluate even those listed here, but briefly to acquaint the reader with some of the previous research done in the field.[17] Several of these works will be evaluated in the Conclusion in light of the results of this study.

Alan Simpson argues in his work *Puritanism in Old and New England* that conversion is the 'essence of Puritanism'. He maintains that the doctrine was a logical development among the English of the Protestant doctrines of predestination, justification by faith, and the authority of the Scriptures.[18]

Edmund Morgan examines Puritan conversion in the context of his discussion concerning requirements for church membership. He traces the growth of the idea of requiring a conversion narrative before one could be admitted to the membership of many New England churches, and argues for a basically uniform 'morphology of conversion'.[19] Patricia Caldwell, in her work *The Puritan Conversion Narrative: The Beginning of American Expression*, argues against Morgan's position (which she previously held) concerning a morphology of conversion. Caldwell claims that, instead of producing 'stereotyped conversion experiences, stiff and formulaic, dutifully conforming to established theological conventions', individuals made significant and varied uses of the 'formula'.[20]

Norman Pettit helped focus attention on the aspect of preparation in Puritan conversion with his book, *The Heart Prepared: Grace and Conversion in Puritan Spiritual Life*.[21] Pettit argues that the Puritans changed the orthodox Reformed theology of the sixteenth century where the sinner was 'taken by storm', emphasizing instead that sinners were to 'prepare' themselves for saving grace. A more recent work dealing with the subject of preparation is Charles Hambrick-Stowe's *The Practice of Piety: Puritan Devotional Disciplines in Seventeenth-Century New England*.[22] Hambrick-Stowe rejects Pettit's assertion that an unregenerate sinner could achieve preparation for conversion, and in the process redefines 'preparation' as a series of spiritual exercises (e.g. daily prayer, meditation, and worship on the Sabbath) by which Christians should prepare constantly and all their lives for final union with the risen Christ.[23]

Lynn Baird Tipson's dissertation entitled 'The Development of a Puritan Understanding of Conversion'[24] is a thorough examination of the concept of conversion held by William

Perkins and his best-known Elizabethan Puritan contemporaries. The study conceives conversion broadly as the whole
process by which God was understood to draw sinful man
back to himself and his service, by which men turned from
resistance to active participation in God's design for the
world. Tipson challenges the widely held belief that Perkins
forced conversion into a series of well-defined stages, and
argues instead that the key to understanding Perkins' view
of conversion is 'the recognition that God's free grace allowed
man's free will to co-operate with it and strengthen an initial
weak faith into full assurance'.[25]

Two other dissertations also focus attention on this crucial
area of Puritan life. James Shields has examined the doctrine
of regeneration as it was understood and taught by seven
English Puritan theologians of the seventeenth century,
noting that in that period 'regeneration was considered
synonymous with conversion, resurrection, sanctification,
and vocation or calling'.[26] Sidney Rooy's work discusses the
theology of conversion of representative Puritans to elucidate
the development of the theology of missions in the Puritan
tradition.[27] Rooy notes that the conviction that persons must
be brought to personal conversion 'dominates the Puritan
message'.[28]

An award-winning book by Charles Cohen focuses on the
Puritan experience of conversion to examine how ministers
elaborated the psychological imperatives of faith and how
their listeners modified and internalized them. Through all
extensive use of primary source material, Cohen attempts to
emphasize and understand what conversion meant to the men
and women of that century instead of searching for hidden
meanings in their lives and actions.[29]

Numerous other studies focusing on this general topic
could be cited as well.[30] What then does this book purport to
do? How does it differ from these other treatments?

First, it adds Baxter's voice to the chorus of Puritans whose
views on conversion have received a thorough examination.
We demonstrated earlier that a comprehensive analysis of
Baxter's views is a significant lacuna in this field of study.

In light of Baxter's significance, our picture of the Puritan understanding of conversion cannot be complete without investigating his views.

Second, this study attempts to view conversion in its various aspects by studying Baxter's views holistically. Because conversion is intrinsically related to other doctrinal and practical issues, to gain an accurate picture of his teaching, we must examine it in its complete context.

The book contains two main sections. Part One explores Baxter's theology of conversion, followed by Part Two which investigates his practice of 'soul-winning'. The Puritans would have disdained the modern practice of separating theology from practice; in fairness to Baxter and his Puritan heritage, I have chosen to treat both together in this study. It is hoped that this holistic approach will shed more light on Baxter's understanding of conversion as we are able to examine it both in theory and in practice.

Chapter One provides the historical background for our treatment. A brief summary of Baxter's life and ministry positions the study of his theology in its proper context. Particular attention is given to Baxter's own conversion experience. What light does it shed on the debate over a 'morphology of conversion'? Did his own experience perhaps affect his theological formulations?

Chapter Two analyzes the theological foundation of conversion. In order to appreciate how Baxter arrived at his conclusions, this chapter begins with an explanation of his theological method. How did he use Scripture? What use did he make of natural theology? Next, his teaching concerning the need for conversion and the basis for conversion are set forth. Why is conversion necessary? How did Baxter view man's predicament? What was the effect of Christ's death? Did he die for all men, or only for the 'elect'?

Chapter Three considers Baxter's understanding of the doctrine of Justification.

Chapter Four looks at the process of conversion. What does it mean to become a 'true Christian'? How did someone actually become 'converted'? What role did preparation play in the process? Was humiliation a necessary step? Was there a 'morphology of conversion'? What kind of assurance could the Christian expect? This chapter elucidates Baxter's perceptions on these key issues.

The second section of the book begins with Chapter Five, which describes Baxter's teaching and practice regarding the presentation of the gospel. How should the gospel be shared? What method(s) should be employed? In what manner should the presentation be made? How did he appeal to the unconverted to 'turn and live'?

Chapter Six examines the church and conversion. How did Baxter's concern for adult conversion impact his view of the Church? How did he relate the ordinances of baptism and the Lord's Supper to conversion? How did he work within the concept of a national church to seek the conversion of the unregenerate in its midst? How did he attempt to keep conversion piety within the framework of the national church?

The Conclusion summarizes the findings of the investigation and evaluates their significance for Baxter studies and for our understanding of Puritan conversion. Secondary literature is assessed in light of the results of this research on Baxter.

Because this study centers upon one man, the dates of his life span form natural chronological boundaries, in this case 1615–1691. The method for handling the material is logical rather than chronological, though the study attempts to be sensitive to the issue of development in Baxter's thought.[31] Since this study is concerned with Baxter, the focus is on the writings of Baxter himself. He was a prolific author, with the most accurate bibliography of merely his published writings listing one hundred forty-one titles,[32] while other scholars argue for yet more.[33] Many of these writings fall outside the bounds of the topic under consideration and are not examined.[34]

What is the significance of this study? What contribution might it make? First, it will deepen our understanding of Puritanism as a whole. The twentieth century witnessed a renewed interest in the subject of Puritanism, a movement which often has been misunderstood and misrepresented. This study seeks to join the many others which are helping to reshape long-held misconceptions of Puritanism.[35]

Second, this study will add to our understanding of the Puritan view of conversion. Earlier citations have demonstrated that there is no consensus as to what the Puritans taught concerning conversion. Debate continues on issues such as preparation, the legitimacy of a 'morphology of conversion', and the relationship between faith and assurance. This study will shed further light on these and other related issues, particularly for the period of Puritanism which Baxter represented.

Third, this study will hopefully help clear up some of the confusion surrounding judgments of Baxter's views.[36] 'His opinions,' said Stoughton, 'have been a battle-ground for critics ever since he left the world.'[37] Recent studies have labelled his beliefs as Pelagian,[38] moderate Arminian,[39] Amyraldian,[40] improved Amyraldian,[41] and faithful Calvinistic.[42] In his own day, Baxter was accused variously of being a Papist, a Socinian, and an Arminian.[43]

It is to his day, England of the seventeenth-century, and his life, beginning in 1615, that we now turn.

1

THE LIFE AND MINISTRY
OF RICHARD BAXTER

I am sensible that in speaking of him I shall be under a double disadvantage: for those who perfectly knew him will be apt to think my account of him to be short and defective, an imperfect shadow of his resplendent virtues; others, who were unacquainted with his extraordinary worth, will, from ignorance or envy, be inclined to think his just praises to be undue and excessive. (Dr. William Bates, *A Funeral Sermon ... for Richard Baxter* [1692], 86).

Richard Baxter was born November 12, 1615, at Rowton, a village in Shropshire, England.[1] It was his destiny to live through most of the seventeenth century, a watershed in English history. Before his death in 1691, Baxter witnessed the Civil War, the beheading of Charles I, the Commonwealth under Oliver Cromwell, the Restoration of the monarchy under Charles II, the persecution of Nonconformity, the Great Ejection, and the struggle for toleration which culminated in the Act of Toleration of 1689. Baxter was no passive observer of these events, no idle bystander. As a prominent religious leader, he actively participated in the numerous political and ecclesiastical struggles of his day.

When viewed in light of his later influence, Baxter's early years were far from auspicious. No one could have guessed that this boy, born to Richard and Beatrice Baxter, would amount to much of anything. He was forced to live until the age of ten with his maternal grandfather because of his father's gambling debts.[2] His early schooling proved a great disappointment. In six years he had four different schoolmasters, all of them 'ignorant'. More deplorable yet was the discovery that two of the four were immoral.[3]

After his father's conversion, young Richard returned to his parental home at Eaton Constantine.[4] Unfortunately, however, his return brought no improvement in his educational environment. The vicar there, who was over eighty and 'never preached in his life', brought forth a motley assortment of substitutes to fill in for him: among them a day-labourer, a stage-player, and a common drunkard.[5] The condition of the area clergy and churches was so low that little or nothing could be expected from them in the way of spiritual nurture.[6]

The crude and meaningless manner of his confirmation at age fourteen only made matters worse. The bishop did not examine any of the boys who were present as to their spiritual condition. Instead, he quickly lined them up and passed down the line, laying his hands on them and uttering a few words of a prayer that neither Baxter nor the other boys could decipher. 'And yet,' Baxter laments, 'he was esteemed one of the best bishops in England.'[7]

Despite the aforementioned lack of piety in the established church, young Richard was not left without spiritual guidance. It pleased God to make his father 'the instrument of my first convictions, and approbation of a holy life, as well as of my restraint from the grosser sort of lives'.[8] Baxter struggled with numerous sins in his youth: lying, gluttony (especially of apples and pears), theft (of fruit), addiction to play, covetousness, love of romance stories, idle chatter, pride, and irreverence for his parents.[9] A turning point in his spiritual pilgrimage was when he overheard his 'friends' call his father a Puritan. He says that, 'it did much to cure me and alienate me from them; for I considered that my father's exercise of reading the

Scripture was better than theirs, and would surely be better thought on by all men at the last; and I considered what it was for that he and others were thus derided.'[10]

Through his father's example and particularly by the reading of Edmund Bunny's *Resolution*,[11] Baxter recounts that at about age fifteen 'it pleased God to awaken my soul.'[12] He says,

> The same things which I knew before came now in another manner, with Light, and Sense and Seriousness to my Heart. This cast me first into fears of my Condition; and those drove me to Sorrow and Confession and Prayer, and so to some resolution for another kind of Life: And many a day I went with a throbbing Conscience, and saw that I had other Matters to mind, and another Work to do in the World, than ever I had minded well before.[13]

He proceeds, however, to make a most remarkable admission: 'Yet whether sincere conversion began *now*, or *before*, or *after*, I was never able to this day to know.'[14] Richard Sibbes' *The Bruised Reed and Smoking Flax* (1630), a book his father purchased from a peddler, also greatly encouraged Baxter during this time. 'And thus,' Baxter concludes, 'without any means but books, was God pleased to resolve me for himself.'[15]

Baxter passionately desired university training but had to settle for preparatory school at Wroxeter and private tutoring at Ludlow Castle under Richard Wickstead.[16] Wickstead, however, all but neglected Baxter. Undaunted, Baxter made good use of the excellent library there.[17] Baxter also refers to 'one intimate companion' he made while at Ludlow,

> who was the greatest help to my seriousness in religion that ever I had before, and was a daily watchman over my soul. We walked together, we read together, we prayed together.... He was the first that ever I heard pray *ex tempore* (out of the pulpit) and that taught me so to pray. And his charity and liberality were equal to his zeal, so that God made him a great means of my good, who had more knowledge than he, but a colder heart.[18]

Unfortunately, Baxter's companion fell prey to strong drink, and became a 'fuddler, and railer at strict men'.

Baxter next placed himself under the tutelage of Rev. Francis Garbett, the minister of Wroxeter. Garbett was a strict Churchman, and directed Baxter's reading to theology, the Schoolmen, and the controversialists against Nonconformity. In 1634, on the advice of Wickstead, he set aside his preparations for the ministry and accepted an appointment to court life at Whitehall in London.[19] There he lived at the home of the Master of Revels, Sir Henry Herbert, a brother of the poet George Herbert. Within a month he grew disenchanted with the lax moral standards of the court,[20] and when he learned his mother had been stricken by serious illness, quickly returned home in December, 1634.[21] His mother died the following spring.

From the age of twenty-one to about age twenty-three, Baxter was so persistently sick that he did not expect to live. Even though he 'recovered' after two years, these sicknesses and expectations of death remained with him to varying degrees of severity throughout his life.[22] Yet, in God's providence, they also provided a source of motivation to him:

> ...my own soul being under the serious apprehension of the matters of another world, I was exceeding desirous to communicate those apprehensions to such ignorant, presumptuous, careless sinners as the world aboundeth with.... I knew that the want of academical honours and degrees was like to make me contemptible with the most, and consequently hinder the success of my endeavours. But yet, expecting to be so quickly in another world, the great concernments of miserable souls did prevail with me against all these impediments; and being conscious of a thirsty desire of men's conversion and salvation, and of some competent persuading faculty of expression, which fervent affections might help to actuate, *I resolved that if one or two souls only might be won to God it would easily recompense all the dishonour which for want of titles I might undergo from men....*[23]

This burning desire to be used in the conversion of others led him to seek ordination within the Church of England, though he feared he might not be considered qualified because of his lack of academic credentials. He was, however, accepted and episcopally ordained in 1638 after subscribing to the necessary doctrines and teachings of the Church of England.[24]

Baxter had no scruples with Conformity when he was ordained. After beginning his public preaching ministry, however, and having greater opportunity to look afresh at the implications and meaning of his subscription and conformity to the doctrines and teachings of the Church of England, he concluded:

> Subscription I began to judge unlawful, and saw that I sinned by temerity in what I did. For though I could still use the Common Prayer, and was not yet against diocesans, yet to subscribe, *ex animo*, that there is nothing in the three books contrary to the Word of God was that which, if it had been to do again, I durst not do. So that subscription, and the cross in baptism, and the promiscuous giving of the Lord's Supper to all drunkards, swearers, fornicators, scorners at godliness, etc., that are not excommunicate by a bishop or chancellor that is out of their acquaintance – these three were all that I now became a Nonconformist to.[25]

But most of this he kept to himself until the *Et Cetera* Oath of 1640 required all ministers of the Church of England to swear that they would 'never give any consent to alter of the present government of the Church by archbishops, bishops, deans, archdeacons, *et cetera*, as it now stands established and ought to stand.' Not being able to subscribe to this in good conscience, Baxter, and many others, chose to reject English episcopal polity and assume a Nonconformist stance.[26]

Immediately after his ordination, Baxter served for nine months as a schoolmaster in Dudley while preaching in vacant pulpits on Sundays. In the autumn of 1639 Baxter left Dudley for the position of curate in Bridgnorth, where he remained for nearly two years. Baxter acknowledges that his labors there were 'not so successful as they proved afterwards in other places', with the parishioners proving to be a 'very ignorant, dead-hearted People'.[27] Baxter said that the experience at Bridgnorth 'made me resolve that I would never more go among a people that had been hardened in unprofitableness under an awakening ministry'.[28] His desire was soon fulfilled.

While Baxter was at Bridgnorth, the parishioners of Kidderminster[29] threatened to petition Parliament against their vicar and his curate on charges of incompetence and drunken-ness.[30] To avoid the scandalous consequences of exposure from such a petition, the Vicar of Kidderminster agreed to dismiss the curate and offered to give up his pulpit to any lecturer whom the parishioners might select.[31] The parishioners formed a 'selection' committee of fourteen members, and in March, 1641, they invited Baxter to be their lecturer.[32]

Baxter accepted the position of lecturer at Kidderminster in 1641. Here in a township of three or four thousand, Baxter exercised his pastoral ministry first for fifteen months, and then, after a five year interruption because of the English Civil War, for fourteen years. It is ironic that the very thing for which Baxter is now renowned, his pastoral work, was not foremost on his heart when he accepted the charge. In fact, one of the great attractions of this position to him was that at Kidderminster he would have no official pastoral responsibilities![33]

Initially, some among the townspeople opposed and maligned him.[34] Before long, however, Baxter began to win the townspeople over through his love and generosity. He interested himself in the affairs of his parishioners, he loved their children, he gave any money he could spare to the poor, he cared for the infirmed, and he distributed many useful books.[35]

During this time Baxter was assailed by various doubts. At one point he even questioned whether he were a 'Christian or an infidel'.[36] These doubts caused him to dig to the very foundations of his faith, and to examine seriously the reasons of Christianity. Baxter emerged triumphant from the process, saying: 'And at last I found that ... Nothing is so firmly believed as that which hath been sometime doubted of.'[37]

When the Civil War broke out in 1642, Baxter was forced to withdraw from his parish. Though loyal to the monarchy, he had already intimated his sympathy with the Parliamentary party, regarding it as the champion of religion and liberty. Baxter's sympathies with Parliament inflamed the Royalists of the town against him. The entire county had declared openly its support for the king, and Kidderminster was entirely under the influence of Royalist families living there. So despite his efforts to remain aloof from the struggle, after one of the townspeople had publicly denounced him as a traitor, Baxter found he could only remain there at the risk of losing his life.[38]

When he left, Baxter fully expected to return within a few weeks, thinking the war would come to a speedy end. Actually, he was away for nearly five years. He first went to Coventry, where he preached once a week to the soldiers.[39] Cromwell twice urged him to become a chaplain to his troops, but Baxter declined, a decision he later regretted.[40] When he visited the Parliamentary army at Naseby, he felt condemned that he and other ministers had allowed it to develop tendencies towards what they regarded as sectarianism and disloyalty. Accordingly, when Colonel Whalley offered Baxter the chaplaincy of his regiment, he accepted it.

Beginning in the summer of 1645, Baxter worked for two years to encourage pure and undefiled religion and to restrain the army from hasty and too radical reforms in Church and State. His primary motive in accepting the chaplaincy appears to have been his desire to stem the growing tide of religious and political errors he saw in the Parliamentary Army, particularly their Antinomianism.[41] He set himself daily to 'find out the corruptions of the soldiers, and to discourse and dispute them out of their mistakes, both religious and political'.[42] With the leaders of the army, however, Baxter's efforts proved fruitless. Being unable to accomplish any lasting or large scale reversal of opinion among the Parliamentary soldiers and because of another serious bout with ill health, Baxter resigned his Chaplaincy.

For five months Baxter languished near death at the home of friends. There he took up his pen and wrote most of *The Saints Everlasting Rest*.[43] This work won him immediate fame, being read to the 'profit of many'. Baxter says: 'Weakness and pain helped me to study how to die; that set me on studying how to live.'[44] He had stated earlier that his sicknesses proved to be, throughout his life, 'an invaluable mercy.'[45] The many benefits[46] included greatly weakening temptations, a strong contempt for the things of the world, a great appreciation for time, and last, but not least, Baxter claims that his weakness 'made me study and preach things necessary, and a little stirred up my sluggish heart to speak to sinners with some compassion, *as a dying man to dying men.*'[47]

After recovering from his illness, he returned to his ministerial duties at Kidderminster in June 1647,[48] where his life became a model of ministerial consistency and faithfulness. He labored successfully by visiting his parishioners in their homes,[49] giving them public and private instruction, and becoming their friend as well as their pastor.[50] The key to his method was personal care of individuals, based upon intimate knowledge of their daily lives, prompted and sustained by an unaffected and impartial love for all.[51] At first he was content to catechize only 'in the Church', and to talk with individuals 'now and then'. He discovered, however, that for his preaching to be fruitful he must follow it up with direct personal discourse with every family. In addition to his regular parish work between 1647 and his 'silencing' in 1660, he still found time to write and publish fifty-seven books, including *The Reformed Pastor, A Treatise on Conversion,* and *A Call to the Unconverted.*[52]

He also served as the catalyst in forming the Worcestershire Association of Ministers in the area around Kidderminster. This association was composed mostly of men who espoused no religious party but were content to be 'mere catholics'.[53] They met together regularly for mutual edification and to co-operate in furthering the gospel in their county.

Baxter's success at Kidderminster is legendary. Initially, he recorded the names of all his converts, but they became so numerous that he was obliged to discontinue the practice.[54] In speaking of his accomplishments, Baxter is quick to give God the glory:

I must here, to the praise of my dear Redeemer, set up this pillar of remembrance, even to His praise who hath employed me so many years in so comfortable a work, with such encouraging success! O what am I, a worthless worm, not only wanting academical honours, but much of that furniture which is needful to so high a work, that God should thus abundantly encourage me, when the reverend instructors of my youth did labour fifty years together in one place, and could scarcely say they had converted one or two...[55]

Baxter recognized God's mercy in this 'encouraging success' because he was 'naturally of a discouraged Spirit'.[56]

He readily points out the numerous 'advantages' Kidderminster afforded him for a successful ministry. He first cites the fact that he came to a people that never had any awakening ministry before, 'for if they had been hardened under a powerful ministry and been sermon-proof I should have expected less.'[57] He also mentions his youthful vigour, his moving voice, his overall acceptance by the people, the diligence of his assistants, the unity and zeal of the godly people of the town,[58] his use of private meetings, his wide distribution of Bibles and other reading materials, his single status, his practice of medicine among them, and the fact that the town was not too large for his range.[59] Kidderminster's dominant industry, that of carpet-weaving, proved to be of peculiar importance: 'And it was a great advantage to me that my neighbours were of such a trade as allowed them time enough to read or talk of holy things; for the town liveth upon the weaving of Kidderminster stuffs, and as they stand in their loom, they can set a book before them, or edify one another.'[60] A final advantage Baxter lists was his length of service.[61]

Baxter grieved when King Charles I was beheaded in 1649. He later preached before Cromwell, the Lord Protector of the newly formed Commonwealth. After the service, the Protector asked him to a meeting. Cromwell proceeded to enter into a lengthy exposition and justification of his policy and the changes in the government which he said God had made. Baxter's reply was blunt: 'I told him that we took our ancient monarchy to be a blessing and not an evil to the land.'[62]

While he wrote freely upon Cromwell's faults, Baxter forthrightly acknowledged that under his rule religion had prospered: 'I bless God who gave me, even under an usurper whom I opposed, such liberty and advantage to preach his Gospel with success, which I cannot have under a king to whom I have sworn and performed true subjection and obedience.'[63] Baxter believed no previous era in English history had afforded such opportunities for the spread of the gospel.

After Oliver Cromwell's death in 1658 and the short rule by his son, Richard, Parliament voted on May 1, 1660 to recall Charles II. Baxter was in London at the time, working for religious reconciliation and concord. On the day before this crucial decision, April 30, Baxter preached before the members of the House of Commons in St. Margaret's, Westminster. His subject was Repentance; his text, Ezekiel 36:31.[64] He also preached on May 10th at St. Paul's Cathedral before the Lord Mayor. The day had been appointed by the House of Commons as a Day of Thanksgiving for General Monk's success, and the prospective restoration of the monarchy. The point of Baxter's sermon was too obvious to be missed. Titled *Right Rejoicing,* his text was Luke 10:20, 'Notwithstanding in this rejoice not, that the spirits are subject unto you; but rather rejoice, because your names are written in heaven.'[65]

After his coronation, King Charles II made Baxter one of his chaplains. He preached before the king[66] and for a time, exercised considerable influence at Court. Charles would later offer him the bishopric of Hereford, which he declined rather than give up his Nonconformist views, saying he was 'fully resolved against the lawfulness of the old diocesan frame'.[67] These days at Court proved to be the calm before the storm. Twenty years of brutal oppression soon begun, during which Baxter was harassed by spies, fined, and imprisoned under the rule of this same king.

At the Savoy Conference in 1661, he served as the leader for the Nonconformist Party and produced for them a revision of the Book of Common Prayer.[68] The conference proved a bitter disappointment, with the bishops failing to budge from their position on the prayer book.[69] On May 19, 1662, the Act of Uniformity established the extreme Episcopal polity as orthodoxy and officially removed from their ecclesiastical assignments or places of ministry all who disagreed and refused to 'conform'. Baxter possessed episcopal ordination and was not opposed to the Prayer Book in principle. But he refused to conform to a Church established on terms intended to exclude rather than include. Not waiting until the August 24th deadline when the Act would be enforced, Baxter let it be known immediately that he would not conform, leaving the Church of England on May 25th.[70] Two thousand of his fellow ministers followed soon thereafter.

The disappointment of his 'silencing' was somewhat tempered by an unexpected but blessed event: on September 10, 1662, Baxter married Margaret Charlton.[71] His decision to marry was startling when viewed in light of his clear teachings concerning clerical marriage.[72] Baxter records that his marriage caused quite a stir:

> The unsuitableness of our age, and my former known purposes against Marriage, and against the conveniency of Ministers Marriage, who have no sort of necessity made our marriage the matter of much publick talk and wonder... [73]

> And it everywhere rung about, partly as a wonder and partly as a crime.... And I think the king's marriage was scarce more talked of than mine.[74]

In the earlier period of his ministry, Baxter had resolved not to marry so that he might pursue his pastoral and ministerial duties without interruption.[75] After his ejection, however, having no public charge, he thought himself sufficiently free to take a wife.[76] It was a good decision: Margaret proved 'the meetest helper that I could have had in the world'.[77]

During the three years of his residence in London, two before and one after his final ejectment, Baxter spoke in various places as opportunities presented themselves. He preached once a week in London at Dr. William Bates' Church, St. Dunstan's-in-the-West, where the people gave him a small stipend. He lectured also at St. Bride's, Fleet Street, at a church in Milk Street, and every Sunday at Blackfriars.

In July 1663 he moved from London to the country village of Acton, that he might devote himself more fully to study and writing. Yet people continued to desire his preaching and teaching. Despite the recently enacted Conventicle Act,[78] Baxter held meetings in private houses, where he enjoyed the company of 'divers godly faithful friends'.

During his residence at Acton, the Great Plague of London burst forth with tremendous fury. Beginning in December 1664, this pestilence raged for over a year. Yet Baxter recognized God's providence even in this horrible event. Many of the ejected ministers seized the opportunity of preaching in the neglected or deserted pulpits with good results:

> when the plague grew hot most of the conformable ministers fled, and left their flocks in the time of their extremity, whereupon divers Nonconformists, pitying the dying and distressed people that had none to call the impenitent to repentance, nor to help men to prepare for another world, nor to comfort them in their terrors, when about ten thousand died in a week, resolved that no obedience to the laws of mortal men whatsoever could justify them for neglecting of men's souls and bodies in such extremities.... Therefore they resolved to stay with the people, and to go into the forsaken pulpits, though prohibited, and to preach to the poor people before they died; also to visit the sick and get what relief they could for the poor.[79]

The conditions were ripe for a good response:

> The face of death did so awaken both the preachers and the hearers, that preachers exceeded themselves in lively, fervent preaching, and the people crowded constantly to hear them. And all was done with so great seriousness, as that, through the blessing of God, abundance were converted from their carelessness, impenitence, and youthful lusts and vanities; and religion took that hold on the peoples hearts as could never afterwards be loosed.[80]

To make matters worse, scarcely had the plague ceased when the great London fire began. Seeing earthly goods go up in flames only increased Baxter's awareness of the vanity of this world.[81]

Initially, no action was taken against Baxter for his preaching at Acton. But his services became so popular, with people crowding in and out of his house to hear, that it could no longer be ignored. The authorities issued a warrant for his arrest in June 1669 on charges of keeping conventicles contrary to law. Baxter was imprisoned for six months in the New Prison at Clerkenwell.[82] When someone suggested that his views might change somewhat due to his imprisonment, Baxter replied, 'truth did not change because I was in a Gaol.'[83]

After being released from prison, Baxter settled back into his writing ministry, moving to a new home in Totteridge to escape the continual threat of arrest at Acton. Because he defended the practice of occasional attendance and communion in the parish churches where the gospel was preached, it was erroneously reported that he had conformed.[84] The Earl of Lauderdale, on order from Charles II, offered Baxter a bishopric, or the presidency of one of the universities, in Scotland. Baxter graciously declined.

In 1672, the Royal Declaration of Indulgence for Non-conformists and Recusants was announced. In November, after some hesitation, Baxter secured his license as a mere Nonconformist without 'the title of Independent, Presbyterian, or any other party'.[85] After having been 'silent' for ten years, he again undertook weekday lectures.

But this reprieve proved to be short-lived. In 1673, Parliament withdrew the Indulgence, and Baxter subsequently moved to Bloomsbury, London, where he continued his pulpit ministry.[86] He considered that the 'vows of God were upon him', and that he must preach whenever and wherever Divine providence opened a door for him. Therefore, despite continual harassment and persecution, he continued to preach the gospel.

He lectured at various churches in the city, but did most of his work in the parish of St. Martin's, Bloomsbury, holding his meetings in St. James's Market-house. With the help of wealthy friends, Baxter erected a larger building in the neighborhood for the carrying on of his work. But persecution once more reared its ugly head, and Baxter was subject to the constant irritation of hostile surveillance. Through it all he patiently bore persecution, imprisonment, and the seizure of his property.[87] He grieved most for the loss of the library he had carefully collected.[88]

His wife, Margaret Charlton, died in June 1681, at the age of forty. They had lived together in beautiful harmony for nineteen years. She had been his companion in tribulation, his comforter in sorrow. Baxter buried her in her mother's tomb at Christ Church, London.

The coming of James II to the throne upon Charles II's death in 1685 boded ill for the Nonconformists, especially for Baxter. James was a pronounced Roman Catholic who saw his strongest opponents among the Nonconformists. Baxter was again imprisoned, this time for eighteen months, beginning in 1685.[89] His prison sentence was based upon the fallacious charge that his *Paraphrase of the New Testament* was an attack on the established church and the state.[90] The unjustness of his trial is legendary in English history.[91]

Baxter appeared for sentencing on the 29th of June. Lord Chief Justice Jeffries wished him to be publicly whipped through the city, but the other judges would not consent that a man to whom a bishopric had been offered should be punished as a felon. Baxter was fined five hundred marks and imprisoned until it was paid.

He refused to pay the fine imposed upon him, however, because he knew that it most likely would be repeated and enforced every time he attempted to preach, or whenever he wrote anything that could possibly be objected to by the Court. He also refused, on principle, to petition for his release from an unjust imprisonment. On November 24, 1686, James II released Baxter from his imprisonment. The King undoubtedly hoped that Baxter would then help him in his growing conflict with the Church. But the King underestimated Baxter; he refused to take any part against his brethren in the English Church.

Upon his release, Baxter continued his writing ministry, as well as assisting Matthew Sylvester in his ministerial labors. He continued to preach until his body could no longer take the strain, with Bates observing that the last time he preached he 'almost died in the pulpit'.[92]

Even on his deathbed, Baxter did not abandon his calling. He was the same in his life and death; his last hours were spent preparing others and himself to appear before God.[93] To some who came to visit him, he remarked,

> You come hither to learn to die; I am not the only person that must go this way. I can assure you that your whole life, be it never so long, is little enough to prepare for death. Have a care of this vain, deceitful world, and the lusts of the flesh. Be sure you choose God for your portion, heaven for your home, God's glory for your end, His Word for your rule; and then you need never fear but that we shall meet with comfort.[94]

A few hours before his departure, Baxter was asked how he was. His reply? 'Almost well.'[95] On December 8th, 1691, the great preacher entered into that 'everlasting rest' of which he had so often and so confidently spoken.

He was buried in Christ Church, Newgate Street, where he had placed the remains of his wife and her mother. Eayrs notes that 'Never had there been such a private funeral'.[96] A great multitude of persons attended, many of them ministers, conformists as well as nonconformists, all of whom were eager to testify of their respect to this great man.

Baxter's philanthropy was evidenced in his death as in his life. In his will, written two years before his death, he directed the executors to give his books to needy scholars, and he left his estate for the benefit of the poor. Dr. William Bates gave the following epitaph at Baxter's funeral:

> Love to the souls of men was the peculiar character of Mr. Baxter's spirit. In this he imitated and honored our Saviour, who prayed, died, and lives, for the salvation of souls. All his natural and supernatural endowments were

subservient to this blessed end. It was his meat and drink, the life and joy of his life, to do good to souls.[97]

Numerous others could testify firsthand to the truth of those words.

With this we conclude an all too brief biography of Richard Baxter. To provide a basis for us to understand his views on conversion, we next turn to his teachings on the theological foundation for conversion, examining in order his theological method, his beliefs concerning man's sin and God's grace, and his teaching on the atonement of Christ.

2

THE THEOLOGICAL FOUNDATION
FOR CONVERSION

'I never thought that my faith must follow the major vote;
I value Divines also by weight, and not by number' (Richard
Baxter, *Aphorismes of Justification* (1649), 'Appendix', 12).

'Christ's sufferings render satisfaction, because they
demonstrate the justice, wisdom and mercy of God, and
enable Him to attain to the ends of government in a better
way than by executing the law and destroying the world'
(Richard Baxter, *Catholick Theologie* (1675), II, i, 41).

'And therefore I conclude that when God saith so expressly
that Christ died for all, and tasted death for every man,
and is the Ransom for all and the propitiation for the sins
of the whole World, it beseems every Christian rather to
explain in what sense Christ died for All men, than flatly to
deny it' (Richard Baxter, *Universal Redemption of Mankind*
(1694), 286).

Baxter's Theological Methodology
Before exploring Baxter's teaching on the atonement and
justification, we must first examine his method of approaching

theology, for herein lies the 'key' to understanding his theological formulations.[1] Baxter believed that a proper method was necessary to achieve a clear understanding of truth.[2] A faithful system of theology will not add to the Scripture, but merely draw out what is already there. Such formulation should not be left to the novice; it required the work of a 'skillful hand'.[3]

Baxter was far from alone in his pleas for a 'right method'. Throughout the seventeenth century the Puritans absorbed themselves in an 'engrossing preoccupation' to methodize their theology.[4] Baxter's statements merely reflect this typical Puritan concern about using a proper method to arrange truth.[5] The glory of methodized theology was that it could be 'thoroughly understood' and 'kept in memory'.[6] Method was the art of memory. The correct method could make any subject more intelligible, and hence more indelible on the hearts of learners.

The Puritan concern over 'method' derives from the work of the French humanist Petrus Ramus (1515–72).[7] His method was accepted at Cambridge in the 1570s and became identified with Puritanism through the work of the great commentators.[8] Ramus's contribution to the Puritans in terms of their theological formulations was due to his emphasis on system and method of a particular kind. Miller asserts that the 'crowning achievement' of the Ramist system was its 'doctrine of method',[9] i.e. its technique of organizing ideas so as to make their content and their truth both coherent and memorable.

The Ramist method was one of systematic dichotomy. According to Ramus, the essential work of method is to define carefully the terms, arranging the material into dichotomies, each of which is carefully defined again. This process continues, moving from universal principles to specifics.[10] One could therefore understand every reality by dichotomizing one's statements about it. When theology had been developed along these lines, it was proudly hailed as 'analytic' and 'methodically arranged'.[11] This concept of arrangement appealed to Baxter's logical mind. He says, 'I could never from my first Studies endure Confusion.... I never thought I understood any thing till I could anatomize it, and see the parts distinctly, and the Conjunction of the parts as they make up the whole.'[12]

Baxter faced two issues in beginning his theology: what material to include, and how to arrange it. He desired to begin by examining the nature of God and Man, believing that they should be given greater emphasis than were commonly accorded them.[13] Initially he hesitated, fearing how 'uncouth' it would seem to many if he began his Body of Divinity in this manner. 'But,' Baxter says, 'the three first Chapters of Genesis assured me, That it was the Scripture-Method.'[14] It only seemed logical to him to begin as Scripture did, with creation, before proceeding to redemption.

In response to the second challenge, that of arrangement, we see Baxter's resourceful mind at work. Though in full agreement with those who followed Ramus's emphasis on order and arrangement, Baxter parted ways with them over the principle of dichotomizing. Despite their noble efforts, in his eyes their results were less than satisfying.[15] The right way to arrange, Baxter asserted, was to *trichotomize*: 'I had been Twenty Six Years convinced that Dichotomizing will not do it; but that the Divine Trinity in Unity, hath expressed itself in the whole Frame of Nature and Morality.'[16]

Baxter believed that not only his subject matter but also his method had come directly from Scripture: 'There is a method of Scripture theology, which is the most accurate that ever the world knew in morality. I have drawn up the body of theology into schemes, in which I doubt not but I have shown, that the method of theology contained in the holy Scriptures, is more accurate than any logical author doth prescribe.'[17] Thus, through the use of trichotomizing, Baxter claimed to have accomplished the methodological goals of clarity and fidelity to Scriptural teaching.

But there is far more to Baxter's method than simply subdividing material into three parts instead of two. To focus on this part of Baxter's scheme is to focus on the external trappings and miss the heart of his system. Baxter believed the key theme in Scripture was the Kingdom of God, and that therefore the idea of the Kingdom should be taken as one's starting point in constructing a system of theology. He argues: 'Theology is the Doctrine of the Kingdom of God: A Kingdom is a State of Government: Government is by Laws: He therefore that will understand any thing in Divinity, must understand the Laws of God.'[18]

The Kingdom of God and his government of man, being the central theme in Scripture, must therefore become the central focus for our theology. Thus the fall of man and the plan of redemption must be seen from a 'political' framework. A failure to follow this 'political method' would lead to erroneous conclusions about God's relation to his creation. But Baxter went even further. Having seen that the Kingdom of God is the central theme in Scripture, Baxter next argued that we must understand Scripture in terms of what we know about kingdoms. He therefore took seventeenth century political thought as his frame of reference from which to interpret Scripture. God should be thought of as a governor, and the gospel as part of his legal code.

The primary influence on Baxter's thought at this point appears to have been Hugo Grotius (1583–1645), particularly through his work *De Satisfactione*.[19] Baxter admired Grotius, because he felt that Grotius was at least theologizing according to the right method (political theology), even if as an Arminian he did not always come to the right conclusions.[20] As we shall soon discover, Grotius also had a profound impact on Baxter's view of the atonement.

Another major influence on Baxter's thought was George Lawson (d. 1678). Baxter greatly profited from Lawson's insight into politics, which Baxter claimed 'contributeth not a little to the understanding of Divinity'.[21] He maintained that Lawson's *Theo-Politica* had 'reduced Theology to a Method more Political and righter in the main' than any that he had studied before, and hailed it as the 'soundest' and 'most abounding with Light' of any that he had seen.[22] Baxter openly acknowledges his debt to Lawson: 'I must thankfully acknowledge that I learnt more from Mr. Lawson than from any Divine ... that ever I conversed with.... Especially his instigating me to the

Study of Politicks, (in which he much lamented the Ignorance of Divines) did prove a singular Benefit to me.'[23]

Baxter summarizes the impact that Grotius and Lawson made on his turning to a political method in theology:

> I must be so grateful as to confess that my Understanding hath made a better Improvement (for the sudden sensible increase of my Knowledge) of *Grotius de Satisfactione Christi,* and of Mr. Lawson's Manuscripts, than of any thing else that ever I read; and they convinced me how unfit we are to write about Christ's Government, and Laws, and Judgment, &c., while we understand not the true Nature of Government, Laws and Judgment in the general; and that *he that is ignorant of Politicks and of the Law of Nature, will be ignorant and erroneous in Divinity and the sacred Scriptures.*[24]

Baxter steadfastly held to this last point. The theologian who desires to be accurate must use the political method. To fail to use it is to distort Scripture and theology.

Baxter brought these emphases together in what he considered his most prominent work: *Methodus Theologiae* (1681).[25] Unfortunately, others did not agree about its significance. Written in Latin to appeal to the scholarly community (the only Latin work Baxter penned), it was ignored, its influence being 'negligible'.[26] Powicke argues that perhaps the only man who both read and admired it was Sir Matthew Hale.[27] Nuttall remarks that Philip Doddridge, who read Baxter's works with 'abundance of pleasure', found the *Methodus Theologiae* to be 'unintelligible'.[28]

We will see how Baxter made use of the political method when we examine his theological formulations. It remains at this juncture to leave Baxter for a moment in order to point out the tragic results of this approach when used by those following him. Once one works on the principle that political theory (or anything else for that matter) provides the framework from which to view Scripture, the Bible 'loses' its ability to judge that framework. When a theologian takes something in his or her own experience as the absolute, the Bible ultimately ends up being relativized in light of that experience.

Those who followed Baxter in the use of this method ultimately became Unitarians.[29] Unitarians began forcing ideas about the unity of God into mathematical concepts of unity. In order to be rational, they claimed, one had to be a Unitarian. Thus the doctrine of the Trinity was relativized by mathematical notions of unity. The English Presbyterian Church died by turning to Unitarianism, following Baxter's approach and making something outside of Scripture, in this case mathematics, the absolute.[30] As Packer says, 'It is sadly fitting that the Richard Baxter Church in Kidderminster today should be – Unitarian.'[31]

We conclude this treatment of Baxter's theological methodology by examining three other elements of his thought which will prove important to our examination of his theology: his view of reason, his eclecticism, and his belief that 'holiness was the essence of Christianity'. Baxter placed a great emphasis on reason, believing that God made man's mind such that its assent was only evoked by evidence. Yet De Pauley certainly overstates the case when he says that Baxter argues 'for the authority of reason as well as that of scripture'.[32] Baxter did give a high place to reason, but he clearly did not place reason as a judge over revelation, asserting, 'if there were nothing in Scripture but what the Reason of man could comprehend, it were not so like to be the product of the infinite wisdom of God. Let reason, therefore, stoop to the wisdom of our Maker; and when he hath let us know that it is he that speaketh, let us humbly learn, and not proudly expostulate with him about the rest.'[33]

Baxter's anthropology did not allow him to place too great an emphasis on man's unregenerate reason.[34] It is not the Christian religion that is unreasonable, it is those who deny its truth:

There is evidence of truth in Scripture, and there are sound reasons for the christian faith, before the Holy Ghost persuades men to believe them. The Holy Ghost is not sent to cure the Scripture of obscurity or any defect, but to cure men's eyes of blindness ... not ... to make our religion reasonable, but to make sinners reasonable ... for the believing it ... nor doth he cause us to believe by enthusiasm, or without reason, but he works on man as man, and causeth him to believe nothing but what is credible; and his causing us to believe is by showing us the credibility of the thing.[35]

Baxter's belief that God works on 'man as man' (i.e. as a reasonable creature)[36], combined with his copious reading of the Scholastics,[37] caused him to make great use of painstaking, detailed, 'reasoned arguments' in both his sermons and theological treatises.[38]

Another key factor in understanding Baxter's formulations is to recognize that he was 'eclectic' in his theology. He felt free to *draw from* any system, as well as to *criticize* it.[39] He was never concerned about 'holding the party line'. He belonged to the 'School of Truth'.[40] He complained bitterly against those whose sole concern was the protection of their particular theological system, saying sarcastically,

when a man hath read once what is the opinion of the divines that are in most credit, he dare search no further, for fear of being counted a novelist or heretic, or lest he bear their curse for adding to, or taking from, the common conceits! So that divinity is become an easier study than heretofore. We are already at a *ne plus ultra*. It seemeth vain, when we know the opinion is in credit, to search any further.[41]

Baxter did not hesitate to set forth any opinion he thought was true, nor to oppose any he thought false. He refused to be swayed by the majority opinion simply because it was held by more people.[42] He told his critics that if they found him asserting anything for which he did not give evidence, to point it out to him, and he would retract it.[43]

The final factor we mention only briefly here, as we will return to it frequently in the ensuing discussion. Baxter believed that holiness was the essence of Christianity;[44] therefore, anything which detracted from holiness must be opposed and opposed strenuously.[45] This provided the basis for his lifetime battle with Antinomianism.[46] He came into contact with the Antinomians in the army – we will see in the following discussion how his theology was formulated largely in reaction to them.

Having laid this foundation, we are now prepared to study Baxter's actual theological formulations which provided the basis for his teaching on conversion. We first examine his views on the need for conversion: the nature and fall of man.

The Nature and Fall of Man

Baxter insisted that when God created man, he created him both soul and body. The soul is a unity in essence, but has three faculties: a vital activity, or power; an understanding, or intellect; and a will.[47] These comprise the soul's natural image of God. Thus in the nature of man the nature of God is revealed in some measure.[48]

Because God is Creator, man must respond to him as such. Baxter trichotomizes God's dealings with man: he is man's Lord or Owner, his Ruler or Governor, and his Father or Benefactor.[49] Man stands accountable to respond properly to God in each of these relations. As Lord (*Dominus*), God has an absolute right to order his creation as he chooses, and none may call him to account.[50] Man may not always understand God's ways, yet, 'when we find that it is indeed revealed, our reason must presently submit, and undoubtedly conclude it reasonable and good.'[51]

The second part of God's relation to man is that of being his Governor or Ruler. This relation is based on the first, but applies only to the rational creatures.[52] Having made man a 'rational free agent', God now chooses to govern him by 'moral means, and not ... as inanimates and brutes'.[53] Since God could only rule man according to his nature, Baxter stated what to him seemed obvious: 'God would not have made him rational, if he would not have governed him accordingly.'[54]

God's moral government thus has three parts. He makes laws for men, then teaches them and persuades them to keep the laws, and finally executes the laws by judging, and giving reward or punishment as is due.[55] He motivates man to obey by use of the two supreme motivations: love and fear. 'Take away all reward and punishment,' Baxter claimed, 'and you take away duty in effect ... for a rational agent will have ends and motives for what he doth.'[56]

The third of God's three relations to man, that of loving Father or bountiful Benefactor,[57] rests on the other two. God displays his willingness to be our Benefactor through his act of creation, by becoming our governor, and by making us capable of seeking after happiness as our end.[58] In God's relation to man as Benefactor, 'All is from love, and in a way of love, and for the exercise and demonstration of love.'[59] Thus we can see the glorious truth that,

> Though all God's three essential principles or faculties, power, wisdom, and goodness, appear in each of his three grand relations, owner, ruler, and benefactor, yet each one of these hath most eminently some one of God's essential principles or faculties appearing in it; viz. his power most appeareth in his propriety, his wisdom in his rule, and his goodness or love in his benefits given us.[60]

Here we see Baxter's political method at work. Using his political framework, he interprets the divine attributes as governmental attributes, manifesting themselves in God's legislation and execution of his laws.[61] Since man is a rational being, government by law is the only government consistent with man's nature.

In addition to creating man a rational agent, God also made him 'a free self-determining agent'.[62] This is also necessary if he is to follow God's Sapiential Rule. When asked what this free-will is that makes us fit to be subjects, Baxter replies, 'It is a will made by God, able to determine itself, by God's necessary help, to choose good, and refuse evil; understood to be such, without any necessitating predetermination by any other.'[63] Therefore, as the act of a free agent, duty is rewardable, while sin is punishable.[64]

Baxter believed the creation of man with free-will brought tribute to the Creator: 'And that it is a great Honour to God, to make so noble a Nature, as hath a Power to determine its own elections.'[65] He had strong words for those who denied that man was a free agent:

And he that dare say that God Almighty who made all the World, is not Able to make a Creature that can determine his own will to this object rather than to that, under Divine Universal Influx, without Divine pre-determining pre-motion, on pretence that his wit doth find a contradiction in it, is bolder against God, than I shall be. And if God *can do it*, we have no reason to doubt whether it be done.[66]

The fact that man was not fixed 'by necessity in love and obedience, but left with a power of loving and obeying, which he could use or not use', made man a befitting subject of God's moral Government by laws.[67]

When God created Adam, he actuated with him the Covenant of Nature (or Works).[68] Life was promised and death threatened to Adam by virtue of his actions.[69] The Law of Nature proclaimed the reality of rewards and punishments: the wages of sin was death, while the result of obedience was life. Adam, being created in the image of God, had an original righteousness. Holiness was the natural constitution of man.[70] Adam's powers, at the beginning of his existence, were in a right state. He therefore had not a hypothetical, but a *true* power to stand.[71]

Baxter felt this was an important safeguard in protecting God from being said to be the cause of sin. 'There is,' he claimed, 'a great difference between God's *permitting* sin (after great means against it) and his *causing* it.'[72] God did not cause Adam to sin; he make him a free agent and put life or death in his choice.[73] Baxter rightly saw that the holiness of God's nature would not stand with the charge that God was the author of sin.

When Adam and Eve were tempted, sin resulted because of the failure of the will to rule over the sensitive appetite. Since the will is the 'master-commanding faculty of the rational soul', if it is 'right', then man is 'upright and safe'.[74] Thus sin always begins with the failure of the will to rule by reason the sensitive appetite. Baxter set forth a detailed anatomy of temptation in his *Christian Directory*. The devil first works on the sensitive appetite, then on the imagination, then on the passions or affections.[75] When fantasy has 'inflamed' the passions, they 'violently urge the will and reason'.[76] When the will is 'infected' and reason is 'blinded' by sensuality and passion, an act of sin results.[77]

The problem is with the will. If it did not neglect its duty in 'commanding the understanding to meditate on preserving objects and to call off the thoughts from the forbidden thing',[78] man could stand in spite of temptation. 'It seemeth,' Baxter argued, 'that all sin beginneth in the wills omission of what it was able to have done.'[79] The will fails to will *what* and *when* it should, and sin results.

Adam, being the 'universal Head and Father of all mankind',[80] passed on his sinfulness to his posterity by imputation on the basis of natural derivation. It was in him that all mankind sinned since all mankind is propagated from him and was seminally in him. God dealt with Adam not only as an individual person, but also as 'a whole mankind', since he and Eve were then the whole world.[81] We are guilty of death because of our natural interest in Adam's sin as his descendants. As soon as our persons exist, they are guilty persons.[82]

As Adam was sinful, he could give us no better than he had himself, and 'therefore being a son of death, he could not beget sons of life; being guilty, he could not beget persons that are innocent; nor bring a clean thing from himself, who was unclean.'[83] Thus, our original nature is a guilty nature, because Adam 'cannot convey to us the right to felicity which he lost'.[84] Baxter laments that our nature is therefore 'vitiated with Original sin, and unhappy in the miserable effects'.[85] Both Adam's guilt and depravity were transmitted to his posterity. Those who deny original sin 'go against plain Scripture, reason, and the experience of mankind'.[86]

Baxter also asserted that all parents' sins were imputed to their children on the grounds of physical descent. He recognized this as a logical exigency if he was going to assert that physical descent was the ground of the imputation of sin.[87] We are therefore guilty not only of Adam's sins, committed while were were seminally in him, but also of our parents' sins, committed while we were seminally in them. This was obvious, for if 'the very guilt and corruption derived from Adam, had not been my next Parents first, it had never been mine, no more than my nature: For I had it not immediately from Adam, but from them.'[88]

Baxter believed he had done the Church a great service by explaining this teaching.[89] It cleared up confusion about how we received our depraved natures, and enabled Christians to answer most of the attacks made on the doctrine of original sin. It was not God who made us sinners, but Adam and our parents.[90] Baxter confessed that he was not able to maintain man's guilt from Adam's sin without this teaching.[91] And did not common experience testify to this? Did not the children of ungodly parents have an 'additional pravity in their natures', much more than mankind in general has merely from Adam's sin?[92] Baxter's conclusion is terse: 'From hence it appears, that it is a sad thing to be born of evil Parents, and a blessing to be born of those that fear God: and accordingly to be acknowledged.'[93]

In addition to the guilt transmitted to all of Adam's posterity by propagation, we all have an 'inherent pravity of our own' and 'at age our actual sin'. Both of these, Baxter claimed, are our unrighteouness, as well as Adam's sin imputed to us.[94] The result is that,

> The three Faculties of mans Soul are all vitiated by sin. 1. The vital active Power is so far dead to God and Holiness, as to need the cure of quickening, and strengthening, and exciting Grace. 2. The Intellect is so far blinded, as to need the cure of illuminating grace. 3. And the Will is so far turned by Enmity from God, to the inordinate Love of carnal self-interest and Creatures, as to need the cure of converting, sanctifying Grace.[95]

Where then does this leave mankind? Is man's will still free? Baxter answers the question forthrightly: 'No man of brains denieth, that man hath a will that is naturally free ... but it is not free from evil dispositions. It is habitually averse to God and holiness, and inclined to earthly, fleshly things; it is enslaved by a sinful bias.... If you had a will that were freed from wicked inclinations, I had no need to write such Books as these to persuade you to be willing.'[96] Thus he could assert that it is more proper to say that an unbeliever *will not* repent and believe, than that he *cannot*.[97]

Man still has physical ability. His inability is not physical but moral. Man has not lost his capacity to make choices, for that would be to cease to be a man. What he has lost is his inclination to make *right* choices.[98] Thus Baxter could say, 'Even in the point of believing, [the will] hath natural power and liberty to act otherwise than it doth, even to turn itself from the act of unbelief to the act of faith. But being indisposed and ill-disposed, it *will not do* that which it hath a natural self-determining power to do; till God assist it or turn it by his grace.'[99] This fact demonstrates why man is guilty and deserving of punishment. If a man breaks a law because he is *physically* unable to keep it, nature teaches that man is not guilty. If however, he breaks a law merely because he was disinclined to keep it, he is breaking it by his own deliberate choice, and is therefore guilty and liable to punishment.[100] 'For morally to be unable to believe,' he argued, 'is no more than to be unwilling to believe.'[101]

The tragic fact of total depravity makes sin a terrible reality.[102] Sin is manifested in each individual by his turning away from God's rule to his own self-rule, caused by an 'inordinate self-love'.[103] Man has turned from loving God as his ultimate end and chief good to loving himself as the source of his happiness. It is not wrong to seek happiness; indeed, God has placed that legitimate desire within man. Sin results from seeking happiness in the wrong way.

Thus we conclude Baxter's treatment of man created and fallen.[104] We next proceed to Baxter's interpretation of the Divine plan to remedy man's hopeless situation.

The Basis for Conversion: The Grace of God and the Work of Christ
In our previous discussion about man created and fallen, we discussed the Covenant of Works (Baxter's Covenant of Nature). A covenant is an arrangement by which two parties give themselves to each other to form a relationship. In the

Covenant of Works, Adam was promised life on the condition of perfect obedience. When this covenant became invalid due to the Fall, God in his mercy enacted a new covenant with Adam: the Covenant of Grace.[105] This is a single covenant between God and man, though administered in different ways. Baxter, as we might expect, uses political imagery when discussing the Covenant of Grace: 'The New Covenant is Christs Law of Grace; his Instrument by which he giveth Title or Right to the Benefits promised, and conveyeth Right to the Fruits of his Sacrifice and Merits; And his Law by which he governeth the Church as a Saviour, in order to Recovery and Salvation.'[106] On the basis of Christ's satisfaction, accepted by the Divine Lawgiver, this new law of grace has been announced. The risen Christ, now enthroned as King, governs the world by it.

Baxter followed in the footsteps of his Puritan predecessors in his use of Covenant Theology.[107] But, as we shall see, his 'political method' caused him to put his own particular twist on how the Covenant of Grace is administered now. In order to present his views equitably, we must first look at how he developed the views he came to hold and to teach to others.

Originally he held to the extreme positions of supra-lapsarianism[108] and the justification of the elect from eternity. He also maintained the doctrine of a limited atonement. Later, after seeing firsthand how the Antinomians 'abused' these doctrines, he retreated to a mediating position which denied reprobation and maintained a universal atonement. We already have alluded to Baxter's emphasis on holiness as the essence of Christianity. Here we can better appreciate why his theology developed along the lines it did. Anything which contributed to Antinomianism was against holiness, therefore against God, and therefore to be opposed. The formulation of his theology of justification cannot be comprehended apart from this background. Baxter's theology was reactionary, and if it tended to extremes, it was because the other position was abhorrent to him.[109]

What did the Antinomians teach? They laid such an exclusive stress on the completeness of a believer's justification that they were accused of denying the obligation of the moral law – hence the name of 'Antinomians'.[110] The attempt to lead a good life or practice good works detracts from God's glory by failing to trust solely in his unmerited gift of salvation. Believing himself justified from eternity, and perfect in the sight of God, the antinomian may be led by his confidence in God's immutable decree of election into libertinism. While libertine practice was rare, in Baxter's view, any theology which left the door open for such abuse undercut the very foundation of Christianity.[111]

Baxter first encountered Antinomianism when he served as a chaplain in the Army:

> When I was in the Army Antinomianism was the predominant Infection. The Books of Dr. Crisp, Paul Hobson, Saltmarsh, Cradock and abundance such like, were the writings most applauded; and he was thought no spiritual Christian, but a Legalist, that savoured not of Antinomianism, which was sugared with the Title of Free Grace; and others were thought to preach the Law and not to preach Christ.[112]

Baxter lamented the fact that the soldiers were 'just falling in with *Saltmarsh, that Christ hath repented and believed for us, and that we must no more question our faith and Repentance, than Christ*'.[113] Baxter says this awakened him 'better to study these points'.[114] Study them he did, with the result being a modification of some of his previously held theological positions.[115] We first look at Baxter's views on the atonement.

We have already seen how Baxter was influenced by Grotius to adopt a 'political method' in theology. Baxter likewise adopted Grotius' concept of the atonement.[116] Often called the Governmental Theory, it teaches that Christ secured a change in God's law rather than satisfying it as it stood. God wants to forgive sin, but he cannot simply ignore it or he will not be seen as a good Governor. The cross then becomes the means by which God is able to forgive sin. It is the removing of a barrier by a gracious God who wants to forgive everyone anyway.[117]

The fundamental difference between Baxter and traditional Calvinists at this point can be boiled down to one concept:

the idea of law.[118] Standard Reformed teaching maintained that Christ satisfied the law in the sinner's place through substitution; Baxter asserted that Christ satisfied the Lawgiver and so obtained a change in the law.[119] Baxter says, 'Christ's sufferings render satisfaction, because they demonstrate the justice, wisdom and mercy of God, and enable Him to attain to the ends of government in a better way than by executing the law and destroying the world.'[120] Thus the wisdom and mercy of God are seen in that he still attained the ends of the law and government, but in a better way than by executing the law.[121] The law is therefore but a means to an end, and God may justly change his law provided the same end is attained.[122]

Baxter summarizes the effects of Christ's death:

1. That Christs Death doth *demonstrate Gods justice and hatred of Sin.*
2. In it an *Example* is given for the *deterring of Offenders.*
3. And for *preserving the Lawgiver*, and the *Law* from contempt.
4. And a demonstration made of unspeakable Love to Men.
5. And in and by these,
      1) The Lawgiver satisfied.
      2) And the chief Ends of the Law are attained.[123]

He concludes: 'Thus *satisfaction of Justice* is the sum of these most immediate Effects. And the whole work together may well be called A Satisfactory Penalty.'[124]

While indebted to Grotius for his basic formulation, Baxter differed from him in two key points. First, Baxter maintained an Anselmic component in his formulation.[125] Whereas Grotius had argued that satisfaction is rendered to God, not as God, but only as Governor, Baxter correctly asserted that Christ offered satisfaction to God as God.[126] Second, Grotius shifted to the Arminian position and maintained that all men are now able to fulfill the new law obtained by Christ's death. Baxter refused to accept this view, still retaining the traditional Reformed emphases of unconditional election and irresistible grace. He was able to maintain this distinction because of his 'trinity of relations' between God and man. As Governor, God freely offers amnesty to all who will fulfill the conditions of the new covenant; as *Dominus*, God effectually gives faith to the elect to guarantee their salvation.[127]

This last point raises the question of whether the atonement was limited (Christ died only for the elect) or unlimited (Christ in some sense died for all men). We have noted that Baxter initially held to a limited atonement.[128] His encounter with the Antinomians caused him to rethink his entire theological system, and the doctrine of the limited atonement was another element he abandoned. He expresses his new conviction on the matter in his work *Universal Redemption*: 'And therefore I conclude that when God saith so expressly that Christ died for all, and tasted death for every man, and is the Ransom for all and the propitiation for the sins of the whole World, it beseems every Christian rather to explain in what sense Christ died for All men, than flatly to deny it.'[129] Yet as we have mentioned previously, Baxter believed in unconditional election. How did he reconcile these two seemingly contradictory ideas?

Baxter came to hold a position similar to what is commonly referred to as Amyraldian or 'hypothetical universalism'.[130] Brian Armstrong, in his work, *Calvinism and the Amyraut Heresy*, states that the essence of 'hypothetical universalism' is that before the decree of election there was the decree to redeem the world in Christ. Though none but the elect will be saved, through Christ's death God has redeemed all men 'hypothetically or potentially'.[131] This is in contrast to the strict Reformed understanding that God's decree to give faith to the elect precedes his decree to send Christ to redeem them, and that therefore the atonement is limited to the elect.[132]

Again we see Baxter's political theory at work. In Baxter's system it was critical that one maintain a universal atonement, for it was at the very cornerstone of God's new design of Government: 'He [Christ] hath laid the Foundation of his new right of Rectorship ... God being minded to change the Government of the World, *did lay the whole Foundation of the New Government in Christs Universal Redemption*, even as he laid the Foundation of the Old Government, in the Creation of

Man after his Image.'[133] Based on this premise, Baxter deflected criticism about his formulation back to those who argued for a limited atonement: 'And it is no small flaw or errour in their Theology, that deny the Foundation of the whole Government [of Christ], and then cry out, that we make Christ to dye in vain, if he bring not all infallibly to Heaven that he dyed for.'[134]

Because Christ died for all, if any perish it is only because they did not take the remedy offered in Christ.[135] Christ's death has provided for common grace to be extended to all men. If men will but use this common grace, they can draw nearer to Christ than they are now. No man shall be damned for the lack of a Savior to die for him, but for the abusing or refusing of his mercy.[136]

Baxter rightly anticipated that such statements would bring the accusation of Arminianism. He vehemently denied that this was the case with his formulation. 'I avoid the Remonstrants extream,' he asserted, 'I say not that all have sufficient means or Grace to believe, or to Salvation.'[137] Likewise Baxter rejected the idea that God had promised to give men special grace, if they would use their common grace well. Baxter maintains, 'God hath not thought meet to make any such Covenant with Unbelievers; nor to engage himself to them, but when he giveth the first Special Grace for Repenting and Believing he doth it as not pre-engaged to do it; and therefore as *Dominus Absolutus.*'[138]

Baxter believed that his teaching on universal redemption safeguarded the justice of God. 'Do you think,' he argued, 'that it will be the way of glorifying the justice of God in judgment, to have the world know that he condemneth the world, merely because he will condemn them, for that which they never had any more true power to avoid than to make a world? 2. Or will their conscience in hell accuse them or torment them for that which they then know was naturally impossible and caused by God?'[139] This truth also displayed the horrors of hell. Hell is hell precisely because those who are there are those who refused the mercy that was offered them. We cite Baxter's comments here at length:

The consciences of the damned in Hell (which will be God's executioners) will everlastingly torment them for refusing that pardon and Salvation that was so dearly purchased for them, and that Redeemer that expressed so much Love to them, and for not performing so reasonable and easie a condition as Faith. They shall not then have the discovery of an impossibility in the condition, or that Christ never died for them, and never was their Redeemer, and consequently that it was no Sin of theirs to refuse a Redeemer, that was not their Redeemer, and satisfaction that was none for them, I say, they shall not have such discoveries to ease their consciences, and lessen their torments, and make Hell as no Hell to them.[140]

Each man's own conscience will bear witness against him that he rejected the mercy of God which was freely offered.

Most interpreters place Baxter in the Amyraldian school of thought.[141] In light of current theological terminology, it seems equitable to do so. We would argue, however, that it should be done with two caveats. The first regards how Baxter came to hold this position. Most scholars simply assume that Baxter read Amyraut's work and adopted his views.[142] But this is simply not the case! Baxter candidly says that he had developed these views before he read anything from Amyraut or his school. In the Preface to *Certain Disputations of Rights to Sacraments*, Baxter answers the charge, made by Ludovicus Molinaeus,[143] that Baxter was Amyraldus's 'only proselyte in England'.[144] Because this point often is misunderstood, we cite Baxter at length as he proceeds to prove Molinaeus guilty of two mistakes. As to the issue of him being the *only* proselyte, Baxter asks,

Whether this Learned man know the judgement of all England? I meet with so many of Amyraldus mind in the point of Universal Redemption, that if I might judge of all the rest by those of my acquaintance, I should conjecture that half the Divines in England are of that opinion.... Its famously known that Bishop Usher was for it, that Bishop Davenant, Bishop Carleton, Bishop Hall, Dr. Ward, Dr. Goad, Mr. Balcanquall, being all the Divines that were sent to the Synod of Dort from Britain, were for it: and Davenant, Hall, and Ward, have wrote for it:... And many yet living do ordinarily declare their judgment that way. And are not these more then *unus Baxterus*?[145]

Baxter thus argues that he is not the *only* proselyte; numerous others held to a universal atonement.

Baxter proceeds to argue that if he *were* the only one who held this position, then Amyraldus did not have even *one* proselyte. Why? Because Baxter had written in favor of Universal Redemption before he had ever seen any of Amyraldus's writing! He says,

When this *unus Baxterus* did write a Book for Universal Redemption[146] in this middle sense, before he ever saw either *Amyraldus, Davenant*, or any Writer (except Dr. *Twiss*) for that way, and was ready to publish it, and stopt it on the coming forth of Amyraldus, and was himself brought to this judgement, by reading Dr. *Twiss*,[147] and meditating of it, and had in print so long ago professed these things, whether this Learned man should after all this publish to the world, that I am *Amyraldus* proselyte?[148]

Lest the reader think that Baxter is merely denying the source of his views to escape criticism, Baxter goes on to tell why he took the time to straighten out the matter: 'I speak but as to the truth of the report; for as to the reputation of the thing, I should think it a great benefit if I had the opportunity of sitting at the feet of so judicious a man as I perceive Amyraldus to be.'[149]

The second caveat is that Baxter's final formulation differed from Amyraut's. Baxter helped shield his view from the criticism of inconsistency (leveled against the Amyraldian position) with his emphasis on God as both *Dominus* and Rector. God's general benevolence to the world is part of his governing; his special love to the elect is part of his secret plan as *Dominus*. Man should not speculate about God's secret will – he should instead live under the light of God's revealed will. Man's role is not to question, but to obey the laws set forth by his Governor. Because of this modification, Packer has titled Baxter's viewpoint an 'improved Amyraldianism'.[150] We would concur with this appellation, as long as it is not presented in such a manner that infers that Baxter learned this doctrine directly from Amyraut. Perhaps the term Baxterianism is a worthwhile one after all!

Holding to a universal atonement had other attractive features to Baxter. He argued that one had to believe that Christ died equally for the entire race in order to give authenticity to the invitation to come to him. Baxter tells us that Archbishop Ussher held to universal redemption and that during a conversation with Baxter, Ussher had stated, 'we cannot rationally offer Christ to sinners on any other grounds.'[151] Because the offer was genuine, Baxter taught, the doctrine of universal redemption was a 'rich mine of consolation'.[152]

Baxter's doctrine of the atonement was 'packaged' in the political method. The governmental theory of the Atonement fit the political method like a hand in a glove, and the fact of an unlimited atonement provided the foundation upon which Christ could exercise his rule as governor. But there are yet more pieces to the puzzle. The Amyraldian scheme wedded together the concepts of universal atonement and election. We now turn to Baxter's teachings on the second of these concepts, that of election. Baxter speaks of election in terms befitting the strictest of Calvinists:

> And if besides all the mercy that God showeth to others, he do antecedently and positively elect certain persons, by an absolute decree, to overcome all their resistances of his Spirit, and to draw them to Christ, and by Christ to himself, by such a power and way as shall infallibly convert and save them, and not leave the success of his mercy, and his Son's preparations, to the bare uncertainty of the mutable will of depraved man, what is there in this that is injurious to any others?[153]

Though Christ has died for all men and offers eternal life if they will but believe in him, only the elect actually will do so.[154]

God's gift of special grace to the elect was decreed from eternity.[155] The decree of election was by necessity free, not based on any foreseen merit in the elect.[156] God, of his own good pleasure, absolutely decreed from eternity to give to certain definite, chosen individuals saving faith in Christ. They are elected, 'not *a Posteriore*, upon the foresight of their Faith: but *a priore* before and without any moving cause or condition in themselves.'[157] Baxter asserts the truth that it is *specific individuals* who are the objects of election, 'as against the Arminian Conceit, that it is only Believers in General, or All men Conditionally if they will Believe ... without determining infallibly of any certain Individuals till he foresaw that themselves would make the difference by Believing.'[158]

Baxter's statements on election are straightforward and precise. Faith is only given to the elect; the non-elect will not be saved. Yet despite Baxter's clarity at this point, some interpreters misinterpret his position.[159] A common maxim assigned to Baxter's views is 'that the gospel net is sure to catch all the elect, and free to catch as many more as it can'.[160] This erroneous view is put forth in Irvonwy Morgan's work, *The Nonconformity of Richard Baxter*:

> Where Baxter really differed from the Calvinists of his day was in the fact that he did not believe that God willed that anyone should be damned, but he thought that God did will that the elect should be saved, as a kind of extra grace, as it were. *The elect were lucky, but many others would be saved as well*, and those who were damned, were damned not because they could not be saved, but because they would not be saved.[161]

Baxter nowhere asserted that 'many others would be saved as well'. Morgan misread Baxter at this point. Baxter believed that Christ's death provided every man with an opportunity to be saved if he *would* choose Christ, but Baxter knew that only the elect would so choose.

The election of men to salvation is absolute and not conditioned on God's foreknowledge of their repentance. The same cannot be said, however, for damnation. God predestinates men to destruction 'only on the foresight of their wilful sin'.[162] Since so much of damnation consists in sin itself,[163] it is therefore primarily the work of the sinner himself;[164] there is 'no Act of God in the execution, so far no man can prove any Positive Act of Volition or Decree'.[165]

So even though Baxter held to election, he clearly denied reprobation. Claiming that the word 'reprobation' is never used at all as an act of God,[166] Baxter aptly summarizes his views on this subject:

> The conceit and supposition of many, that Election and Reprobation are such perfect contraries ... and that God willeth in the one just as he doth in the other, End and means, for matter and order, is a gross mistake ... many more have shewed, that God predestinateth men to Faith, and perseverance, and to Glory, and not only to Glory upon the foresight of faith and perseverance: But that he predestinateth or decreeth men to damnation, only on the foresight of final impenitence and infidelity, but not to Impenitence or Infidelity it self.[167]

Baxter does note, however, that 'election implyeth that some are not elect'[168] but asserts that God is free to deal with his creation as he sees fit. If he gives grace to some and not to others, who can call him into question? None will perish but those who refuse God's mercy.[169]

To anticipate our forthcoming discussion on Justification, it remains here briefly to mention two other key issues in Reformed theology. The first of these is effectual or irresistible grace. God has not only decreed the elect to salvation, but also, as a fruit of Christ's death, has infallibly and unconditionally given them faith as well.[170] Election is therefore completely of God, unaffected by any act of man. The second issue is that of the perseverance of the saints. Baxter has this to say: 'To others he giveth his Spitit [sic] to work in such seasons, manner and measure, as shall infallibly prevail, 1. For to bring them to Faith; and 2. To further Sanctification and Perseverance. In a word he useth such means with all his Elect as shall infallibly succeed, to bring them to Faith and Perseverance; and so much with all the World, as shall leave them without excuse.'[171] Baxter found comfort in the fact that 'Christ is the author and finisher of our faith' and that 'the certainty of the salvation of his elect doth lie more on his undertaking and resolution infallibly to accomplish their salvation, than upon our wisdom, or the stability of our mutable free-wills'.[172]

Yet Baxter was troubled by the fact that he could not find the doctrine of perseverance clearly taught in the ancient church.[173] Therefore, even though he himself maintained it, he refused to make it a fundamental of the faith or a necessary belief for the concord of the Churches.[174] Baxter ends with his own resolution: 'For my part I will labour as earnestly as I can to make sure both that I am sincere and justified and shall persevere, and I will be none of those that shall command, commend, or encourage causeless troublesome fears.'[175]

3

CONTROVERSY REGARDING JUSTIFICATION

The part of Baxter's theological formulation which drew the most criticism was his teaching on justification. We have noted his contact with Antinomianism in the army which caused him to reformulate his basic theological positions. He abhorred the fact that many of the soldiers were following the Antinomian Saltmarsh in affirming that 'Christ hath repented and believed for us, and that we must no more question our faith and repentance, than Christ'.[1] If this is true, then man is totally passive.[2] Repentance and faith have nothing to do with justification. Faith becomes merely the belief that we have already been justified.[3] If men are 'bound to Believe that Christ Believed for them, and Repented for them',[4] then they may attain complete assurance of justification without ever having actually repented themselves. No sin could ever make them doubt their justification.[5]

Baxter recoiled in horror from such assertions and set himself to answer this erroneous teaching.[6] A careful study of Scripture, especially Matthew 25, led him to his new formulation.[7] He published these new ideas in a book, *Aphorismes of Justification*, a work which cost him 'more than any other' by putting him upon 'long and tedious Writings'.[8] He only intended it to be against the Antinomians, but it sounded strange to many others who read it.[9]

Baxter benefited from the comments of many, among them John Warren, George Lawson, Christopher Cartwright, John Wallis, and John Tombes. The insight they shared with him, plus the tedious study he engaged in to answer their objections, proved a great advantage to Baxter.[10] Even though he publicly retracted the *Aphorismes* because of 'the crudity and unfitness of many expressions',[11] he later claimed that he felt 'the main doctrine of it sound'.[12]

What truths did Baxter 'discover' about justification? How did he formulate them? Clearly Baxter wanted to present the doctrine of justification in such a way that it would not lead to Antinomianism. At this point his dependence on the political method proved extremely useful. Note his following comments:

> It was the Army and Sectarian Antinomians (more fitly called Libertines) who first called me in the year 1645 and 1646 to study better than I had done the Doctrine of the Covenants and Laws of God, of Redemption and Justification: I fetcht my first resolving thoughts from no Book but the Bible, specially Matt. 5, and 6, and 25. *Grotius de Satisfactione* next gave me more light. While I was considering many mens friendly Animadversions on my Aphorismes, and answering some (that more differed from each other than from me), it increased light, especially the Animadversions of Mr. George Lawson.[13]

Here we see the importance of understanding Baxter's use of the political method. Without this background, the significance of the above statement can be overlooked all too easily. When Baxter sat down to read his Bible, he did so with the outlandish statements of the Antinomians still ringing in his ears. Undoubtedly several questions were plaguing his troubled mind. Was this the end result of Reformed theology? Does Calvinism ultimately lead to Antinomianism?

Others had argued against antinomian license by maintaining that works would always follow genuine faith, but Baxter's dependence on the political method led him to package his formulation somewhat differently. When he read Scripture through the magnifying glass of political theology, the light dawned on him.[14] Using the political method, he framed the scene of the Last Judgment found in Matthew 25 in terms of seventeenth-century English political structures.[15] We must think of the Last Judgment happening just as judicial process happens here: the evidence is examined, and *there* and *then*, on the basis of the evidence being examined, a determination is made.

Works, then, the prescribed expression of faith, are absolutely necessary for justification at the last judgment. What better way to thwart the Antinomian's false teaching? To say simply that works followed genuine faith seemed to be too weak to counter the Antinomians. But if works were necessary for justification at the final judgment, this would certainly offset their lack of emphasis on the Christian's obedience. This led to Baxter's formulation of two justifications. The first happens when a man believes, but the final justification takes place at the Day of Judgment. Note his mention of the two justifications when he discusses the conditions of the Covenant of Grace: 'whosoever will Repent, Thankfully and heartily accept Jesus Christ to be his Saviour, Teacher, King and Head, believing him to be the Redeemer, and will Love him (and God in him) above all, and obey him sincerely, to the Death, shall *upon his first acceptance be Justified* and Adopted, and *upon his perseverance be justified at Judgment*, saved from Hell, and Glorified.'[16] We now look at Baxter's teaching on each of these justifications.

The 'first' justification took place as a result of repentance and faith. What, in Baxter's view, was faith?[17] We have already noted how he taught that God infallibly would give faith to His elect. But how was one to distinguish true faith from false faith? How could a man know if his faith was genuine?

John English has shown that Puritan theologians discussed faith in three different aspects: *notitia* (knowledge of facts), *assensus* (consent or persuasion), and *fiducia* (trust or confidence; an act of the will).[18] English notes there was no unanimity on which of these were necessary for there to be 'true faith':

The faith which justifies is defined in different ways by different Puritan theologians. Several Puritan divines think of justifying faith in terms of assent to the promises of God plus a hesitant application of them to one's self, a combination which is called 'weak faith.' Other theologians identify justifying faith with 'strong faith,' that wholehearted application of the Gospel promised to one's self which excludes all fear of punishment and all doubt concerning one's salvation. Still other Puritan divines state that *fiducia* or the individual's reliance upon the mercy of God is true justifying faith.[19]

Baxter clearly falls among those who defined saving faith primarily as *fiducia*. His concept of faith combined both the understanding and the will.[20] He distinguished between a historical belief and true saving faith,[21] between 'bare opinion' and 'practical trust'.[22]

True faith is an act of all three faculties of man, the vital power, the understanding, and the will.[23] True faith will always result in action.[24] The object of one's faith must be Christ in all of his offices as Prophet, Priest, and King. We must accept Christ as both our Savior and Lord.[25] Not to do so is to fail to believe in the Christ of Scripture.[26] Until one has this faith, one has no part in Christ. Words mean nothing. 'In vain do you boast of Christ,' Baxter claimed, 'if you are not true believers.'[27] Faith without works is dead.[28]

A failure to grasp this trusting aspect of faith had led to the Antinomian error. They do not understand, Baxter asserts, 'that receiving Christ as Lord is an essential act of justifying Faith, nor that the refusal of his Government is an essential part of damning unbelief.'[29] In the *Aphorismes of Justification*, Baxter remarks that Saltmarsh mistakes faith for nothing but a 'persuasion more or less of God's love'.[30] Baxter saw this deficient view of faith as the Antinomian 'master-point'.

Where then does repentance fit in? Repentance is the other side of the coin of faith. 'One is denominated from the object turned from,' Baxter asserted, 'and the other from the object turned to.'[31] The combination of repentance and faith, given by God to the elect but exercised by them in their persons, resulted in the first justification.

So far so good. But Baxter raised eyebrows with what he had to say after this. The standard Reformed position held to only one justification – at the moment of belief. Works should follow as the fruit of faith, but they in no way were a part of justification. Baxter argued for a second justification which would take place at the judgment. In this justification works did matter. The believer had to demonstrate his own obedience or 'evangelical righteousness' to be justified on that final day. This avowal of two justifications is no part of the mainstream Reformed perspective. Calvinists consistently have emphasized that there is only one justification, and that takes place here and now when the individual believes. What takes place at the final judgment is simply a ratification of what took place long before. Most were quite uncomfortable with mention of 'our own evangelical righteousness'.

Was Baxter's position substantially different from the standard Reformed perspective, or were the differences merely verbal? Some quickly answer yes, that Baxter's position was fundamentally different from the standard reformed teaching that works are the fruit of faith.[32] I am convinced that, while there were unique features in Baxter's formulation, when seen in light of his entire theology, the differences were *largely* verbal.[33] I will attempt to demonstrate this by means of a five-fold approach. I will first highlight why Baxter's formulation seems different. Second, I will verbalize what I believe Baxter was trying to protect in his formulation. Third, I will examine where Baxter in one sense failed in his formulations. Fourth, I will show that, when seen in light of his entire theological system, his position was substantially the same as the 'orthodox' position. Finally, in light of this discussion I will proceed to critique those interpreters of Baxter who have claimed a great divergence in his teaching.

Baxter has been charged, both in his day and since, with significant departures from Reformed orthodoxy in his teaching on justification. Did he in fact make such departures, or did he teach substantially the same thing but phrase it in a different manner? Why does his teaching seem different? The first reason can be found in Baxter's use of terminology. He uses the term 'justification' in more than one sense: sometimes in the orthodox sense[34] and sometimes in the same manner as others would use the term sanctification.[35]

This dual usage is made clear by his response to someone's assertion that 'we are justified only by the first act of faith; and all our believing afterwards to the end of our lives are no justifying acts at all'. Baxter concedes, 'if the question be only about the name of justifying, if you will take it only for our first change into a state of righteousness by pardon, it is true.'[36] But he goes on to emphasize the necessity of continued acts of faith to bring us safely to the ultimate justification at the final judgment.[37] Allison perceptively notes Baxter's ambiguity in his terminology for justification: 'To justify, for Baxter, can mean variously: to forgive initially, to judge in final judgment, to make righteous, to treat as righteous, to give faith and repentance, or any of a number of combinations of the same.'[38] The problem is that Baxter does not always bother to tell the reader in which sense he is using the term, and therefore his formulations were ripe for being misunderstood. This will become clearer as we proceed.

Baxter placed his greatest emphasis on the final justification, the justification that will take place on Judgment Day. He describes what will take place:

> This is the day of the believers' full justification. They were, before, made just, and esteemed just, and by faith justified in law; and this, to some, evidenced to their consciences. But now they shall both, by apology, be maintained just; and, by sentence, pronounced just actually, by the lively voice of the Judge himself; which is the most perfect justification...[39]

Baxter elsewhere calls this final justification 'the chief and most eminent Justification'.[40] It is plain he was formulating this in terms of his political theory. He says that to deny 'Justification by sentence of Judgement' (among other things) 'is to deny Principles in Politicks'.[41]

Two things must be said in response to Baxter's formulation. First, his concept of a justification in judgment is not outside the mainstream of Reformed thinking. James Buchanan, whose treatise on *Justification* is regarded as a classic in Reformed circles, acknowledges that in Scripture justification is used in more than one sense. He makes a distinction between actual and declarative justification, noting the context of the final judgment on the last day. Buchanan says, 'No one will be actually justified then, who was not justified before: but every believer will be justified *declaratively*, when he is openly acknowledged and acquitted by the sentence of the Judge.'[42] I maintain that Baxter would have little quarrel with this statement.

Second, others have argued, as Baxter did, that the primary sense of justification in the New Testament is eschatological. New Testament scholar George E. Ladd maintains that justification in Paul is an eschatological doctrine.[43] He explains:

> God is the righteous lawgiver and judge; and it is only in the final judgment when God will render a judicial verdict upon each man that his righteousness or his unrighteousness will be finally determined. Only God, who has set the norm for human conduct, can determine whether a man has met that norm and is therefore righteous. The issue of the final judgment will be either a declaration of righteousness that will mean acquittal from all guilt, or conviction of unrighteousness and subsequent condemnation.[44]

Therefore, although justification has already taken place in the present, it 'primarily means acquittal at the final judgment'.[45] This seems to me to be little different from what Baxter was trying to emphasize.

Another point of controversy in Baxter's formulation was his alleged denial of the imputation of the active obedience of Christ to the believer. But as we shall see, this was not as much of a denial as it was a refusal to affirm what the Antinomians were claiming by their interpretation of the doctrine.[46] Watson explains:

> The Antinomian doctrine which Baxter was opposing said that Christ so represented the elect that his righteousness is imputed to us as ours; as if we ourselves had been what

he was, that is, perfectly obedient to the law of God, and had done what he did as perfectly righteous. Yet, as Baxter rightly observed, it is nowhere stated in Scripture that Christ's personal righteousness is imputed to us.[47]

Baxter lamented the fact that others, 'seeing the pernicious consequences of this [Antinomian] opinion, deny all imputed righteousness of Christ to us, and write many reproachful volumes against it.'[48]

In light of these two extremes, Baxter gives what he believes is the correct sense of Christ's imputation. Christ's obedience was important in that by it our perfect obedience is no longer necessary for our salvation.[49] Thus while we receive the benefits from his obedience, we ourselves are not 'reputed the legal performers ourselves ... or by divine estimation or imputation, to have ourselves in and by Christ fulfilled the law.[50] To deviate from this position in either direction was to err:

> They heinously err, who deny Christ's Righteousness to be so far imputed to us, as to be reputed the meritorious Cause of our Pardon and Right to Life.... And they heinously err, and subvert the Gospel, who say, that Christ's Righteousness is so imputed to us ... [that God] reputeth us to have been perfectly holy, righteous, or obedient in Christ, as our Representer, and so to have our selves fulfilled all righteousness in and by him, and in him to have satisfied Justice, and merited Eternal Life.[51]

Baxter acknowledges the doctrine of justification by imputation, but denies that this is by the direct imputation of Christ's active righteousness. He attacks those who 'divide Christ's Performance into little Parcels, and then say, This Parcel is imputed to me for this use, and that for that use, and by one he merited this, and by the other that.... When ... it was only the entire performance that was the Condition of the Benefits.'[52]

What was he trying to protect in his formulations? One issue was the nature of saving faith. The fact that a great deal of the controversy revolved around the true nature of saving faith is made clear from the following challenge issued by Baxter: 'If you would but grant me, that Justifying faith, as faith, is an Accepting of Christ for King, and Prophet as well as for a Justifier, and consequently that it is a resigning our selves to be ruled by him, as well as to be saved by him, I shall then be content for peace sake to lay by the phrase of Justification by works, though it be Gods own phrase.'[53] Baxter realized that his definition of faith, if properly appropriated, would lead to the same results as what he was striving for in his other formulations.[54]

Another point Baxter wanted to protect was the scriptural teaching on man's responsibility. The Antinomians so stressed the sovereign grace of God in Justification that any activity of man was seen as 'salvation by works'. Some even characterized the act of faith in this manner. While their efforts were noble, the Antinomians failed to do justice to another truth clearly revealed in Scripture – that of human responsibility. Scripture teaches that humans must make a commitment. Does that response save one? No, Baxter would answer, but one cannot be saved without it. A man only moves as God moves him. Psychologically the man is doing something, but theologically God is doing it.

The Antinomians had lost this tension, however. The denial of any necessary human action in salvation, while for worthy reasons, was misplaced. Baxter realized that there were conditions given in Scripture that a man had to meet before he could be justified: repentance and faith. 'I say,' claims Baxter, 'these conditions must needs be performed, and that by our selves: and who dare deny this?'[55]

But even though the gift is conditional, it is but the condition of *receiving* it that is required on man's part (and that is even 'wrought by him in our selves').[56] Until the condition be performed, no man can be certain that the benefit shall be his.[57] Baxter says: 'Faith is neither sufficient, nor is Faith without Christs legal righteousness: And Christ is sufficient *Hypothetically*, but will not be effectual to our Justification without Faith (and repentance.)'[58] Note that the Antinomians were teaching that Christ *was* effectual to our justification without our faith and repentance.

This was why Baxter attacked the Antinomians so fiercely. They denied that each individual must personally believe and repent in response to Christ's call. The necessity of faith and repentance is so obviously taught throughout Scripture that Baxter had no sympathy for those who denied it. Indeed, he felt that in the teaching of the Antinomians that 'Satan transformed himself into an angel of light'.[59] This helps put into perspective his following statement concerning the dangers of Antinomianism:

> For I profess considerately, that I do not know in all the body of popery concerning merits, justification, human satisfactions, assurance, or any other point about grace, for which we unchurch them, that they err half so dangerously as Saltmarsh, and such antinomians, do in this one point, when they say, That Christ hath repented and believed for us; meaning it of that faith and repentance which he hath made the conditions of our salvation. And that we must no more question our own faith, than we must question Christ the object of it.[60]

This statement is even more remarkable when seen in light of Baxter's attacks on the papists! The papists were dangerous, but the Antinomians were deadly.

Baxter argued that this sense of man's responsibility applies not only to a man's first believing, but to his ultimate justification in judgment as well. If it is only those who persevere who shall be saved, then one's certainty of salvation is only as good as one's perseverance. Note Buchanan's comments on this issue:

> Some have imagined that the doctrine of a free Justification now by grace, through faith alone, is inconsistent with that of a future judgment according to works.... But there is no real inconsistency between the two doctrines. They relate to different parts of the divine procedure; and are equally necessary, – the one for the immediate relief of the sinner's conscience, – the other for the regulation of the believer's conduct.[61]

Baxter would give his wholehearted agreement. If he tended to place more emphasis on the final 'justification by works', it was because the Antinomians forced him to do so.

Baxter was attacked for affirming that 'faith is imputed to us for righteousness'. But note what he was and was not saying in affirming it. The reason he used the terminology, he tells us, is that he found it throughout Scripture.[62] In fact, he claimed, 'nothing in Scripture is more plain then that Faith it self is said to be accounted to us for Righteousness; and not only Christs own righteousness: He that will not take this for proof, must expect no Scripture proof of any thing from me.'[63] He asks tersely, 'Whether Scripture phrase or mans invented phrase be the better and safer in a controvertible case? And next Whether you should deny or quarrel at the Scripture saying, that [faith is imputed to us for righteousness] and not rather confute our misexpounding it, if we do so?'[64]

Calvinists disliked Baxter's terminology because it suggested that faith was in some way meritorious. Baxter emphasizes that when he uses the term, he is not using it in this way: 'And that faith is imputed for Righteousness, plainly meaneth but this, that Christ having merited and satisfied for us, all that is now required on our part to denominate (or primarily constitute) us Righteous, is to be true Believers in him, or true Christians.'[65] Baxter had similar problems with his use of the term 'evangelical righteousness'. Here let us not misunderstand what Baxter was saying. What he is calling our 'evangelical righteousness' is simply our enacting the conditions set out by God: 'I say that the performance of these conditions is our Evangelical righteousness.'[66] To those who attacked his terminology, Baxter retorted, 'Yea, while they make Faith, Repentance and Holiness but Signs and Evidences of our right to Life-eternal, they thereby allow it some place in Justification.'[67]

Just what will take place on the Day of Judgment? Will the thrust of that day be to judge Christ's performance? Absolutely not, replies Baxter. On that day the issue will be 'whether we have part in him or not, and so are to be justified by the gospel covenant, through his merits against the legal covenant; and whether we have fulfilled the conditions of the pardoning covenant or not'.[68] He says:

> In Judgement, if you be accused to have been finally impenitent, or an Infidel, will you not plead your personal faith and repentance, to justifie you against that accusation? or shall any be saved that saith, (I did not repent or believe, but Christ did for me?) If it be said that (Christs satisfaction is sufficient; but whats that to thee that performedst not the conditions of his Covenant, and therefore hast no part in it?) Will you not produce your faith and repentance for your Justification against this charge, and so to prove your Interest in Christ? Nay is it like to be the great business of that day to enquire whether Christ have done his part or not?[69]

We see clearly then what Baxter was trying to protect. The Antinomians said faith and repentance were unnecessary. Baxter insisted that they were necesssary.

I would also argue that Baxter has picked up on a Scriptural emphasis often missed by those who maintain the perseverance of the elect. Baxter would argue, as would any Calvinist, that Scripture teaches the perseverance of the elect.[70] But Scripture is also full of warnings about the dangers of falling away, about making one's calling and election sure, about living a life of holiness.[71] Baxter argued that since these are found in Scripture, they must be there for a reason. God, in his wisdom, knew that man would need not only the motivation of love but also that of fear to persevere.

This brings us back to the mystery of divine sovereignty and human responsibility. Baxter knew that God would cause all the elect to persevere. But how would he do it? Baxter was certain that one of the means was the giving of warnings. He cautions, 'take heed of separating what God hath joined. If God, by putting in your nature the several passions of hope, fear, love, &c. and by putting a holiness into these passions, by sanctifying grace, and by putting both promises and dreadful threatenings into his word: I say, if God by all these means hath given you several motives to obedience, take heed of separating them.'[72] But God commands no duty which he is not ready to help us to perform, so 'that he that commandeth us to Believe, Repent and Love him, doth by effectual grace cause all his Elect to Believe, Repent, and Love him, and sincerely to obey him, and persevere herein.'[73]

Baxter's sad experience showed him that even some who appeared to be strong believers would ultimately fall away.[74] This helps explain why Baxter asserted that 'many holy, watchful, and obedient christians, are yet uncertain of their salvation, even then when they are certain of their justification and sanctification; and that because they are uncertain of their perseverance and overcoming; for a man's certainty of his salvation can be no stronger than is his certainty of enduring to the end and overcoming.'[75] He took very seriously the 'danger of falling away'. Again, the Antinomians would have asserted that if a person were indeed one of the elect, then nothing he does after his justification matters, as God will infallibly bring him to heaven. We see Baxter's 'contingency in the midst of certainty' clearly in the following passage:

> Let me also give you this warning, That you must never expect so much assurance on earth, as shall set you above the possibility of the loss of heaven, or above all apprehensions of real danger of your miscarrying.... God hath decreed that none of his elect shall finally or totally fall away and perish; and therefore their so falling and perishing is not future; that is, it is a thing that shall never come to pass. But God never decreed that it should be utterly impossible, and therefore it still remaineth possible, though it shall never come to pass.[76]

Despite the truth of perseverance, Baxter warns that a man in a relapsed state should be wary about venturing his salvation 'wholly on this supposing that he were certain that he was once sincere'.[77] 'Though he have no reason to think that God is changeable,' Baxter acknowledges, 'or justification will be lost, yet he hath reason enough to question whether ever he were a true believer, and so were ever justified.'[78]

When Baxter maintained that 'evangelical righteousness' was no less necessary for man's salvation than the righteousness of Christ, he was attempting to formulate his theology in such a way that it did not relieve man of his responsibility (though God would provide the will and the power for the work).[79] It was the same emphasis that he made to men in saying, 'YOU must turn,' knowing full well that God caused the elect to turn.[80]

Why then did Baxter's formulation 'fail'? Why was it attacked by even those outside of Antinomian circles? We find the key again in Baxter's use of the political method. We have noted his emphasis on the final judgment, and his use of the term 'justification' for what takes place at the judgment. To those who held to a single justification at the moment of belief, this teaching sounded as if it had come from Rome. His use of the term 'evangelical righteousness' was also misunderstood. His opponents connected righteousness to the concept of merit; whereas Baxter explicitly denied that anything man did was meritorious in the same sense as Christ's works.

The political method caused Baxter to focus primarily on God as Rector. God, in His wisdom, knew that man needed not only love, but also fear to motivate him.[81] God rules by his laws, threatenings, and promises, which he will bring to pass. 'It is not a painted fire that he threateneth,'[82] Baxter warned. Judgment is a necessary part of government. Laws are mere shadows if they are not executed. Here his dependence on the political method caused him to overlook the radically different nature of the relationship between God and unbelievers and God and believers. Though he recognizes one of God's relations to man is that of Benefactor, Baxter seems to focus inordinately on God as Governor. Thus, instead of relating as a child to a Father, Baxter too often paints the Christian life as a subject relating to a Governor.[83] For Baxter, the primary reason for good works seems to be because God has ordered us to do them as necessary to our final justification.[84]

The Westminster Confession[85] provides the balance that Baxter lacked in his formulation:

> God doth continue to forgive the sins of those that are justified; and although they can never fall from the state of justification, yet they may by their sins fall under God's fatherly displeasure, and not have the light of his countenance restored unto them,

until they humble themselves, confess their sins, beg pardon, and renew their faith and repentance.[86]

This is not to say that Baxter ignored the emphasis on God as Benefactor or Father. In his *Divine Life*, Baxter penned rapturous thoughts about our relation to God as our loving Father.[87] But overall, he seems to have taught a view of the Christian life that called Christians to relate to God more as Ruler than as Father.

Baxter's theology must always be interpreted in light of his battles with Antinomianism.[88] Baxter was running from Antinomianism at a time when most Calvinists were running from Arminianism.[89] His 'narrow escape' from the perils of Antinomianism caused him to attack anything which seemed to support it.[90] If he did indeed run to the other extreme, it was only because he felt compelled to flee from Antinomianism.[91] His theology tended to emphasize what the Antinomians denied, and thus seemed to lack balance.[92]

Given all the confusion in Baxter's formulations, why do I argue that his position was substantially the same as the 'orthodox' Reformed position? A dominant reason is that Baxter refuses to give any merit whatsoever to man in any of these necessary actions on man's part. 'No work or act of man is any true proper cause of his justification,' Baxter avows, 'neither Principal or Instrumental. The highest Interest that they can have, is but to be a condition of our Justification.'[93] Lest he be misunderstood, he states it even more strongly: 'No man can say that he is a Co-ordinate Con-cause with Christ in his Justification: or that he hath the least degree of a satisfactory or Meritorious Righteousness, which may bear any part in co-ordination with Christs righteousness, for his justification or salvation.'[94]

Not only does Baxter give no merit to man in the 'Second Justification', he also maintains that 'Perseverance in Faith, and a State of Justification was intended infallibly and certainly to be given to them [the elect].'[95] 'To purpose all persevering believers to salvation,' Baxter says, 'and not to purpose faith and perseverance absolutely to any particular persons, is to purpose salvation absolutely to none at all.'[96] God gives the actual gifts of faith and perseverance, not merely legal rights to them.[97] Salvation is certain for the Elect, because it is for these that Christ died with a 'Special Intention of bringing Infallibly, Immutably, and Insuperably ... to Saving Faith, Justification, and Salvation,'[98] which is what 'our Divines mean by the word (Irresistible)'.[99]

Listen again to Baxter's description of the Day of Judgment in this light:

> But the turning point of the day [of judgment] is yet behind;
> 1. Our allegation of Justification by Christ and the Covenant may be denied. It may be said by the Accuser, that the Covenant justifieth none but penitent Believers, and giveth plenary Right to Glory to none but saints and persevering Conquerors, and that we are none such. Against this Accusation we must be justified or perish; else all the rest will be uneffectual. And here to say, that it is true, I died an impenitent Person, and Infidel, Hypocrite, or Ungodly, but Christ was a penitent Believer for me, or sincere and holy for me, or that he died to pardon this,] all this will be false and vain. Christ's Merits and Satisfaction is not the Righteousness it self which must justifie us against the Accusation; But our own personal Faith, Repentance, sincere Holiness and Perseverance], purchased by Christ, and wrought by the Spirit in us, but thence, our own acts. He that cannot truly say, The accusation is false, I am a true Penitent, Sanctified persevering Believer must be condemned and perish. Thus Faith and Repentance are our Righteousness by which we must thus far be justified.[100]

Note that even though our faith and perseverance were 'purchased by Christ, and wrought by the Spirit in us', it is the fact that they are our *own* acts which justifies us against the charge that we were not a persevering believer. Even though the continuation of our pardon is given but conditionally, 'we shall certainly perform the condition.'[101]

Therefore, when seen in the light of election, perseverance, effectual grace, and giving no merit to man, we conclude that Baxter's teaching on justification is substantially the same position as the standard Reformed position, though in places extremely poorly and even dangerously worded.[102] Because of his political theology terminology, Baxter seemed to be asserting that works count decisively towards a salvation which is not absolutely certain yet. But when viewed in light of the remainder of his theology, the contingency disappears.

Many seem to agree with this conclusion. Fisher indicates that substantially Baxter's position was orthodox, but that he employs different phraseology.[103] Baker stops short of asserting that Baxter made sanctification essential for salvation, instead saying he had a tendency in this direction.[104] Muller cites Bunyan and Baxter as representing 'the limits to which the federal structure could be stretched ... [and delineating] the points beyond which Reformed theology cannot go without becoming on the one hand a metaphysical determinism and on the other a pious voluntarism.'[105] McIntyre says Baxter moved 'toward' the other extreme from Antinomianism and that his writings appear to have 'at least a tincture of legalism'.[106] Clifford argues the differences are primarily from 'terminological ambiguities'.[107]

Yet others charge Baxter with severe departures from Reformed orthodoxy in his teaching on Justification. Allison makes a serious charge when he asserts that, 'according to Baxter, the imputation of our own faith is the formal cause of justification.'[108] Here is what Baxter has to say on the issue:

> No act of mans, no not faith itself can justifie as an act or work ... and therefore it is not faith as faith, that is, as it is an apprehension of Christ or recumbency on him, that Justifyeth: nor yet as an Instrument thus acting. *The nature of the act is but its aptitude to its office or justifying Interest, and not the formal cause of it.* No work or act of man is any true proper cause of his justification, neither Principal or Instrumental. The highest Interest that they can have, is but to be a condition of our Justification...[109]

Allison has misread Baxter at this point. Baxter did not teach the 'error' with which Allison charges him.[110]

Leo Solt charges Baxter with the error of teaching Christians to work '*for* life and salvation and not *from* life and salvation'.[111]

Solt failed to see that in Baxter's formulation, the '*for* life' was nothing more than performing the conditions of the covenant. Baxter emphasized that while Christ would do his work, and enable his people to do theirs, it is wrong to say that Christ does their work for them. 'He [Christ] believes not, repents not,' Baxter said, 'but worketh these in them; that is, enableth and exciteth them to do it.'[112] This was simply another of Baxter's attempts to counter the Antinomian teaching that Christ has done all the work and we merely need to recognize that fact. Was Baxter's statement poorly worded? Without a doubt. Is it heretical? No, not when seen in light of what he was trying to protect in his formulation. This again comes down to the issue of Baxter wanting to protect man's responsibility under the umbrella of God's sovereignty.

Much ink was spilled over the controversy concerning justification, and most of it was spilled in vain. Baxter's reformulation of justification in terms of the political method confused his opponents and caused them largely to misinterpret what he was teaching. He in no way was advocating that anything man did was meritorious; he was, however, insisting that man had to do something! Christ would not repent and believe for the Christian. Though God would give the gift of faith to the elect, they still had to exercise it.

We thus conclude this journey through Baxter's teaching on the theological foundation for conversion. We have seen his views on man, created and fallen. We have observed Baxter's teaching on the atonement of Christ and on election and perseverance. We have analyzed the controversy which arose over justification. Having laid this foundation, we are now prepared to examine Baxter's teaching on conversion.

4

THE PROCESS OF CONVERSION

'If therefore you care whether you are saved or damned, it concerneth you to make both your calling and election sure, 2 Pet. 1. 10. Make but your calling sure, and you need not make any question of your election. Make sure that you are converted, and hold fast what you have, and then you may be certain you shall be saved. You begin at the wrong end, if you would first ask whether you are elected, that you may know whether you shall be saved; but you must first try whether you are converted and saved from the power of sin, and then you may certainly gather that you are elected and shall be saved from hell. Will you begin at the top of the ladder and not the bottom?' (Richard Baxter, II:496, TCon [1657]).

'Faith entereth at the understanding; but it hath not all its essential parts, and is not the gospel faith indeed, till it hath possessed the will. The heart of faith is wanting, till faith hath taken possession of the heart' (Richard Baxter, II:623, DP [1658]).

'But I understood at last that God breaketh not all men's hearts alike' (Richard Baxter, *Reliquiae Baxterianae*, I, 7).

'Except ye be converted, and become as little children, ye shall not enter into the kingdom of heaven.'[1] The Puritans took these words of Jesus Christ quite seriously. Should anyone question the need for conversion when we have such a clear statement telling us of its necessity?[2] If you believe Christ, you must believe that salvation is impossible without conversion.[3] Not only Christ's words but all of Scripture is directed to convert men from sin to God. Would God have made conversion the main thrust of his Word, unless it was necessary?[4] A man may profess to be in Christ, but as long as he remains unconverted, he is not a 'true christian'.[5]

Man needs to be converted because all men by nature are children of wrath. As long as a man remains unconverted, he is loathsome and abominable to God.[6] Man's denial of this fact only increases his danger. If a man in the midst of trouble puts his eyes out, does that make him safe because he can no longer see the danger?[7] The unconverted man lacks pardon for his sins. Should he not live in fear, when one unpardoned sin will condemn him as surely as one stab in his heart will kill him?[8] Surely the unconverted are in a pitiful state: they are slaves of Satan, they cannot truly please God, they live in continual danger of damnation.[9] They have no grounds for even an hour's peace and comfort, but instead have reason to live in continual terror.[10]

How then is a man to escape such a dangerous condition? In chapter 2 we examined Baxter's teaching on sin and on the atoning death of Christ to satisfy for man's sin. Christ died for all, but until an individual actually exercises faith and repentance, he or she remains under judgment. We saw how Baxter emphasized election, effectual grace, and perseverance. How did these concepts actually work themselves out in the lives of people? How did someone actually become converted? We have seen how the basis for conversion was provided in the grace of God and the death of Christ. We now turn to Baxter's teaching on the efficient cause of conversion: the Holy Spirit.

The Efficient Cause of Conversion: The Holy Spirit

Baxter acknowledges that the word 'conversion' can be used in an active sense to indicate what man does, or in a passive sense to indicate the change that occurs.[11] Even though Scripture often speaks of conversion in the active sense as man's act ('except ye convert yourselves'), it is proper to translate it as passive ('be converted'), because God is the one who causes man's will to turn.[12] Baxter explains further:

> So that conversion actively taken, as it is the work of the Holy Ghost, is a work of the Spirit of Christ, by the doctrine of Christ, by which he effectually changeth men's minds, and heart, and life from the creature to God in Christ: conversion, as it is our work, is the work of man, wherein by the effectual grace of the Holy Ghost, he turneth his mind and heart, and life from the creature to God in Christ. And conversion as taken passively, is the sincere change of a man's mind, heart, and life from the creature to God in Christ, which is wrought by the Holy Ghost, through the doctrine of Christ, and by himself thus moved by the Holy Ghost.[13]

Even when conversion is referred to in the active sense, it is still not man doing the work; he is only moving as he is being moved by the Holy Spirit. But yet man does have a part. It is not the Holy Spirit that does the believing, it is the man himself who believes (though that belief is caused by the Holy Spirit).

Without the Holy Spirit's regenerative work there is no salvation.[14] Until he does his work, man is dead, blind, and indifferent.[15] Through him man is illuminated and converted.[16] We took note in our previous discussion that Baxter distinguished between common grace, given to all men as an effect of Christ's death, and special grace, given only to the elect. How did the Spirit convey special grace? How did he bring the elect to faith?

Baxter taught that the Spirit's actual working was a mystery. While he normally worked through means, the Spirit has freedom to work outside of the normal means if he so chooses. God would not have chosen to base so much of his government on the use of means, if he did not intend to work by them ordinarily. 'But,' Baxter asserts, 'God is the Arbitrary Absolute Lord of all means, and therefore he can change and dispose of them as he pleases, and yet work by them.'[17]

However, man must never expect to be an exception to the rule. God ordinarily does not decree the end without the means.[18] 'Christ never meant to carry Sluggards asleep to Heaven,' Baxter avows, 'but to save them in the use of his appointed means.'[19] Never presume that you will achieve the ends without following the means that God has ordained.[20] Those who dispute over election fall prey to this danger, saying, 'if God hath chosen us we shall be saved, and if he hath not, we shall not, whatsoever we do: no diligence will save a man that is not elected, and "it is not in him that willeth, nor in him that runneth, but in God that showeth mercy".'[21] Baxter shows them how foolish it would be to follow the same line of reasoning with their bodies as they do with their souls:

It is as true that God hath decreed how many years and days you shall live, as that he hath decreed whether you shall be saved. And I will refer it to your own reason, what you would think of the wit of that man that would give over eating and drinking, and say, God hath decreed how long I shall live, and if he have decreed that I shall live any longer, I shall, whether I eat and drink or not. And if he have not decreed that I shall live, it is not eating nor drinking that will keep me alive?... If you will say, If God have elected me, I shall be saved; and if he have not, I shall not, whatsoever, I do; and therefore I may spare my pains; it is no wiser than to give over eating and drinking, because God hath decreed how long you shall live; or to give over travelling, because God hath decreed whether you shall come to your journey's end. Will you be thus mad about the matters of your trades and callings in the world?... Why do you not give over ploughing and sowing, and say, If God have decreed that I shall have a crop, I shall have one, whether I plough and sow or not; and if he have not, I shall not, whatsoever I do?[22]

He then reminds them that God ordinarily works through his chosen means.[23] The willful neglect of the ordinary means is a great hindrance to conversion.[24] What are these means the Spirit normally uses to bring the elect to faith?

The Means of Conversion: The Word of God
The primary means (subordinate to Christ and the Spirit) which God has ordained is his word, 'especially the public preaching of this word, which is most eminently the standing ordinance of God for man's conversion and edification.'[25] 'Look through the Scripture,' Baxter challenges, 'and see whether the common way of conversion were not by the hearing the word of God preached.'[26] Therefore men always must strive to attend worship services. If a man is at home when the word of God is preached to the congregation, he cannot expect the blessings of it.[27]

Another means which God has appointed for conversion is the reading of his word, and of books designed to help the reader apply God's word to his or her life. Though this must remain subordinate to hearing the word preached, it yet is an 'excellent means', or else 'God would not have appointed it as he hath done'.[28] Baxter recognized that many had come to faith through reading.[29] The word of God therefore is a means unto conversion in any way it is brought before sinful man: hearing, reading, or any other way it can be made known.[30] The word of God pierces the heart, allowing corruption to flow out and grace to flow in.[31]

Other means ordained by God are serious inquiries of those that can instruct us,[32] confession of sin,[33] earnest prayer to God,[34] and spending time with those who fear God.[35] Baxter particularly emphasized the necessity of keeping company with 'heavenly christians'. 'Company hath a transforming power,' he asserted. 'Commonly men are, or seem to be, such as their familiar company is.'[36]

What then is man's 'responsibility' in conversion? It is simply to use the means which God has given him.[37] God ordinarily works through his means; to think he will do otherwise is rash presumption.[38] A man should not expect special grace unless he is using God's common grace well. 'It is God's ordinary way,' Baxter says, 'to give his first special converting Grace, to predisposed Subjects, prepared by his commoner Grace; in which Preparation some Acts of Man have their part: And the unprepared and undisposed cannot equally expect it.'[39] But this does not mean that God has promised to give men special grace, if they would but use their common grace well. Baxter maintains, 'God hath not thought meet to make any such Covenant with Unbelievers; nor to engage himself to them, but when he giveth the first Special Grace for Repenting and Believing he doth it as not pre-engaged to do it; and therefore as *Dominus Absolutus*.'[40]

Baxter is trying to avoid errors on both sides. He refuses to limit God's sovereignty in giving special grace, but on the other hand he wants to avoid a determinism that makes man a mere cipher. Thus while no act of the unconverted man can in any way obligate God to respond to him, yet it is far better for him to use the means than simply to 'sit still and be careless' until God converts him.[41] Baxter warns that if a man will not use the means God has ordained, God may have to use harsher means to bring that man to faith. God may need to 'fetch you in by some sharp affliction', making you wish you had responded to a more 'gentle' call.[42]

Preparation for Conversion: Consideration and Humiliation
How does the process of turning to Christ actually become a reality? Must man wait passively for God to 'take him by storm'? Baxter would answer with a resounding 'no!' He argues, 'It is not Gods usual way, (nor to be expected) to bring these men to Christ at once by one act, or without any preparation, or first bringing them nearer to him.'[43] In addition to the means mentioned above, Baxter emphasized that men should prepare themselves for conversion through the use of consideration and humiliation.

Consideration is a principal means of salvation.[44] When the Spirit of God comes to effectually convert a man, he causes him to consider.[45] The main reason why preachers fail in calling men away from the vanity of the world to serve God is that they cannot bring them to consideration.[46] When a man has lost his way, nothing keeps him from turning back more than his lack of recognition that he has indeed strayed from the path.[47] Even though God must renew and revive the sinful soul, he has ordained that consideration must do much towards this end.[48]

What then is consideration? How is man to practice it? The first thing to do is to seek knowledge. Who can hate sin until he sees it for what it is, or can love God until he knows him to be lovely?[49] Though a man with knowledge can still be a servant of the devil, no man can be the servant of God without knowledge. 'Man may go to hell with knowledge,' Baxter says, 'but he certainly shall go to hell without it.'[50] A man cannot possibly be saved until he knows the way of salvation. The head is the passage to the heart.[51]

Consideration will do much towards making a man willing to be converted. If a man knew that his everlasting life rested on this decision, would he not regard it as important? Baxter inquires: 'Do you think a man that truly knows what heaven is, and what hell is, can still be in doubt whether he should turn or not?'[52] Therefore, Baxter says, a man must consider what God is, what sin is, what Christ is, and what is the end of rejecting him.[53]

How is a man to do this? He is to search the Scriptures to see whether these things be so or not.[54] Baxter told men he desired that they not take anything from him but what he could prove to them from Scripture to be certainly true.[55] Baxter challenged men to examine these things in the light: 'If we offered you bad wares, we should desire a dark shop; and if our gold were light or bad, we would not call for the balance and the touchstone. But when we are sure the things that we speak are true, we desire nothing more than trial.... Error may be a loser by the light; and, therefore, shuns it. But truth is a gainer by it, and therefore seeks it.'[56]

Baxter stimulated 'consideration' in men's minds by asking a series of questions.[57] He challenged them to 'soberly and considerately' compare the gain and the loss that conversion would bring them.[58] If men would only weigh the two options in the balance, they would certainly resolve to turn.[59]

He recognized that fear alone did not motivate men, so he also emphasized the benefits of conversion.[60] 'The poorest member of the household of Christ,' Baxter exclaimed, 'is in a better condition than the greatest king on earth, that is unconverted.'[61] What benefits might a converted man expect? They are numerous: he now has the special love and communion of the people of God,[62] he is delivered from the power of Satan,[63] he is united or joined to Jesus Christ,[64] he is made a member of the true church of Christ,[65] he has a pardon of all the sins that ever he committed,[66] he is reconciled to God,[67] he becomes an adopted son of God,[68] he has the Spirit of Christ within him,[69] all the promises of grace are his,[70] all his duties are pleasing to God,[71] the angels of God are commissioned to attend him,[72] he becomes a true member of the catholic church,[73] Christ is constantly interceding on his behalf,[74] all things will work together for his good,[75] he is prepared for death and judgment,[76] he now can live a life of peace and joy,[77] he will become useful to others[78] , and finally, all of heaven will rejoice over his conversion.[79]

The unconverted lose far more each day than the pleasures of sin can ever repay. 'Ask any of them that have escaped out of that condition that you are in,' Baxter challenges, 'whether they are willing to return?'[80] Preachers are not calling sinners into a miserable life. Quite the contrary! Baxter concludes with an impassioned appeal:

> I dare say I have shown you enough to win the heart of any man that is not obstinately blind and wicked. If you would be rich, I have showed you the only riches; if you would be honourable, it is only conversion that can make you so; if you would have pleasure, I have showed you the way to pleasure, and how you may be possessed even of your Master's joy. In a word, if you would be happy, I have showed you the only way to happiness; a life of peace and safety hath been offered you; a life of honour and pleasure hath been offered you; and remember that it was offered you. If you refuse it, remember that you might have been happy if you would.[81]

Certainly a reasonable man, one not willfully blinded, would recognize this.

Other things to be considered include the nature of God,[82] man's purpose for being created,[83] the grievousness of sin,[84] and the terms of salvation.[85] Do you not see there is promise after promise? Christ himself offers pardon, life, and salvation if you will but turn.[86]

Baxter laments the fact that he must return to unpleasant doctrines, but the nature of the case requires it. The last thing to be considered is what will be their end if they die unconverted.[87] He goes on to challenge them to consider if it be a condition 'to be rested in one day'.[88] Those who die unconverted are past all hope. Time has run out. Why then the delay? There is no assurance of another day of life, as 'a thousand accidents and diseases are ready to stop your breath'.[89] Until a man is converted, he should live in continual fear. Baxter says, 'every night when you lie down in bed, you should think with yourselves, What if I should die in an unconverted state before the next morning? Methinks the very dreams of this should awake you with terror. Methinks when you rise in the morning, you should think with yourselves, What if I should die in an unconverted state before night?'[90] Why then the delay? If you have a good reason against conversion, what is it? Why do you set yourselves knowingly against God and your own souls? Your own conscience will witness against you that you did not turn to God simply because you did not will to turn.[91]

Having given the things to be considered, Baxter also discussed the manner in which it was to be carried out. Since the devil fights to keep man asleep in sin,[92] the person seeking to be converted must set himself purposely to consider these weighty matters.[93] A man must not wait passively until such thoughts come of themselves into his mind, he must meditate 'oft',[94] 'again and again,'[95] for 'one hour in a day,'[96] or at 'once a day at least.'[97] Salvation or damnation are not issues to be trifled with.[98] The matters of salvation are not to be thought of in the same manner as ordinary trivial business, but with seriousness befitting their importance. A man must guard against laziness and focus his thoughts upon considering these things.[99] Once a man is in this state, he must endeavor to bring his considerations to a resolution. Do not abort the work before it has brought the desired ends.[100] If you resist consideration, God will bring you to it by a 'severer and more dreadful way'.[101]

Consideration should lead to humiliation. Baxter taught that there was a preparatory humiliation that normally occurred before the saving change. This should not be despised, because it helps the sinner draw nearer to God, though it be not a 'full closure' with him.[102] This stage of preparation normally includes the following elements: the fear of being damned; a recognition of the greatness of our sins and the wrath of God; our folly in sinning against God; passions of sorrow (sometimes expressed by groans and tears); and confessions of sin to God.[103] 'This is the end of humiliation,' Baxter asserts, 'to make ready the heart for a fuller entertainment of the Lord that bought it: and to prepare the way before him, and fit the soul to be the temple of his Spirit.'[104]

Baxter cautions his readers not to mistake the nature and the ends of this work.[105] Some go too far and proceed to an indignation against themselves. 'This desperation, and self-execution,' Baxter maintains, 'are no part of the preparatory humiliation ... but the excess and error of it.'[106] The true end of humiliation is simply that the sinner sense his sin and misery so that he can truly trust Christ.[107] The heart that is truly broken will yield readily to Christ.[108]

Men must have a sensible, awakening, practical knowledge of their sin and need.[109] Only this will lead them to Christ and teach them to value him as Saviour. A mere superficial, speculative knowledge of their sin and misery will prepare them but for a superficial, opinionative faith in Christ.[110] Can men take Christ for their Savior, before they 'heartily perceive that they want [need] a Savior'?[111] Since accepting Christ is an act of the will, how can a man be willing to have Christ before a recognition of his sin has made him willing?[112] Man must beware of taking humiliation as an indifferent thing: it is God's normal way of bringing his elect to faith.[113]

As might be expected, the Antinomians criticized this emphasis on preparation. They maintained this took the focus off Christ. Baxter's response shows this is not the case: 'We persuade men to believe that they are sick, that they may go to the Physician: And they rail at us for persuading men to delay going to the Physician till they think they are sick.'[114] Baxter displays how ludicrous the teaching of the Antinomians is at this point:

> So that the preaching of these men according to the Doctrine must be thus: (Come presently to Christ; stay not to hear the Gospel or to consider of it, or to understand the meaning of it, before you Trust Christ as your Saviour: Presently cast your selves upon him before you know who he is, or what he hath done for you; and trust him for the pardon of your sin before you perceive that you are sinners, or feel any need of pardon: Stay not for a will, but Take him or Accept him for your Saviour before you are willing of him, or willing to be saved.) Do you think this is the only Gospel-preaching?[115]

In fact, Baxter claimed, the Antinomians were the ones who were 'making light' of Christ and salvation. How can they value Christ as Savior before they see their sin? When men are truly humbled, however, then they are ready to come to Christ on his terms.[116]

Baxter recognized that this teaching was open to misuse, so he warned about errors to avoid in humiliation. A major error is to focus on the outward expression instead of the inward reality. It is not the measure of outward sorrow and anguish that shows sincerity, not the amount of tears. The key lies in the judgment and will.[117] Men must avoid two dangers at this point. Some can 'weep abundantly' during a sermon or a prayer, and think they are truly humbled, but yet are not. Others think they have no true humiliation because they do not have great pangs of sorrow, and 'freedom of tears', but yet their hearts are contrite.[118] To the 'tender consciences' who feared a lack of sincerity because they had no tears, Baxter says: 'Show me, if you can, where the Scripture saith, He that cannot weep for sin, shall not be saved, or hath no true grace.'[119]

What then is the proper balance? 'There is more humiliation in a base esteem of ourselves,' Baxter asserts, 'than in a thousand tears; and more in a will or desire to weep for sin, than in tears that come through ... passionate tenderness of nature. If the will be right, you need not fear.'[120] But this truth has caused some to run to the other extreme, and argue that sorrow and tears are unnecessary. While Baxter acknowledges that grief and tears are not necessary, he says 'certainly God made not the affections in vain.'[121] Sorrow of some kind is necessary, and it is not a good sign for there to be no tears from them that easily weep over other things.[122]

Baxter acknowledges that some men go to an extreme in humiliation, especially those among whom melancholy prevails. He warns them not to 'dwell too much at home', (i.e. engage in searching self-introspection) and neglect the rest of their duty.[123] But those who so err are few. Most men's problem is that they do not take self-examination seriously enough![124] It is far more dangerous to examine yourself too little than too much. Though one must avoid excess, Baxter notes that for the most part, it is 'a sign of an honest heart to be much at home, and a sign of a hypocrite to be little at home and much abroad'.[125] Again Baxter pleads for a balance: 'we must be careful to avoid both extremes; and neither neglect the study of ourselves, nor yet exceed in poring on ourselves.'[126]

Those who are not converted do not need words of comfort. They need 'plain dealing' about their sin.[127] We must not speak peace before God has spoken it. The heart cannot be melted into godly sorrow by 'the bubbles of a frothy wit, or by a game of words'.[128] The searching light of sacred truth must shine on man and illuminate him for what he is. Baxter says, 'We would not have you think one jot worse of your condition than it is.'[129] But you must see it as it really is!

The key is to remember the end of humiliation. The reason why you must strive for deeper sorrow is so that you may obtain the ends of that sorrow.[130] Sin must become odious to you and self must be taken down, so that Christ may be valued.[131] This is God's normal means of preparing the soul for grace.

Baxter emphasized that there was no merit in this activity. A man cannot force God's hand, cannot make him give special grace if the man humbles himself properly.[132] Baxter reminds them not to think they can merit anything from God, even though they should weep 'tears of blood'.[133] God is *Dominus*. He gives grace when and where he so chooses. Though he normally works through his appointed means, he remains free to work outside them.[134]

The Channel of Conversion: Faith and Repentance

Baxter taught that conversion was a process. Often it is long after the initial desires come before a man reaches a sound resolution. While God may suddenly turn the heart at a sermon, the normal situation finds men sticking long under conviction and 'half purposes' before they are finally converted.[135] There usually passes a period of time between a man's first discovery that he needs Christ to the point where he exercises faith and repentance. The key is that faith and repentance must be *thorough*. 'There is no promise in Scripture,' Baxter warns, 'that you shall be pardoned if you almost repent and believe.'[136]

What then is faith?[137] It is certainly more than mere opinion.[138] God will not be mocked. He knows the difference between head faith and heart faith.[139] True faith results in action.[140] The Antinomians fail to understand these things. They think they already have faith in Christ, but their 'common belief' will never save them. This is the 'most common delusion of unconverted men among us, that they verily think that they truly believe in Christ already'.[141] Baxter illustrates the difference between mere opinion and saving faith:

> Christ is known among us to be the able Physician of souls; we all confess and praise his skill, and know that he can save us. We all hear of the freeness of his cure, that he takes nothing, but doth it as soon for the poorest beggar as the greatest prince: but knowing all this, and speaking well of him, will cure no man; no, but you must go to him believingly, and beg his help, and take him for your physician, and trust your souls upon his blood and Spirit, and apply his means...[142]

Likewise, a true faith can be recognized by the other saving graces which accompany it: repentance, hope, love, humility, and a heavenly mind. The 'faith' which is separated from these is not true faith, but only an opinion with which presumptuous men deceive themselves.[143]

Repentance is the other side of the coin of faith. There can be a counterfeit repentance just as there exists a counterfeit faith. True repentance is a change of the whole soul – the judgment, the will, and the life, and not of any one of these alone.[144] Counterfeit repentance only changes a man's opinion, and not his heart and life.[145] True repentance involves both a turning from sin and a turning to God, and setting our hearts and hopes on heaven.[146] This second component must not be overlooked. True repentance does not come from fear alone, but also from the love of God. The heart is not changed to God without love.[147]

Baxter often referred to the actual act of turning as 'closing with Christ'. This is the sum of conversion, with the rest being only preparation for this.[148] The person must not covenant with Christ until he feels 'the scales turn by a true resolution'.[149] Christ must be believed in with all a man's heart, soul, and strength.[150] Baxter recognized this could not be done in a perfect degree, but it must be done with a predominant, prevalent degree.[151] 'Faith entereth at the understanding,' Baxter asserted, 'but it hath not all its essential parts, and is not the gospel faith indeed, till it hath possessed the will. The heart of faith is wanting, till faith hath taken possession of the heart.'[152]

Do not mistake a change of opinion for true faith, Baxter warned. A change of opinion is different from the renewing of the heart.[153] Make sure there is no secret reserve in your heart. If the devil cannot keep you from a change and reformation, he will try to deceive you with a superficial change and half-reformation.[154] This 'half-conversion' deceives men by strengthening false hopes that they have exercised true faith, when in fact it is but an opinionative faith.[155] One must not trust counterfeit graces that do not effectually convert the soul.

The Result of Conversion: Can the Christian Expect to Realize Assurance of Salvation?

Baxter crossed swords with the Antinomians over the nature of assurance of salvation. The Antinomians followed Calvin who defined assurance into the essence of faith.[156] Baxter followed many other Puritans, including the Westminster Assembly, in teaching that assurance was not necessarily of the essence of faith. While one might receive direct assurance from the Holy Spirit, the more normal path to assurance was through inference. Assurance was derived from a practical syllogism: all who manifest the signs of grace have eternal life; you manifest the signs of grace; therefore, you have eternal life. The changes in an individual's life became proof that he or she had been converted.

The Antinomians objected to this emphasis on signs, asserting that it drew men away from Christ to themselves. How can a man have assurance when the basis of that assurance is the signs of grace in him, signs which most certainly are imperfect?[157] Baxter countered their arguments by an appeal to the conditional nature of the covenant of grace. If pardon, justification, and adoption are all given to men in the gospel only conditionally, i.e. not fully realized until they believe, then until the condition be performed, no man can have any certainty that the benefit is truly his.[158] Since God has said it is those who believe who will be saved, no man can know that he will be saved until he first knows that he believes.[159]

It is not we who discourage assurance in men, Baxter argued. The Antinomians were the ones who left men no ground for true assurance of salvation, because they took away the difference between the worthy and the unworthy.[160] How can a man know if he is godly except by examining his life? The Antinomians argued from an uncertainty to a certainty. The wrong place to begin is to say, 'I am justified and godly, and therefore my wilful sins of drunkenness, fornication, oppression, lying, malice, &c. are consistent with justification.'[161] The correct way to argue is from a certain truth, and to say, 'I live in ordinary, wilful, heinous sin; therefore I am not justified or sincere.'[162] Assurance can be no more tenable than the certainty of the sincerity of one's faith and repentance.[163]

This does not mean that the believer will live a perfect life. There are many sins which can dwell with true grace, but which cannot exist with the assurance of the sincerity of that grace.[164] If a man lives in gross sin, and is certain that he is justified, and that no sin can make him question it, he has fallen prey to 'the antinomian devil transforming himself into an angel of light'.[165] The difference between true assurance and blind presumption is that the former will cause men to hate sin more, while the latter causes men to sin with less remorse, because they sin with less fear.[166]

The key in examining one's life lay in not judging oneself by a few extraordinary actions, but by the main design and scope, by the tenor of one's heart and life.[167] To judge a good man by his worst actions or a bad man by his best actions is to misjudge them. Simon Magus, when professing his faith at his baptism, seemed more righteous than Simon Peter when he was denying Christ.[168] Judge your heart by that which has been your chief love, by that which has been the main design of your life. While not every sin should lead to doubting, certainly gross sins or a notable decline in your spiritual life should cause you to question your sincerity.[169]

One should make use of 'infallible signs of sincerity', and not take those for certain which are not.[170] The infallible signs are few:

1. Are you heartily willing to take God for your portion?
2. Are you heartily willing to take Jesus Christ as he is offered in the gospel? that is, to be your only Saviour and Lord, to give you a pardon by his bloodshed, and to sanctify you by his word and Spirit, and to govern you by his laws?
3. Are you heartily willing to live in the performance of those holy and spiritual duties of heart and life, which God hath absolutely commanded you?
4. Are you so thoroughly convinced of the worth of everlasting happiness, and the intolerableness of everlasting misery, and the truth of both; and of the sovereignty of God the Father,

and Christ, the Redeemer, and your many engagements, to him; and of the necessity and good of obeying, and the evil of sinning, that you are truly willing; that is, have a settled resolution to cleave to Christ, and obey him...

5. Doth this willingness or resolution already so far prevail in your heart and life, against all the interest and temptations of the world, the devil and your flesh, that you do ordinarily practise the most strict and holy, the most self-denying, costly, and hazardous duties that you know God requireth of you...[171]

If so, then you can be assured of your salvation. These five marks express the gospel description of a true Christian.[172]

The key is not a particular feeling, but is rather a sincere disposition to serve God fully. The main point to be tried is the matter of one's willingness. While affections and duties are not to be ignored, they are not safe marks by which to try one's state.[173] Yet Baxter recognizes that a man's willingness and choice cannot be perfect. 'When I mention a hearty willingness,' Baxter clarifies, 'I mean not a perfect willingness.'[174] How then can a man know? Baxter sums it up: 'Yet your willingness must be greater than your unwillingness, and so Christ must have the prevailing part of your will.'[175] A true willingness will demonstrate itself in actions.

What then of direct assurance? Many other Puritans, while emphasizing inferential assurance, still held to direct assurance (assurance as part of faith) as a genuine possibility. Baxter acknowledged that it was possible, but argued that it was quite rare. While God could 'bestow assurance on whom he pleaseth', it was not to be thought this is his normal way of operating.[176] This leads us to Baxter's teaching on the witness of the Spirit.

It is the Spirit dwelling in the believer that witnesses that he is God's son.[177] How is the witness of the Spirit to be recognized? Baxter lists three elements: 'the Spirit witnesses first and principally, by giving us those graces and workings which are our marks; and then, secondly, by helping us to find and feel those workings or marks in ourselves; and then, lastly, by raising comforts in the soul upon that discovery.'[178] Men should not expect an inward witness of the Spirit, i.e. a direct discovery of their adoption, without first discovering the signs of grace within themselves. Do not expect an inward voice to say, 'Thou art a child of God, and thy sins are pardoned.'[179]

Two sorts of errors arise from this false notion of the Spirit's witness. Some languish in doubt their entire lives waiting for this kind of witness which the Spirit ordinarily does not give. Others more dangerously err, by 'taking the strong conceit of their fantasy for the witness of the spirit'.[180] They are deceived in this, however. It is certainly not the Spirit of God who would give assurance to one who had exercised merely opinionative faith. The Antinomians emphasize this 'inner witness' and thereby cherish presumption, and destroy true faith and assurance. Baxter summarizes their errors:

> They mistake the meaning of the Witness of the Spirit, As if it were but an inward Inspiration and Impulse equal to a voice, saying, *Thou are Elect and Justified*; Whereas it is an Inherent Impress, and so an objective Evidencing witness, even the Divine Nature, and Image of God, and the habit of Divine Love, by which Gods Spirit marketh us out as adopted.... Hereby they destroy the assurance and comfort of most (if not almost all) true Christians in the world; because they have not that inspiration or certain inward word of assurance, that they are Elect and Justified. I have known very few that said they had it.[181]

We see again how Baxter's formulation is designed to protect against the Antinomian errors. While it is only by the Spirit that a man can come to assurance, it is only by the fruits that he may know that he has the Spirit.[182] This, not immediate revelation, is the true witness of the Spirit.[183]

Baxter warned against an inordinate preoccupation with assurance. Some Christians were so busy inquiring whether or not they had saving grace that they neglected to exercise that grace! 'They spend so much time in trying their foundation,' Baxter said, 'that they make but little progress in the building.'[184] They are like musicians who spend all day tuning their instruments, and never getting around to playing.

A man should instead focus on his duty.[185] The first duty is not to ask whether Christ be yours or not, but to take him that he may be yours.[186] The Scripture so often guarantees salvation to all true believers, that if you can only be sure that you are a true believer, you need not doubt your salvation.[187] But not all doubts about one's salvation are bad. In fact, it would be better if some men had doubted *more*, that 'they might have believed, and been settled better'.[188] Again men tend to run to extremes. The Antinomians endeavor to dispel all doubts, calling upon men simply to believe they are justified. Some err in the other direction. They 'command doubting or commend it, as if it were a duty or a benefit'.[189] Men must find a balance between not dealing negligently with their souls, but yet not vexing their souls with 'needless scruples'.[190] Baxter admits he would rather have Christians suspect and search too much rather than too little, 'because there is a hundred times more danger in seeing sin less than it is, or overlooking it, than in seeing it greater than it is, and being over-fearful.'[191]

When a man doubts his salvation, he should labor to discover the true cause of his doubt.[192] Different doubts require different cures. A common cause of doubt is a melancholy temperament.[193] Another cause is a misunderstanding about afflictions.[194] Other men doubt their salvation because of ignorance about the true application of the covenant of grace.[195] An overarching cause of doubt is sin.[196] In this last instance, God's wisdom prevents him from giving assurance to the disobedient. If he were to give assurance and peace to those living in willful sin, he would not encourage the ends of his government.[197] 'Think not,' Baxter warns, 'those doubts and troubles of mind, which are caused and continued by wilful disobedience, will ever be well healed but by the healing of that disobedience.'[198]

Another major cause of doubt was not knowing the time of one's conversion. Baxter admits that this was a major reason for his early doubts about salvation:

[I doubted] Because I could not distinctly trace the workings of the Spirit upon my heart in that method which Mr. Bolton, Mr. Hooker, Mr. Rogers and other divines describe; nor knew the time of my conversion, being wrought on by the forementioned degrees.[199]

But since then I understood that the soul is in too dark and passionate a plight at first to be able to keep an exact account of the order of its own operations; and that preparatory grace being sometimes longer and sometimes shorter, and the first degree of special grace being usually very small, it is not possible that one of very many should be able to give any true account of the just time when special grace began, and advanced him above the state of Preparation.[200]

According to Baxter, not knowing the time of one's conversion is not the exception, but the rule among Christians.[201] This is because conversion is normally a process over time. Men seldom yield to the first conviction or persuasion.[202]

Since so few can assign the time and manner of their conversion, it is not a safe way to determine whether or not one is a true Christian. The key, Baxter asserts, is what condition you are in now. Is special grace present or not? If it is, then it does not matter when it came. He that wants to know whether or not he is a man does not try and remember when he was born, but instead discerns the rational nature in himself at present.[203] Baxter gives this advice: 'Find Christ by his Spirit dwelling in your hearts, and then never trouble yourselves, though you know not the time or manner of his entrance. Do you value Christ above the world, and resolve to choose him before the world and perform these resolutions? Then need you not doubt but the Spirit of Jesus is victorious in you.'[204]

Ordinarily it is only the stronger sort of Christians who attain assurance.[205] Few Christians have assurance at the first because few are strong at first.[206] Even once assurance is realized, it is mixed with imperfections, often being clouded and interrupted.[207] Therefore, do not be overly preoccupied with assurance. It is the erroneous expectation of unseasonable assurance that has caused men to turn to the Antinomians, and 'frame an assurance of their own making'.[208] If assurance of salvation is so rare among true Christians, then it is possible to be a true Christian without assurance. Those who begin with the question of election begin at the wrong end. Instead, you must first examine whether or not you are converted. If you are, then you may 'certainly gather that you are elected and shall be saved from hell'.[209]

There is a difference between absolute certainty and probable certainty. When you cannot attain to a full certainty, do not despise the comforts that probability can provide for you.[210] You can receive much comfort from general grounds: the goodness and mercy of God, the sufficiency of Christ's satisfaction, and the universality and freeness of the covenant of pardon.[211] The love of God was the cause of our redemption by Christ, and that redemption has procured the new covenant. The wise man builds on this threefold foundation.[212] These general grounds may afford you much peace and comfort before you attain to assurance itself.[213]

God has provided other means for a believer's comfort. One such means is to keep company with the cheerful Christians. 'There is no mirth like the mirth of believers,'[214] Baxter claimed. A Christian should also remember God's providences,[215] and practice good works. 'Study well the art of doing good,' Baxter said, and it will help bring you to a comfortable account.[216] The believer who desires assurance should avail himself of the means God has provided for the attaining of assurance.

5

PRESENTING THE GOSPEL: MANNER AND METHODS

Still thinking I had little time to live,
My fervent heart to win men's souls did strive;
I preached, as never sure to preach again,
And as a dying Man to dying Men.
(Richard Baxter, 'Love Breathing Thanks and Praise,'
Poetical Fragments, 1681).

He is no true Minister of Christ whose heart is not set on
the winning, and sanctifying, and saving of Souls (Richard
Baxter, *Compassionate Counsel to all Young-men* [1681], 48).

If evangelists were our theologians or theologians our
evangelists, we should at least be nearer the ideal church
(James Denney, *The Death of Christ* [1981 reprint], viii).

What is the minister's primary task? Baxter's response was
clear and concise: evangelism[1] must be the first and greatest
priority of the minister. He claimed, 'the work of conversion
is the great thing we must first drive at, and labour with all
our might to effect.'[2] The saving of souls must be the main
end of the minister's study and preaching.[3] Baxter confessed
that he often was forced to neglect the work of building up

the Christians in his congregation, because of the 'lamentable necessity' of the unconverted.[4] He exhorted his fellow ministers to engage themselves in the great work of converting souls regardless of what else they had to leave undone.[5]

Baxter decried what he termed 'false apprehensions' of the doctrine of election which left men saying, 'if God hath chosen us, we shall be saved, and if he hath not, we shall not, whatsoever we do.'[6] As we have seen, he asserted that God elects no man to the end without means, but to the ends and means together.[7] We have noted how he emphasized the means of hearing the word of God preached,[8] reading the Word, and reading books written to help one apply it.[9] Baxter also taught that another means which God has appointed for obtaining his grace is to seriously inquire of those who are able to give guidance for salvation, both ministers and private Christians. He said a great deal about the responsibility of these two groups in evangelism. Before examining his teaching on the practice of evangelism, it will serve us well to focus on the responsibility that Baxter maintained all Christians, especially Christian ministers, had – to share the gospel with the lost.

Baxter never tired of reminding his fellow ministers of their obligation to fulfill their calling to evangelize. He continually referred to Christ's commission to his ambassadors to preach the gospel to every reasonable creature, without exception or restriction.[10] Baxter spoke of his own proclamation as 'obey[ing] the voice of God',[11] and reminded pastors that God had appointed their voices to be the means of arousing and reclaiming the lost.[12]

He reminded them that they would be judged for how well they fulfilled this task.[13] He challenged them to, 'Let not the blood of souls ... be required at thy hands.'[14] He compelled ministers to examine their own lives by focusing on the judgment they would incur if they neglected their responsibility: 'I am afraid, nay, I am past doubt, that the day is near when unfaithful ministers will wish that they had never known that charge; but that they had rather been colliers, or tinkers, or sweepers of channels, than pastors of

Christ's flock! when, besides all the rest of their sins, they shall have the blood of so many souls to answer for.'[15]

But this was not all that the ministers needed to remember. In addition to not neglecting their responsibility to proclaim the gospel, they must not forget God's role in the process. They were to plant; only God could bring the fruit. Ministers were to cast the seed at God's command, but only God could bring the increase.[16] This reminder that it was the power of the Holy Spirit working through the Word of God that converted men should help the minister keep his role in proper perspective.[17]

Baxter also taught that each 'individual Christian' had the responsibility to witness.[18] The profession of true religion is such a great duty that only a foolish man would try to conceal his faith or keep it to himself.[19] Baxter stands amazed that anyone could be genuinely converted and not be telling others about salvation through Jesus Christ:

> Shall the Holy Ghost make such a change on the heart of a sinner, and shall not the tongue partake of it, or express it? Can Christ and his Spirit dwell in the heart, and the tongue conceal so blessed an inhabitant? Can a man have a taste of heaven upon his heart, and the kingdom of God begun within him, and yet not express his life or joy?... What! have the love of God shed abroad in their hearts, and say nothing of it? have the pardon of sin in the blood of Christ, and say nothing of it!? What! see many hundred souls in danger of damnation, and say nothing, but let them perish?[20]

Obviously the answer to these questions is 'no'. A person who has experienced new life in Christ cannot but speak of what he has seen and heard.

Baxter emphasized the responsibility to witness to one's family and servants. He encouraged fathers to help children and servants learn that 'they have a higher Father and Master that must be first served'.[21] He challenged them to avoid making family duties into meaningless routines, but to use them as opportunities to speak about God, heaven, hell, and holiness.[22]

One of the great hindrances to conversion was parental neglect in raising their children in the things of God.[23] The habit patterns developed in youth were hard to break when one became an adult. If parents would only look around they clearly would see that 'most of the world are such as they were taught in their childhood to be'.[24]

Christians must also recognize their responsibility to their neighbors. Believers should speak to their neighbors about Christ, and not stop 'till death hath stopt your mouths, or stopt their ears'.[25] Christians need to go to their neighbors' houses to converse with them concerning spiritual things. 'Take all opportunities that possibly you can,' Baxter exhorted, 'to confer with them privately about their states, and to instruct and help them to the attaining of salvation.'[26] Baxter mentions in his *Call to the Unconverted* that he hopes Christians will give that book or a similar one to their neighbors, in hopes of winning their souls.[27]

Baxter had special words of exhortation for teachers. He reminded them of their tremendous responsibility to influence their students for Christ. 'Let some piercing words fall frequently from your mouths,' he said, 'of God, and the state of their souls, and the life to come.'[28] If they would prove to be the means of students' conversion, many souls would bless them, and they could do no greater good for the church.[29]

Baxter tirelessly reminded Christians that the reason for their conversion was to enter into service for God.[30] He listed the desire to see others converted as one of the marks of genuine conversion. A converted person eagerly shows others the way. He 'prayeth heartily for the conversion of other men: he pleadeth with them, and persuadeth them; and fain he would have their eyes to be opened, and their hearts to be softened and turned to God.'[31] Christians should not focus solely on the benefits of conversion which *they* receive, but should recognize that a major benefit of conversion is that it will make them useful to *others*.

Having looked at Baxter's teaching on the responsibility of all Christians to share the gospel, we now turn to the question, 'How then should evangelism be practiced by ministers and by "private" Christians?' Before looking at how each of these groups should practice evangelism, Baxter would first have us examine the characteristics of a good witness. Baxter continually emphasized that *being* comes before *doing*. In *The Reformed Pastor*, he first challenges the ministers to 'take heed to themselves', to make sure that they themselves are practicing what they are preaching to others. While Baxter did not ever list the qualities of a good witness in the form we are presenting them here, such a list would be fully consistent with his emphasis on being before doing.[32]

Baxter would first call the evangelizer[33] to *be certain of his own conversion experience*. 'See that the work of saving grace be thoroughly wrought in your own souls,' Baxter exhorted. 'Take heed to yourselves, lest you should be void of that saving grace of God which you offer to others.'[34] A cold and careless heart has little chance of warming the heart of another, even if the inclination were there to do so.[35]

Baxter would challenge the evangelizer to *live a godly life*. 'Did professed christians more exactly conform their hearts and lives to their profession and holy rule,' Baxter claimed, 'their lives would ... do more to convince the unbelieving world of the truth and dignity of the christian faith, than all the words of the most subtle disputants.'[36] There is a profession by actions as well as a profession by words.[37] The blameless, humble, loving lifestyle of Christians is a powerful means of winning souls. Every Christian should 'preach' through this kind of example.[38]

Baxter challenged preachers especially at this point, warning them not to allow their lives to ruin what they say with their lips. Good doctrine is often refuted by bad practice.[39] A preacher who did not live a godly life before his people was the greatest hindrance to the success of his ministry.[40] He claimed, 'We must study as hard how to live well, as how to preach well.'[41]

A lifestyle of godliness has many ramifications. Christians must use their time wisely and live in a state of readiness to share the gospel. A believer should be ashamed to fill up his time with 'trifles' that keep him from his business of winning souls for Christ.[42] Baxter challenged Christians not to let souls perish while they minded their worldly business and worldly pleasure.[43] Implicit in this is a willingness to sacrifice. He chastises ministers who would rather see souls eternally perish than have their families live in 'a low and poor condition'. He asks, 'Nay, should you not rather beg your bread, than put such a thing as men's salvation upon a hazard or disadvantage? yea, or hazard the damnation of but one soul?'[44]

Evangelizers should be willing to bear rejection. Baxter knew that the only way to avoid offending the 'guilty and impenitent' was by silence. But 'silent we cannot be', because God has commanded us to speak.[45] He encouraged Christians to bear up under rejection by reminding them 'it is for men's salvation'.[46]

Christians ought to always keep before them the lostness of man. Every time they see the faces of sinners, they must remember that 'they must be converted or condemned'.[47] Baxter challenged Christians to look upon an unconverted man and contemplate that in a few days his soul might be in hell.[48] He believed that keeping the lostness of man in perspective will help the Christian keep a heart of compassion and urgency. If a Christian had only a 'spark' of compassion, it should cause him to labor diligently to save souls from perishing. Recognizing that a lack of compassion hampered evangelistic motivation, Baxter prayed that the Lord would give all Christians 'more compassion to these miserable souls'.[49] Closely related to compassion was the attitude of love. Baxter told ministers that the whole course of their ministry must be carried on in a tender love to their people.[50]

Another interesting characteristic Baxter brings out is *the expectation of success*. He says:

> if you would prosper in your work, be sure to *keep up earnest desires and expectations of success*. If your hearts be not set on the end of your labours, and you long not to see the conversion and edification of your hearers, and do not study and preach in hope, you are not likely to see much fruit of it.... I have

observed that God seldom blesseth any man's work so much as his whose heart is set upon the success [of it].[51]

Remember that God is at work in the hearts and lives of people. You can plant and water with confidence because it is God who has promised to give the growth.

In addition to living a godly life, Baxter believed a good witness would possess certain characteristics in his presentation of the gospel. Whether it involved a preacher exhorting from the pulpit, or a private Christian talking with his neighbor, Baxter taught that several qualities were inherent in a good presentation. He believed mere words without the proper manner to back them up would yield little fruit.

First, and seemingly always foremost in Baxter's mind, was *an attitude of seriousness*. He besought, 'Oh speak not one cold or careless word about so great a business as heaven or hell!'[52] Baxter maintained that few ministers preached with all their might, or spoke about eternal things with the spirit of 'earnest utterance.'[53] He pleads:

> O sirs! how plain, how close, and earnestly should we deliver a message of such a nature as ours is, when the everlasting life or death of men is concerned in it!... Can we believe that our people must be converted or condemned, and yet speak in a drowsy tone? In the name of God, brethren, labour to awaken your hearts, before you come, and when you are in the work, that you may be fit to awaken the hearts of sinners.[54]

Lethargic preaching from a sleepy minister stands little chance of awakening slumbering sinners.

Related to this attitude of seriousness was an attitude of *reverence*.[55] Baxter believed the work of God should be carried out with reverence and in the fear of the Lord, not in a careless frame of mind like everyday affairs often were. He said, 'It beseemeth a believer to have more of the fear of God upon his heart, in his ordinary converse in the world, than hypocrites and formalists have in their most solemn prayers.'[56]

Another important consideration in witnessing was that it be done in *the wisest possible manner*.[57] The work of God should be performed 'understandingly'. God was not pleased in the blind devotion of someone who did not know what he was doing. Thus his constant emphasis that pastors 'study' to be more effective. All discussion of spiritual things should be kept as plain and simple as possible. He said, 'Truth loves the light, and is most beautiful when most naked.'[58] Baxter admitted he had found that it was impossible to speak 'too plainly' to most people.[59]

A good witness *will strive to bring his exhortation to an issue.* If he is drawing a sinner to Christ, he must not leave him until the sinner has confessed that his present state is 'miserable' and 'not to be rested in'.[60] He must lead the unconverted to subscribe to the necessity of Christ and conversion. He must secure a promise that the sinner will 'fall close to the use of means'.[61]

Another key ingredient in being a good evangelizer was *persistence in sharing the gospel.* It is not once or twice that will usually prevail with the unconverted. Frequent exhortation is necessary. 'Weary out sinners with your loving and earnest entreaties,' he said. 'Follow them, and give them no rest in their sin.'[62] Baxter encouraged ministers not to give up on an individual after one try, but to continue trying to reach him: 'A soul is so precious, that we should not lose one for want of labour; but follow them while there is any hope, and not give them up as desperate, till there be no remedy.... Charity beareth and waiteth long.'[63]

Lastly, Baxter would challenge witnesses to remember that it is not their own gifts and abilities on which they are to depend, but upon God.[64] It is God and God alone who can bring fruit from their labors. Prayer is therefore as vital a part of the minister's work as is preaching.[65]

Even though all Christians have an obligation to do all they could for the salvation of others, a minister has a double obligation, because 'he is separated to the gospel of Christ, and is to give up himself wholly to that work'.[66] Baxter argued there were four main ways for a minister to increase his abilities: 'Study[67] and pray,[68] and confer, and practise.'[69]

Baxter emphasized the need for reasoned arguments in preaching. Men are rational creatures, so sermons must reach the will through the mind.[70] Emotion is also necessary at the proper time: 'Every reasonable soul hath both judgment and affection; and every rational, spiritual sermon must have both. A discourse that hath judgment without affection is dead, and uneffectual; and that which hath affection without judgment is mad and transporting.'[71] A man must be made to feel what he knows before he will act on it. Many ministers study only to compose their sermons. According to Baxter, that is not enough. He says, 'in the study of our sermons we are too negligent, gathering only a few naked heads, and not considering of [sic] the most forcible expressions by which we should set them home to men's hearts. *We must study how to convince and get within men,* and how to bring each truth to the quick, and not leave all this to our extemporary promptitude, unless it be in cases of necessity.'[72] Application must come through clearly in each sermon.

Ministers should preach with gravity, with plainness, with convincing evidence, with powerful winning motives, and with fervency.[73] It requires a loud call to waken a deadhearted man.[74] Ministers must beat down men's objections so as to leave them nothing to stand on:

> We must ... find out their common objections, and give them a full and satisfactory answer. We have reasonable creatures to deal with; and as they abuse their reason against truth, so they will accept better reason for it before they will obey. We must therefore see that our sermons be all convincing, and that we make the light of Scripture and reason shine so bright in the faces of the ungodly, that it may even force them to see, unless they wilfully shut their eyes.[75]

Ministers should present their stores of evidence to the unconverted 'as with a torrent upon their understandings', until they are forced to yield to the power of truth.[76]

Baxter believed the public ministry of preaching the gospel from the pulpit was primary, but he also recognized the tremendous benefits of 'private work', i.e. visiting parishioners in their homes[77] to converse with them about spiritual matters. He says, 'I know that preaching of the gospel publicly is the most excellent means, because we speak to many at once; but otherwise, it is usually far more effectual to preach it privately to a particular sinner.... I conclude, therefore, that public preaching will not be sufficient.... Long may you study and preach to little purpose, if you neglect this duty [private work].'[78] The goal of such personal instruction was nothing less than the salvation of all the people in his parish.[79]

Baxter not only asserted that evangelism was the primary task of all ministers, he likewise maintained it should be the focal point of all personal work. He encouraged fellow ministers to speak pointedly to each particular sinner's situation to try and bring home the truth of the gospel, beginning by trying to prepare the person for receiving what they had to say.[80] If the entire family were present, Baxter instructed the minister to take them aside one by one and deal with them in private. People respond better to 'close dealing about their sin' when they are alone with you.[81] Once in private, the minister should begin questioning the individual about the catechism,[82] and if he suspects he is unconverted, question him about his hope for salvation.[83] The minister should close the time by exhorting the sinner concerning the duty to believe in Christ and on his responsibility to use the external means of grace.[84]

Baxter lamented the lack of skill among the ministers for personal work. He comments, 'Alas, how few know how to deal with an ignorant, worldly man for his salvation!'[85] In response to the objection that it would take too much time to learn how to do personal work and would cause the neglect of a minister's studies, Baxter replied: 'I highly value common knowledge, and would not encourage any to set light by it; but I value the saving of souls before it. That work which is the next end must be done, whatever be undone.'[86] Baxter further maintained that if ministers would not waste time in 'vain recreations and employments' or in 'needless sleep', they would have plenty of time for both study and personal ministry.

Baxter stressed that the effectiveness of personal ministry would be greatly heightened if a minister knew his people well:

We must labour to be acquainted with the state of all our people as fully as we can; both to know the persons, and their inclinations and conversation; to know what are the sins that they are most in danger of, and what duties they neglect for the matter or manner, and what temptations they are most liable to. For if we know not the temperament or disease, we are like to prove but unsuccessful physicians.[87]

In line with this, Baxter emphasized ministry to families. He told ministers, 'You are like to see no general reformation till you procure family reformation.'[88]

Another important part of a minister's evangelism was being ready to give advice to inquirers who came for counsel. Ministers must not only be willing to perform this vital ministry, but must instruct their people about the opportunities it provided. Ministers should exhort people publicly to come to them for advice in matters related to their souls. 'We must not only be willing of the trouble,' Baxter claimed, 'but draw it upon ourselves by inviting them hereto.'[89]

Baxter also gives 'private' Christians practical advice about sharing Christ with others. He encourages them to 'pray heartily' for the conversion of others, to 'plead with them', and to 'persuade them' to open their eyes and turn to God.[90] One of the fruits of conversion was an eagerness to prepare oneself to be more effective in evangelism: 'If they [the unconverted] want instruction, you will be more able to instruct them: if they are ignorant or careless, you will have some words to say to them for the awakening of their souls.'[91] He gave a special instruction to private Christians concerning their sharing of evangelistic literature with others. In his *Call to the Unconverted,* he requests: 'That you will seriously read over this small treatise (and if you have such that need it in your families, that you read it over and over to them: and if those that fear God, would go now and then to their ignorant neighbours, and read this or some other book to them of this subject, they might be a means of winning souls).'[92]

Having examined Baxter's teaching on characteristics of a good witness and evangelism by ministers and private Christians, we finally turn to Baxter's use of appeals to the unconverted.[93] What did Baxter appeal to in challenging sinners to be converted?[94] What reasons for turning did he give? He begins by focusing on the nature of God. He challenges sinners to think about the God with whom they will 'have to do'.[95] He asks them to think about those in hell and remember that once death comes, there are no second chances:

> Thousands are under burning and despair, and past all remedy, while patience is waiting yet upon you. Can you forget that others are in hell at this very hour, for as small sins as those that you are yet entangled and linger in? Good Lord, what a thing is a senseless heart! That at the same time when millions are in misery for delaying or refusing to be converted, their successors should fiercely venture in their steps.[96]

He admits that 'it is unpleasant doctrine, but it is necessary, and it is most true! God never yet did prove a liar; if he were not true, he were not God.'[97]

But Baxter's gospel is not only one of judgment and pardon. He knows that Christ came to bring abundant as well as eternal life. He therefore reminds the unconverted man of all the blessings he is missing out in this life as well. He openly challenges sinners, saying, 'If you could show us any probability of a more pleasant and joyful life on earth, than that which serious holiness doth afford, I should be glad with all my heart to heart to hearken to you.'[98] What Christ offers is far better: 'This is the religion, the labour that we invite you to: it is not to despair, nor to ... miserable melancholy ... it is to the foretastes of everlasting joys, and to the beginnings of eternal life.'[99]

Baxter then proceeds to list some of the benefits enjoyed by the converted in this life:

> If you would be rich, I have showed you the only riches; if you would be honourable, it is only conversion that can make you so; if you would have pleasure, I have showed you the way to pleasure, and how you may be possessed even of your Master's joy. If in a word, if you would be happy, I have showed you the only way to happiness; a life of peace and

safety hath been offered you; a life of honour and pleasure hath been offered you.[100]

He also counts it as a special part of the benefits of the converted to live among God's people, in their special love, and to 'have a special communion with them, and interest in their prayers, and may possess among them the privileges of the saints and the ordinances of God'.[101] He appeals to the unconverted man's sense of stewardship, assuring him that when he is converted, he will regret deeply, 'and a hundred times repent it,' that he delayed so long before he yielded.[102]

Baxter brings in an element of urgency by his assertion that the longer the person remains unconverted, the harder it will be to come to Christ later in life. He claims: 'If you stick at conversion as a difficult matter today, it will be more difficult to-morrow, or the next month, and the next year, than it is now.'[103] He challenges them that there is no better time than now.[104] If you cannot turn now with all these helps and means, what hope have you if the means be taken from you? 'If you cannot row with the stream,' he asks, 'how will you row against it?'[105]

Was Baxter's approach effective? He certainly saw great fruit in his personal ministry. We cite once again the oft-quoted passage from his Autobiography:

> The congregation was usually full, so that we were fain to build five galleries after my coming thither.... Our private meetings also were full. On the Lord's Days there was no disorder to be seen in the streets, but you might hear an hundred families singing Psalms and repeating sermons as you passed through the streets. In a word, when I came thither first, there was about one family in a street that worshipped God and called on his name, and when I came away there were some streets where there was not passed one family in the side of a street that did not so; and that did not by professing serious godliness, give us hopes of their sincerity.[106]

As Wilkinson says, 'He had behind him the unquestionable authority that belongs to a successful ministry.'[107] Baxter's ministry not only bore fruit, it was fruit that remained.

6

CONVERSION AND THE CHURCH

The case stands thus. God saith in his covenant, He that believeth shall be saved, and ought to be baptized, to profess that belief, and be invested in the benefits of the covenant; and he that professeth to believe, (whether he do or not,) is by the church to be taken for a visible believer, and by baptism to be received into the visible church (Richard Baxter, I:651, CD:CEccl [1673]).

I had rather let in many that are unregenerate into the church than keep out one that is a true believer, if there be no other remedy. The Lord Jesus that died for them, and sent the ministry for them, and will at last admit them into heaven, will give us little thanks for excluding his weakest members from the church, and from the use of the sacrament and communion of saints, who have most need of them of any that have right to them. For my part, I desire not, nor dare be guilty of, that way of government in the church, as shall grieve those that Christ would not have grieved, and exclude the weak and turn or keep out the infants in grace, from the family of the Lord (Richard Baxter, IV:351, CR [1658]).

We now turn to an examination of Baxter's concept of the church to see how it throws light on his view of conversion. He authored more works on ecclesiology than any other subject he treated.[1] Secondary literature also abounds on this subject, with no other area of his thought receiving as much attention from scholars. This chapter attempts no comprehensive treatment of his views on the church, but will instead examine crucial points where Baxter's doctrine of ecclesiology overlaps with his theology of conversion.[2] We begin by looking at his teaching on the nature of the church.

The Nature of the Church
The universal church has a mystical and a visible component. The Mystical Church has none but true Christians. All who are genuine believers are members of the Mystical Church.[3] This membership in the true church of Christ is one of the many benefits of conversion.[4] The Visible Church, on the other hand, contains 'multitudes of Hypocrites, who profess themselves to be what they are not'.[5] They claim to live under the baptismal covenant but their lives demonstrate their lack of sincerity. Thus a distinction must be made between the membership of the two components.[6]

Baxter explains: 'As all the sincere heart-covenanters make up the church as regenerate, and mystical or invisible; so all that are christened, that is, baptized, and profess consent to all the essentials of the baptismal covenant, not having apostasized, nor being by lawful power excommunicated, are christians, and make up the church as visible.'[7] To become part of the Visible Church one must profess faith in Christ and consent to the baptismal covenant.[8]

What about the believer, who for one reason or another, has failed to be baptized?[9] If he has dedicated himself to the triune God in the same covenant, though without the outward sign, he may be considered a visible christian, though his visibility is incomplete.[10] Can a man lose his membership in the visible church? Absolutely. The man who forsakes his covenant by apostasy, or is excommunicated, ceases to be a visible member of the church. The covenant must be maintained in order to continue one's visible membership.[11]

As members of the universal church, Baxter instructed Christians to present themselves and their services as members of a particular church.[12] Particular churches consist of pastors and people joined together for personal communion in the worship of God. Baxter says,

> There are two sorts of churches, or church forms, of God's own institution. The first is the universal church considered politically as headed by Jesus Christ: this is so of divine appointment, as that it is an article of our creed.... And secondly, there is another subordinate church form of Christ's institution; that is, particular churches consisting of pastors and people conjoined for personal communion in God's worship. These are to the universal church, as particular corporations are to a kingdom, even such parts of it as have a distinct subordinate polity of their own: it is no city or corporation, if they have not their mayors, bailiffs, or other chief officers, subject to the king, as governors of the people under him: and it is no particular church, in a political sense, but only a community, if they have not their pastors to be under Christ...[13]

Observe how Baxter's use of the political method extends even to his ecclesiology! It fit nicely at this point with its emphasis on hierarchical organization.

Christians are to join the particular church where they live, being careful not to violate the common good and peace.[14] Baxter meant by this the local parish church. He says, 'I think Parish Work the best.... I would not be a Member of a Church gathered out of many Parishes, in such a Place as London: Co-habitation is in Nature and Scripture Example, made the necessary Disposition of the Materials of a Church.'[15] Baxter disliked the Independents who 'narrowed' the church more than Christ himself would. He bristled at their accusations of ungodliness in the parish churches, retorting, 'If you gather out the choicest Members that should help the rest, and then complain of Parishes, when you have marr'd them, you do not justly.'[16]

This manifested itself particularly in the Independent's practice of requiring a personal testimony of one's conversion experience before being accepted as a church member. Baxter denounced this practice as 'taking a very few that can talk more than the rest, and making them the Church'.[17] He sarcastically said, 'I do admire how any christian can make himself believe that the love and grace of Christ is confined to so narrow a room, and his church so small.'[18] The Independents thought they were promoting godliness by their actions; Baxter argued they were doing just the opposite.[19] Their practice also meant the shutting out of the worthy, and neglecting the souls of the remainder of the parish, both of which were abhorrent thoughts to Baxter. He says:

> But doubtless the Gospel Church was both more large and pure. Let us therefore take a view of it: And I beseech you remember, that what I say is not to make sin less odious, nor the Church or Godly less esteemed: but to shew you the frame of the visible Church in all Generations, and how it differeth from the invisible; lest you should take on you to be wiser than God, and to build his house after a better rule than his Gospel, and the primitive pattern, and marr all by being wise in your own conceits, and by being righteous overmuch.[20]

Rather than admit only those who could prove their conversion by eloquent testimony, Baxter would accept into fellowship any man until he proved he was unworthy, through immoral living, heretical opinions, or flat ignorance of Christianity.[21] 'I am not for narrowing the Church more than Christ himself alloweth us,' Baxter asserted, 'nor for robbing him of any of his Flock.'[22]

Baxter also disliked the Independents' separatism from the parish churches.[23] He says, 'such excellent Architects are they that they can build Christs house by pulling it in pieces; and such excellent Chirurgeons, that they will heal Christs body by separating the members, and can make as many Bodies as there are separated parts.'[24] Robert Paul argues that Baxter recognized the negative effects which disunity could have on evangelistic endeavours within a parish, saying, 'I have the feeling that it was the concern for evangelism that was at the heart of his persistent opposition to "gathered churches" of any type.'[25] While in agreement with Paul's assessment here, I would argue that more should be said on this issue. It was not only the avoidance of the *negative* influence on evangelism brought about by disunity that caused Baxter to adhere to the parish system, it was also the *positive* influence on evangelism by virtue of the fact that in the parish church all the inhabitants of the town would be present to hear the Word preached.[26]

Did Baxter view the church as a society? Ladell argues he did not: 'Baxter had no conception of the Church as a society or even as a family; his vision was focused upon the soul naked and responsible before its Creator.'[27] While it is true that Baxter focused often on the responsibility of individuals, it is inaccurate to assume on that basis that he did not view the church as a society. He specifically says as much in more than one place. 'Remember,' he exhorts, 'that by a Church is meant, not a mere company of christians, any how related to each other; but a society consisting of an ecclesiastical head and body, such as we call a political society.'[28] Elsewhere he refers to a church as a 'sacred Society',[29] as a 'society dedicated or sanctified to God',[30] and as a 'Society of professed Regenerate ones or Saints'.[31] Ladell could not have been more wide of the mark.

Baxter taught that there were three levels of people in the parish. First were the Communicants, who were the members of the church. Second were the 'Meer Hearers and Catechical Persons', who were candidates for church membership. Comprising the third group were the Aliens, Atheists, Infidels and Papists, Heretics, and the Men of no Church or other Churches, who were outside of the Parish Church.[32] Baxter lamented the situation in countries where the magistrate's laws made every person a *member* of the parish church, even if he were an atheist or infidel.[33]

What made one a true member of a parish church? Baxter's answer is direct and to the point. If a man makes a credible profession of faith, he has the right to membership in a particular church.[34] Baxter discounted the Independent requirements as 'Tyranny and Confusion'.[35] He argues that 'God saith in his covenant, he that believeth shall be saved, and ought to be baptized, to profess that belief, and be invested in the benefits of the covenant; and he that professeth to believe, (whether he do or not,) is by the church to be taken for a visible believer, and by baptism to be received into the visible church.'[36] A pastor must not refuse a man who makes a credible profession of the least degree of grace, even if he cannot 'handsomely utter it'.[37]

Baxter allowed for the possibility that an 'able and willing' individual might be prepared to give a lengthy account of his knowledge, faith, and obedience.[38] But he recognized that most Christians were awed by the prospects of testifying before the pastor and congregation.[39] He therefore did not require that public profession be made before the open congregation in order to gain admittance.[40] The Scriptural examples of the eunuch baptized by Philip (Acts 8) and the jailer and his household baptized at night in their home (Acts 16) further strengthened Baxter's view.[41]

A conversion testimony is unnecessary because 'He that professeth the baptismal covenant, professeth christianity, and godliness, and true conversion.'[42] If a man devotes himself to God through the baptismal covenant, 'no minister may reject him, for want of telling when, and by what arguments, means, order, or degrees he was converted.'[43] Baxter had harsh words for those who demanded a conversion narrative:

They that forsake these terms of church entrance, left us by Christ and his apostles, and used by all the churches in the world, and reject those that show the title of such a profession, for want of something more, and set up other, stricter terms of their own, as necessary to discover men's conversion and sincerity, are guilty of church tyranny against men, and usurpation against Christ; and of making engines to divide the churches, seeing there will never be agreement on any human devised terms, but some will be of one side, and some of another, when they forsake the terms of Christ.[44]

This practice is grievous both to men and to Christ. It serves as the catalyst for further separations in Christ's Church. It is without Scriptural validity.[45]

Baxter thought it ridiculous to ask a man to refrain from covenanting until the church could first see whether or not he would keep the covenant he was going to make.[46] But if the man seems not to understand the words he utters, he should be examined by the pastor more carefully to determine his true state.[47] Likewise, if he commits a horrible sin before he is baptized, the baptism should be stopped, because the man's life contradicts his own profession.[48]

To summarize, pastors are guilty of two extremes. Some believe that the visible church must be constituted only by such persons as can give a narrative of their conversion or the work of grace on their hearts. Baxter argues that this is more than the early church required of the baptized.[49] Others think the church should be seen as the school of Christ, where he teaches the way to true regeneration. Therefore if a man merely is willing to learn, he should be baptized, even if he professes no special saving faith or repentance.[50]

Both of these views are wide of the mark. The first view 'introduceth Church tyranny, and injustice, and is founded in the want of Christian charity, and knowledge, and tendeth to endless separations and confusions'.[51] But the second view was even worse, for it 'confoundeth the Catechumens with the Christians, and maketh all [those] Christians who are but willing to learn to be Christians'.[52]

Baxter gives his opinion as to the true conditions of admittance into the church and a state of Christianity:

A true belief in God the Father, Son and Holy Ghost, and a Devoting of our selves sincerely to Him, as our reconciled Father, our Saviour, and our Sanctifier, in a resolved Covenant, or Consent, renouncing the Devil, the world, and the flesh (expressly or impliedly) is the whole and the only condition of our Communion with the Church mystical or the living body of Christ (which is called The Church, in the first and most famous sense).[53]

All truly baptized Christians must be taken as church members.[54] A man cannot search another's heart, and therefore must believe his testimony, if credible.[55] Baxter believed that this confusion over the requirements for church membership was 'the great controversie which hath troubled the Church'.[56] He wondered at those who could not recognize that the church, since the days of the apostles, had always baptized the adult upon a personal profession of faith and repentance. He who knows not this, Baxter argued, 'knows little for what the church hath practised.'[57]

The pastor has the key role in the church. A group of Christians meeting together does not automatically constitute a particular church. A true church is a society of Christians joined together with a pastor in a certain relation. 'And it is no particular church,' he says, 'in a political sense, but only a community, if they have not their pastors to be under Christ...'[58] Baxter gives the role of the pastor:

> A Minister of the Gospel is an Officer of Jesus Christ, set apart (or separated) to preach the Gospel and thereby to convert men to Christianity, and by Baptism to receive Disciples into his Church, to congregate Disciples, and to be the Teachers, Overseers and Governours of the particular Churches, and to go before them in publick worship and administer to them the special Ordinances of Christ, according to the word of God; that in the Communion of Saints, the members may be edified, preserved, and be fruitful and obedient to Christ; and the Societies well ordered, beautified and strengthened; and both Ministers and People saved; and the Sanctifier, Redeemer and Father Glorified and Pleased in his People now and for ever.[59]

The first task of the minister is to preach the gospel to unbelievers for their conversion. Nothing must be allowed to thwart this great obligation. The second task is to baptize those who solemnly covenant with the Triune God. The third task is to congregate the baptized into particular churches for worship. The pastor then has the task of shepherding the flock.

Not every man is capable of fulfilling such tremendous responsibilities. Baxter lists the qualities he thinks are necessary in a man who feels he is called to pastoral ministry: '1. Natural wit and capacity. 2. Acquired improvement, and so much knowledge as must be exercised in the office. 3. If apt to teach and able signified no more than to read what is prescribed by others, a child, fool, or an infidel, were apt and able. Ability for competent utterance and exercise.'[60] The approval of other senior ministers is ordinarily necessary, to protect the public good from a man without the gifts and calling to be a minister.[61] A quality ministry is critical – churches rise or fall as the ministry rises or falls.[62]

The Sacraments

Baxter defines a sacrament as a 'solemn dedication of man to God by a vow expressed by some sacred ceremony, signifying mutually our covenant to God, and God's reception of us and his covenant with us.'[63] He was therefore willing to grant that there were five sacraments: baptism, confirmation, absolution, the Lord's supper, and ordination.[64] He recognized that in the strictest sense, as other Protestant divines normally defined the term sacrament, that it was 'an outward sign of Christ's institution, for the obsignation of the full covenant of grace betwixt him and the covenanter, and a delivery, representation and investiture of the grace, or benefits of that covenant'.[65] Based on this common definition Baxter could agree that there were only two sacraments, baptism and the Lord's supper.

The basis of Baxter's sacramental doctrine is the covenant of grace.[66] But it is only the *conditional* promise that God seals by the sacraments, i.e. If thou believe in the Lord Jesus, thou shalt be saved.[67] The mutual nature of the sacraments is expressed in God's promise to perform the promises of the covenant of grace, and on man's part by his acceptance of the terms of the covenant demonstrated by his participation in the sacrament.

The sacraments nurture and strengthen faith, they do not confer grace itself.[68] Partaking of the sacraments presupposes that the individual has experienced conversion, i.e. that faith is already present in the participant. Receiving the sacraments does not give faith, it instead displays one's faith in Christ. Therefore all that is necessary to be admitted to the sacraments is a credible profession of faith.[69]

Baptism

Baptism is the outward seal of the covenant of grace, and is therefore the outward badge of the true Christian. It is like the solemnization of a marriage, or the enlisting of a soldier. Specifically,

> Baptism is a holy sacrament instituted by Christ, in which a person professing the christian faith (or the infant of such) is baptized in water into the name of the Father, the Son, and the Holy Ghost, in signification and solemnization of the holy covenant, in which as a penitent believer (or the seed of such) he giveth up himself (or is by the parent given up) to God the Father, Son, and Holy Ghost, forsaking the devil, the world and the flesh and is solemnly entered a visible member of Christ and his church, a pardoned, regenerate child of God, and an heir of heaven.[70]

Faith must be present before baptism. Baptism does not regenerate, but points to faith already in the baptized (or the parent of a baptized infant). 'Trust not the water of baptism alone,'[71] Baxter warns. Unless a man is born again of the Spirit also, he cannot enter the kingdom of God. Baptism presupposes conversion.

Who then are the subjects of baptism? Only repenting and believing sinners, or the children of such, can be baptized. Baptism is but the expression of a man's repentance and faith, by his making an explicit contract with God.[72] We will examine Baxter's teaching on infant baptism in the ensuing section, but it is worthy of note that he says, 'The full nature of baptism is best to be understood by the case of the adult, who were [sic] capable of more than infants are.'[73] No adult can be baptized without a serious, deliberate profession of faith, repentance, and obedience to Christ.

What was Baxter's position on rebaptism? He taught that the church ordinance should not be repeated, even though the heart covenant was lacking.[74] In a few instances baptism might be repeated where it was not truly received before: when the person made no profession of the Christian faith (nor his parents for him, if an infant); if the profession lacked the full testimony of belief in the triune God; and if no water was used in the ceremony.[75] Laypersons could not baptize even in so-called 'cases of necessity', since baptism is not essential to salvation, and because God has expressly made it a part of ministerial duties.[76] One baptized by a layperson should not be rebaptized however; the error of the layperson does not nullify the validity of the baptism.[77]

In what sense is baptism said to wash away sin? Baptism can be spoken of in this way, Baxter says, because God's covenant, celebrated in baptism, gives pardon of sin through the blood of Christ to all that genuinely consent to the covenant.[78] Too much stress is laid upon the outward washing and not enough upon the nature of the covenant.[79] Thus we see both the inward and outward components of baptism. The term conveys both the inward actions of the heart as well as the outward professions and actions.[80] Therefore,

in this proper sense baptism is the mutual covenant between God the Father, Son, and Holy Ghost, and a penitent believing sinner, solemnized by the washing of water, in which as a sacrament of his own appointment God doth engage himself to be the God and reconciled Father, the Saviour and the Sanctifier, of the believer, and taketh him for his reconciled child in Christ, and delivereth to him, by solemn investiture, the pardon of all his sins, and title to the mercies of this life and of that which is to come.[81]

But the inward reality is what is important. The genuine believer is in a state of salvation before God as soon as he believes.[82] Because the outward washing implies the inward covenanting, Baxter says that it is permissible to 'imitate the fathers, and to say that the truly baptized are in a state of justification, adoption, and salvation, unless when men's misunderstanding maketh it unsafe.'[83]

The believer's covenant with Christ is thus the primary and central significance of baptism.[84] The man who desired to be baptized needed to do three things: understand the meaning of the covenant; heartily accept the covenant and consent to the conditions required of him; and commit himself to the faithful practice of them until death.[85] Baxter gives the words he encouraged the baptismal candidate to use:

> I do heartily take this one God for my only God and chief good; and this Jesus Christ for my only Lord, Redeemer, and Saviour; and this Holy Ghost for my Sanctifier; and the doctrine by him revealed and sealed by his miracles, and now contained in the holy Scriptures, do I take for the law of God, and the rule of my faith and life; and repenting unfeignedly of my sins, I do resolve through the grace of God sincerely to obey him, both in holiness to God, and righteousness to man, and in special love to the saints, and communion with them, against all the temptations of the devil, the world, and my own flesh, and this to the death.[86]

If a man can speak these words sincerely, there is no doubt but that he is a true Christian.

No man can resolve to do these things without the special grace of God. His grace enables man to perform the initial consent, and enables him to fulfill it throughout his life. The baptismal candidate thus must not imagine that he can do all this in his own strength, but instead must rely on the strength of Christ, 'knowing that he hath promised his Spirit and grace for the aid of every true believer.'[87] The covenant must be made deliberately, soberly, and rationally. The man must be in total seriousness and not presume to say these words in jest. There must be no secret exceptions or reserves.[88]

We have alluded to Baxter's emphasis on infant baptism earlier in this section. How does this fit with his strong emphasis on the necessity of faith before baptism? How could Baxter simultaneously maintain that baptism presupposes faith and yet uphold a belief in infant baptism? We now proceed to examine his views on infant baptism in detail.

Infant Baptism

Baxter traces the evolution of his views of baptism in his *Plain Scripture Proof of Infants Church-Membership and Baptism* (1650). He recalls that he had baptized only two children (at Bridgnorth) when he began to have doubts about infant baptism.[89] He set himself to study the point, choosing to forbear the practice until his mind was settled. He was originally tempted towards Baptismal Regeneration, but says, 'I soon discerned the error of this doctrine, when I found in Scripture that Repentance and Faith in the aged were ever prerequisite ... and that to dream of a Physical Instrumentality, was worse than Popish, and to do that in Baptism, which Transubstantiation hath done in the Lords Supper; even to tie God to the constant working of a miracle.'[90] This led Baxter almost to embrace believers' baptism, before his continued study convinced him that the case for infant baptism was sound. His debate with the Baptist Tombes sealed his conviction as to infant baptism.[91] The result of the debate was Baxter's work, *Plain Scripture Proof*, which displayed his true colors to one and all.

The fundamental issue, Baxter claimed, is not infant baptism *per se*, but infant's church membership.[92] If the latter is true, the former must be maintained.[93] Baxter took issue with the Baptists, who denied church membership to infants. Baxter felt this implied that the Old Covenant was better than the New, which certainly was 'most absurd and false' and 'vile doctrine'.[94] He said: 'Nor have you [Tombes] proved to me yet that he [Christ] hath Repealed the Church-membership of Infants; nor shewed me the Scriptures where any such thing is written.... He ... hath not left out the Infants of his people, who as is confessed, were once in.'[95]

Baxter based his case on the covenant. Infants had a right to the baptismal covenant because they became partakers of the covenant through their parents, whose interest in them made their act to be esteemed as the infant's own act. This is evident from both nature and from Scripture.[96] Both bear witness to the principle that children share the privileges and the responsibilities of their parents. Original guilt testifies to this reality, as does the rite of circumcision in the Old Testament.

Baxter lists the differing opinions on infant baptism in his day,[97] and then concludes by agreeing with the Synod of Dort, that 'faithful Parents need not doubt of the Election and Salvation of their Children dying in infancy: The Covenant certainly pardoneth and saveth them.'[98]

This solved Baxter's paradox of simultaneously affirming infant baptism, but yet arguing that baptism presupposed faith. The infants could not exercise faith, but since they are in covenant with their parents, their parents' wills are theirs. Therefore, their parents may dispose of them for their own good, and 'they consent by their parents who consent for them'.[99] If a man dedicate his child, but be a hypocrite himself, the child, like the father, is outside of the covenant.[100] Baxter gave instructions to parents as to their responsibility and subsequent blessing:

> When you enter a child into the christian covenant with God, address yourselves to it as to one of the greatest works in the world; as those that know the greatness of the benefit, of the duty, and of the danger. The benefit to them that are sincere in the covenant, is no less than to have the pardon of all our sins, and to have God himself to be our God and Father, and Christ our Saviour, and the Holy Ghost our Sanctifier, and to have title to the blessings of this life and of that to come.[101]

It should therefore be done with the greatest possible seriousness and reverence.

What were the effects of genuine infant baptism? One effect was acceptance by God. The act of baptism signifies that the child is a beneficiary under the covenant of grace. Baxter says that 'all the children of true christians, do by baptism receive a public investiture by God's appointment into a state of remission, adoption and right to salvation at the present'.[102] During the time before the child comes of age and is capable of actual faith himself, baptism testifies to God's present acceptance of the child.[103]

But this does not mean that baptism brings about spiritual regeneration.[104] While God certainly can regenerate infants, his doing so is not tied to the intrinsic nature of baptism.[105]

To those who appealed to the Church Fathers in their support of baptismal regeneration, Baxter pointed out the necessity of both the internal and external components of baptism. When the ancients referred to sins being washed away in baptism, they meant by baptism not merely the external washing but also the internal covenanting through faith.[106] Baptism does not bring about an internal change, but instead seals the promise of an external relation to God.

All children must make their own decision when of age.[107] Before an individual can be admitted to full adult membership, he should be diligently catechized, and renew and 'own' his baptismal vow. The lack of emphasis on the true nature of confirmation in the English Church has brought dire consequences: 'I confess to you, of the two evils, I think the church is more corrupted for want of such a solemn, serious renewing of the baptismal covenant at age, and by turning confirmation into a ceremony than by those anabaptists, who call people to be seriously re-baptized, as the Afric council did those that had been baptized by heretics.'[108] Baptism in infancy must be complemented at age by the youth's own profession of faith, because the parent's will can no longer go for the child's own will.[109] Baxter refused to set a certain year when a child 'comes of age'. It varied according to the individual, but was marked when the child came to the full or competent use of reason.[110]

As baptism is the sacrament of initiation into the Body of Christ, the Lord's Supper is the sacrament of confirmation and growth in grace. We now turn to Baxter's teaching on this subject.

The Lord's Supper

One must understand the proper ends to which Christ instituted the sacrament of the Lord's Supper. A man must not presume to use it for ends to which Christ never appointed it. The true ends are these: to commemorate the death and passion of Christ; to be the solemn renewing of the baptismal covenant; to be a means whereby the Spirit of Christ might stir us up to greater faith, hope, love, joy, and obedience; to give opportunity for Christians to profess their faith, love, and gratitude to God; and to be a sign and means of the unity, love, and communion of saints.[111] Like baptism this sacrament does not confer grace. It is a dangerous abuse to assume that one will be pardoned and saved merely by the outward exercise alone.[112]

The Lord's Supper should ordinarily be administered every Lord's Day. To omit it is to maim and alter the worship of God.[113] Once a week is not too often for Christians to renew their covenant and commit themselves afresh to obedience.[114] To those who omitted it because its frequent observance had brought contempt, Baxter reminded that there were better means, e.g. teaching and discipline, to keep the sacrament from contempt, than by displacing it.[115]

Only those who have personally owned their baptismal covenant by a credible profession of true christianity may partake of the Lord's Supper.[116] What makes a profession credible? It must be made understandingly, seriously, voluntarily, deliberately, and must not be nullified by contradiction in word or deed.[117] Children and others who do not know what they are to receive, as well as the notoriously wicked, are excluded from the sacrament. The sacrament, Baxter argues, 'belongeth neither to infants nor infidels.'[118] What about those who are uncertain about the sincerity of their faith and repentance? If they are uncertain, they may not partake. If according to their best understanding they are sincere, then they should come in spite of their lack of total certainty.[119]

Two preparations are necessary to this sacrament: a general preparation, which is nothing more than being in a state of grace, and a particular preparation, which calls the believer to examine his present spiritual condition.[120] In his particular preparation, the believer should focus on the following issues: his duty to his own conscience; his duty to God; and his duty to others.[121] He must take a strict account of his life and examine his dealings with God and men, both in secret and public. He should focus especially on those activities of late, since he last renewed his covenant with God. He must listen carefully to hear what God and conscience say about his sins.[122]

When a believer prepares himself for the Lord's Supper, he should be wary of two extremes. On the one hand he should not view his preparation carelessly, as if it were a common work. On the other hand, he should not so greatly fear the sin of unworthy receiving, that he fails to experience the exercise of faith, love, praise and thanksgiving to which Christ invites him in the sacrament.[123] The believer should remember that to partake of the Lord's Supper is a 'delightful business', a 'sweet feast'.[124]

Baxter indicates what qualifications should be present in the celebration of this sacrament:

1. A true belief of the articles of the christian faith concerning Father, Son, and Holy Ghost; the person, offices, works, sufferings, and benefits of Christ. 2. The sense of our sinful and undone condition, as in ourselves, and of our need of Christ: so as humbly to loathe ourselves for our transgressions, with the sense of our present weaknesses to be strengthened, and sins to be forgiven. 3. A true desire after Christ for pardon, and spiritual nourishment and salvation. 4. A thankful sense of the wonderful love of God, declared in our redemption, and in the present offers of Christ, and life. 5. The exercise of holy love and joy in the sense of this unspeakable love. (If these two be not felt before we come, yet in and after the sacrament we must strive to exercise them.) 6. A love to one another, and forgiving wrongs to one another, with a desire after the communion of saints. 7. The giving up ourselves in covenant to God, with resolution for renewed obedience. 8. A patient hope for the coming of Christ himself, and of the everlasting kingdom, where we shall be perfectly united in him, and glorified with him.[125]

Observe that in the receiving of the sacrament the believer must be reconciled not only to God but also to other Christians, forgiving their wrongs and desiring their communion.

The covenant must be renewed often throughout the course of a believer's life. The Lord's Supper is an ordinance particularly instituted to this end. Since there is much in the sacrament that strengthens one's faith, God has appointed the frequent using of it as one of His means to spiritual growth.[126] If a man willfully neglects the Lord's Supper, he starves his faith.[127] If a man engages in wickedness and refuses to repent, he must be barred from the Lord's Table. This brings us to Baxter's teaching on Church Discipline.

The Role of Church Discipline

What are the purposes of church discipline? Baxter lists the following: to awe and preserve the church; to terrify the offenders, bringing them to repentance; and to preserve the order of the church.[128] The first of these is the most important:

> Excommunications and Absolutions in publick are not only nor chiefly for the external Order of the Church, but for the preserving of the peoples souls from sin, and for the warning of others, and for the preserving in their minds a due esteem of the holiness of our Religion, and the necessity of holiness in us, and to convince those without, that God's Laws and Ways and People are more holy than those of the World.[129]

The casting out of the impenitent will cause the rest of the church members more carefully to watch their ways. But this is not meant to imply a lack of concern for the individual under discipline. The purpose of discipline is to bring him to repentance so he may rejoin the fellowship. One of Baxter's complaints about the excommunication administered by the bishops' courts was that it was not reformative, but punitive.[130]

Those who are proven by sufficient witness to have done that which cannot stand with the sincere keeping of the baptismal covenant must be disciplined.[131] The fact that a believer has sinned does not mean his original repentance was not genuine. In fact, one of the marks of genuine conversion is that the true Christian is amenable to discipline! If he willingly submits himself to the loving rebuke of the church, and repents when his error is pointed out to him, it shows his original repentance was sincere.

Baxter was certain his teaching on discipline stood on the authority of Scripture and reflected the practice of the primitive universal church.[132] His belief in the necessity of discipline mirrored his teaching that holiness was of the essence of Christianity. He says,

> Christianity is not a matter of mere opinion: Christ came not into the world only to persuade men to have high thoughts of him, but to save his people from their sins, and to destroy the works of the devil. And when the church of Christ shall be turned into a den of thieves, or a sty of swine, what a great dishonour is it to the Lord! as if we would persuade the world that his servants are not holier than others, and differ but in an opinion from the world.[133]

Evangelism will be crippled so long as those outside the church can see no difference between believers and unbelievers.[134] A lack of discipline brought other problems as well: breeding controversies; hindering the fruits of reformation; and causing people to turn to the papists and the sects.[135] Baxter particularly lamented that a lack of discipline in the parish churches had caused godly believers to 'fly from our churches ... because we will not yield to the healing of our own diseases'.[136]

Baxter gives his method of discipline, based on Matthew 18, in the following passage:

> Expect not that any one lawfully received by Baptism into the Christian Church, should be cast out of it, or denied the priviledge of members, but according to the rules of Christian discipline, by the power of the Keyes, that is; for obstinate impenitency in a gross or scandalous sin, which the person is proved to be guilty of: and this after private and publick admonition, and tender patient exhortation to Repentance.[137]

Baxter continually emphasized this last point. Discipline was to be done in tender love for the offender.[138]

If the offender repents after private admonition, the minister may console him privately with promises suitable to his condition. If he repents only after public admonition, the offender must confess his sin publicly to the congregation, beg the prayers of the church for his situation, and profess his resolution to live in a new obedience to God.[139] When he has made a credible profession of repentance, then it is the pastor's duty to declare him pardoned by Christ, on the condition that his repentance is genuine and sincere.[140] If the offender yet remained impenitent, then the pastor was to openly declare him unfit for communion with the church, and require him to abstain from it.[141]

Both the purpose and method of discipline are brought forth clearly in the following letter written by Baxter to an erring member of his congregation, George Nichols, dated January 28, 1658:

> Because you shall have no pretense to say that wee deale hardly with you, I shall not meddle with that which is commonly called Excomunication against you. But because you have disclaimed yo[r] membership in the Church, and denyed to expresse Repentance of it, even in private (which you should have done in publike) I shall this day acquaint the Church of your sin and seperation (in which you have broaken your covenant to God and us), and that you are no more a member of this Church or of my pastorall charge. I shall do no more, but leave the rest to God who will do more. Only, I shall desire the Church to pray for your Repentance & forgiveness; and therefore desire you this day to be there & joyne with us in those prayers. And then except you openly lament your sin, you shall be troubled with my admonitions no more. From this time forward I have done with you; till either God convert you, or I and my warnings & labours be brought in as a witness against you to your confusion.
>
> Your compassionate friend,
> RICHARD BAXTER.[142]

Observe that since the parishioner had failed to heed private admonition, and had to be admonished publicly, his confession of repentance had to be public before restoration.

Baxter recognized that his fellow pastors were reluctant to enact discipline because of the dislike many in their parishes had for the concept. Baxter himself acknowledges discipline to be a wearisome task. He claimed that if had God left it to his choice, he would preach each week and do nothing more.[143] But as God had commanded ministers to exercise discipline, he would gladly bear the scorn it brought forth.[144] His final judgment on the experiment of church discipline was favorable:

> We knew it to be an Ordinance of Christ, and greatly conducing to the Honour of the Church; which is not a common prophane Society, nor a Sty of Swine, but must be cleaner than the Societies of Infidels and Heathens: And I bless God that ever I made a trial of Discipline; for my Expectations were not frustrate, though the ejected Sinners were hardened: The Churches Good must be first regarded.[145]

Therefore, though some who Baxter cast out never returned, the overall effect was positive.

Baxter's concept of holiness and the necessity for church discipline influenced his view of church polity.[146] He appealed for a 'primitive episcopacy', with a bishop in every parish. His chief reason against diocesan episcopacy was that it undermined church discipline.[147] With only 25 bishops to oversee almost 10,000 English churches, how could discipline possibly take place?[148] Far worse than the numerical disparity was the lamentable fact that the bishops did not even attempt to practice discipline in the congregations under their supervision.[149] This failure of discipline caused endless separations from the parish churches.[150]

Baxter's system would solve these problems. His declaration when applying for a licence under the Declaration of Indulgence in 1672 gives his thought: 'My judgment of Church-government is for that form of Episcopacy which is described in Ignatius and Cyprian and was the usage then of the Christian churches.'[151] Every pastor should have the 'Power of the Keys' in his own congregation.[152] To be a pastor to those who were not under discipline was but 'to be a HALF-PASTOR'.[153] Wood's observation is worth noting at this point: 'That Baxter placed supreme importance upon the pastor's powers over his own congregation can be seen from his willingness in the final analysis, to accept diocesan episcopacy or any other system, if only the pastor had the right to exercise discipline in his parish.'[154]

Nuttall sums up Baxter's views on polity and its relation to church discipline:

> He took up nothing save in terms of its bearing on Christian practice and devotion, and it was with practical consequences that he was always, finally, concerned. His opposition to 'diocesan prelacy,' for example, was fuelled not by abstract notions of ecclesiastical government nor by what he took to be the polity of the apostolic church (though both of these were called in its support), but by dismay at episcopacy's belittling of the minister's responsibility to his people and its inefficiency in parish administration.[155]

Nuttall was exactly right. Again we see how Baxter's passion for holiness affected his ecclesiology.

This concern for discipline led Baxter to organize the Worcestershire Association.[156] The main purpose for its incorporation was the restoration of discipline in adjacent parishes on the lines Baxter was following with such success at Kidderminster.[157] The Association met monthly in five towns. One of the ministers gave a public lecture followed by a period of discussion. The Association considered complaints brought against its member ministers and against members of churches within its jurisdiction.

Baxter published the propositions which the associated ministers agreed upon in his work *Christian Concord*.[158] The ministers agreed that it is the duty of ministers and other Christians to 'admonish and reprove those that live in any known sin'.[159] This must be done with 'tender love' but yet also in a spirit of 'great seriousnesse'. The propositions follow the biblical pattern set forth in Matthew 18 concerning church discipline. A thorough repentance is called for:

> It must not be a slight, unwilling, meer verbal Repentance that must satisfie the Church, either for preventing or taking

off a Censure of casting out, but only such as seemeth free and serious, answerable in some measure to the quality of the fault. Such therefore we resolve to require and expect, that we delude not men's souls, and provoke not God by making a formality or Jest of his Ordinances.[160]

If the person remains obstinate after these several admonitions, he is not only to be debarred from the Lord's Table, but is also to be cast out of the fellowship. If this is not done, the remaining members of the church will grow hardened, the weak will have reason to separate, and the scandal will disgrace the profession of the ministry and will prove an offence to God.[161]

The Teaching Ministry of the Church

We conclude our examination of Baxter's ecclesiology by briefly looking at his views on the teaching ministry of the church. We have noted his concern that children 'own' their baptismal covenant when they reach full age. Therefore the church must be engaged in teaching essential doctrine through the use of catechisms. Baxter believed that catechizing was the chief means by which the church had been reformed in the past and the chief means of hope for the future.[162] In responding to the question, 'What is the use of catechisms?', he says:

> **Answ.** To be a more familiar explication of the essentials of christianity, and the principal integrals, in a large manner than the creed, Lord's prayer, and decalogue do; that the ignorant may the more easily understand it. Every man cannot gather out of the Scripture the greatest matters in the true method, as distinct from all the rest: and therefore it is part of the work of the church's teachers, to do it to the hands and use of the ignorant.[163]

Catechisms were therefore to be formulated skillfully and carefully.[164] Ministers were to labor to see that the ignorant learned both the form and the meaning of the words.[165]

In addition to the teaching that came through preaching and worship, Baxter also emphasized instructional classes.

He held a regular Thursday evening meeting at his house where the group could discuss his previous Sunday's sermon in depth.[166] He held classes for the youth in his parish, and put them through carefully graded stages of instruction.[167] They could then be prepared for the 'owning at age' of their baptismal covenant.

Finally, mention must be made of his personal instruction in the home. He devoted Monday and Tuesdays to catechizing. The families in his parish would be visited a week beforehand and assigned a time to call on Baxter. At the appointed time he would spend an hour with them, teaching them and questioning their understanding of the catechism. He thus was able to see about sixteen families per week and was able to cover the entire parish in a year.

We have now concluded our analysis of Baxter's teaching on the church as it relates to conversion. His doctrine of the church sheds further light on his doctrine of conversion. His ecclesiology matched his soteriology. Holiness is of the essence of Christianity. Both the individual believer and the fellowship of believers should reflect this characteristic.

CONCLUSION

As for me, the Author knoweth not what to call me, unless it be a Baxterian, as intending to be a Haeresiarcha ... (Richard Baxter, *Church-History*, a4).

Thus have I found the old saying true, that reconcilers use [are accustomed] to be hated on both sides, and to put their hand in the cleft, which closeth upon them and finisheth them (Richard Baxter, *Autobiography*, 173).

We have completed our examination of Baxter's teaching on conversion and related topics, and are now prepared to summarize our findings. First, we will discuss this study's significance for Baxter studies in general. Second, we will review Baxter's teaching on conversion. Finally, we will examine how this study has shed further light on the subject of Puritan conversion.

What significance does this study have for Baxter studies? It has reinforced the necessity of understanding Baxter's 'political method' in theology to interpret his position correctly. Without this framework, Baxter's statements are liable to misinterpretation. Packer was the first to emphasize this aspect of Baxter's methodology, using it to defend Baxter against charges that he is 'vague' and 'inconsistent':

> I question the justice of these strictures. I have found in Baxter nothing but the dazzling precision of a man who knows exactly what he thinks and how to say it. I suspect that the impression of obscurity which Baxter's books have given to his critics is due to their failure to grasp the key which unlocks his system: his so-called 'political method', which none of them mentions. When the grounds and nature of this 'method' are understood, the appearance of arbitrariness and confusion vanishes, and everything falls into place.[1]

We would agree with the assertion, except to note that even with this understanding Baxter's teaching on justification is difficult to categorize neatly.

This study has also shown that if Baxter is labelled an Amyraldian, it must be done with two qualifications. The first reflects the truth that Baxter came to hold a position of universal atonement before he had read any writings from those of the Amyraldian school. The second notes that Baxter's final formulation differed from Amyraut's. Baxter helped shield his view from the criticism of inconsistency (leveled against the Amyraldian position) with his emphasis on God as both *Dominus* and Rector. God's general benevolence to the world is part of his governing; his special love to the elect is part of his secret plan as *Dominus*. Man should not speculate about God's secret will – he should instead live under the light of God's revealed will. Man's role is not to question, but to obey the laws set forth by his Governor. Because of this modification, Packer has titled Baxter's viewpoint an 'improved Amyraldianism'.[2] We would concur with this appellation, as long as it is not presented in such a manner that infers that Baxter learned this doctrine directly from Amyraut.

We hope this study will help lay to rest the 'charge' made against Baxter that he was an Arminian. Undoubtedly he had some Arminian bricks in his final theological edifice (e.g. the notion that in the atonement the law was changed and not satisfied), but the foundation was clearly Calvinistic. Though

Christ had died for all men, he died in a special sense for the elect.[3] Only they, who God elected from eternity, would come to faith through God's effectual grace. The truly elect would persevere to the end.

But many assert that Baxter taught the possibility of salvation for those beyond the 'elect'. Morgan says of Baxter's position, 'The elect were lucky, but many others would be saved as well,'[4] and, 'Like Calvin, he believed that the Church was both visible and invisible, but, unlike Calvin, he believed that salvation was possible to all men.'[5] Ladell claims that as Baxter grew older, 'His conception of Predestination, though never extreme, became so moderate as practically to mean nothing. Baxter inclined more and more to his own interpretation of Common and Special Grace, and to insist upon the possibility of Salvation to every man.'[6] Sommerville asserts that Baxter 'implicitly denied the irresistibility of grace',[7] while Bolam argues he 'cleared' predestination.[8]

All the above statements are inaccurate. Baxter did teach that all men could be saved 'if they will', but he knew that God's effectual grace was necessary before man could so will, and that God only gave this grace to the elect. We concur with Shields' conclusion: 'In reality he stood for a moderate Calvinism which was to be approached from an experiential perspective.'[9]

Another disagreement in Baxter studies concerns the issue of fear as a primary motivation in preaching. Powicke says, 'Baxter, as we know, employed fear as his chief instrument; and, in his hands, it was an instrument of terrific force.'[10] The latter statement we can readily agree with – it *was* an instrument of terrific force. But the former statement stands in need of revision. Baxter did not employ fear as his chief instrument. Listen to him make an appeal to the unconverted:

> For as there is enough in your misery to drive a sober man from it, so is there enough in the hope that is set before you, to draw any believing heart to embrace it. The gospel is a joyful message, and bringeth glad tidings of salvation to all that entertain it.... *Fear is not the principal affection of a true convert; and therefore terrifying arguments are not the principal means;*

yet these must be used, or else God had never put such an affection into man's heart, nor such terrifying passages into his word; and we all feel the need and usefulness of it; for in reason he that is in danger should know it. But yet, *it is love that must be the predominant affection; and therefore it is the discovery of the amiableness of God, and the wonderful gain that comes by godliness, that must be the principal argument that we must use with you.* For we know that men will not be directly affrighted into love, though they must be affrighted from the contrary that hindereth it: do not think that God hath no better argument to use with you, than to take you by the throat, and say, Love me or I will damn thee.[11]

Elsewhere Baxter says that fear is not 'of the right strain, if love be not its companion'.[12] Love must draw, as well as fear drive. Powicke of all men should have recognized this.[13]

A final issue to which we call attention is Baxter's classification. What terminology should be used in describing him? Nuttall has demonstrated that while Baxter is usually considered a Presbyterian, he in fact never was one.[14] Baxter expressly denies the label: 'It pleaseth the Prelatists to say truly of me that I am no Presbyterian.'[15] Rooy has shown that Baxter's objection to labels was that 'the taking of the name of a party tended to division in the church'.[16]

We have designated Baxter's position as 'Puritan' throughout this dissertation. Where exactly does he fit in the Puritan tradition? One scholar argues that he should be placed outside the tradition, saying, 'neither Baxter nor Bunyan, usually thought of as distinguished representatives of Puritanism, thought of themselves as Puritans. Baxter says that people so described his father...'[17] Hall argues that 'contemporary usage of the word Puritan was confined to the period 1564–1640'.[18] He quotes Baxter's statement on the eve of the Restoration as the basis for his assertion: 'Any man that was for a spiritual serious way of worship ... was called commonly a Presbyterian as formerly he was called a Puritan.'[19]

Hall is correct when he observes that Baxter says people called his father a Puritan. But to suggest on the basis of the aforementioned quote by Baxter that 'contemporary usage of the word Puritan was confined to the period 1564–1640' is inaccurate. In 1680, Baxter noted that the godly were reproached as 'Presbyterians and Puritans'.[20] In 1681 he could write that the godly people were reproached by the vulgar, 'as lately by the word Puritans'.[21]

To infer further that the 1640 'terminus' means Baxter should not be called a Puritan heightens the error. We might remember William Haller's assertion that, 'Who was the first Puritan and who may prove to be the last are questions one need not try to answer. There were Puritans before the name was invented and there will continue to be Puritans long after it has ceased to be a common epithet.'[22] Yet the accusation that Baxter falls outside of the Puritan camp demands an answer. Is it true, as Hall asserts, that Baxter never considered himself a representative of Puritanism?

As in the case of the issue over Presbyterianism, we must note at the outset that Baxter disliked all party names.[23] His self-designation was that of a 'meer nonconformist',[24] 'meer Christian', or a 'Catholick Christian'.[25] Yet in *The Poor Man's Family Book* he takes the position of the Puritan in the following dialogue between Sir Elymas Dives, a malignant Contradicter, and Paul, a Teacher:

> E. But you are the most censorious generation of men in the world. You make a sect and party for religion, of precise and self-conceited people, and then none must be saved but your precise party; and how empty will heaven be, if none be there but puritans!
>
> P. 1. I suppose you will grant, that if we should never so much flatter ungodly persons with the hopes of salvation, their case might be the worse, but it could be never the better.[26]

He used statements such as 'we Puritanes',[27] and 'we called *Puritans* and *Non-conformists*'.[28] He was 'bold' in speaking for the Puritan movement because others stigmatized him as a 'total Puritan' and because all the Puritans whom Baxter knew 'are of this mind'.[29]

Baxter clearly considered himself a representative of Puritanism. Why he did not ascribe to this designation more often is indicated by his following confession:

> I will add, that if to be serious in the belief of the Christian Faith, and the Life to come, and in seeking it above this world, and in constant endeavors to please God, whoever be displeased by it, is it that maketh a man a *Puritan*, because he is not a *formal Hypocrite*, then I would I were worthy of the Titles which your *Pseudo-Tilenus* and his Brother give me, who say, I am *Purus Putus Puritanus*, and one *qui totum Puritanismus totus spirat*: Alas I am not so good and happy... [30]

Baxter was reluctant to use the name not because he does not agree with the Puritan position but because he considers himself unworthy of such a noble appellation!

Nuttall's conclusion is well put: 'Baxter's title for himself was a "meer Catholick"; the only description which fits him throughout his ministry, and which he would not have repudiated, is Puritan.'[31] With this we are in total agreement. But what is his exact place within this tradition? Can we say, along with Flynn, that Baxter was 'the most representative Puritan in history'?[32]

In terms of his ministerial practice, we would argue that Baxter is well deserving of this description. His work at Kidderminster has remained to this day a model of ministerial fidelity. He has been called 'the greatest of all English preachers',[33] 'the great apostle of evangelical fervency,'[34] and 'the most successful preacher and winner of souls and nurturer of won souls, that England has ever had'.[35] Clearly Baxter's ministerial efforts make him worthy of Flynn's appellation.

But in terms of his view of the atonement and his teachings on justification, he can hardly be styled the most representative Puritan.[36] His concept of an unlimited atonement in an 'improved Amyraldian' scheme did not square with the emphasis of a limited, substitutionary atonement taught by the majority of the Puritans. Though we have argued that Baxter's position on justification was substantially closer to the orthodox position than some have claimed, his views at this point cannot be said to be representative. Baxter clearly stands outside the Puritan mainstream when these teachings are considered.

In terms of his views on conversion, however, he appears to have been 'orthodox Puritan'. This study began by asking the question, 'What understanding of conversion [the process of becoming a 'true Christian'] did the Puritan pastor Richard Baxter have?' Having completed our examination of Baxter's teaching on conversion and related topics, we are now prepared to answer this question. Baxter taught that conversion was a process. Men lie dead in sin and cannot respond until God moves them to do so through effectual grace. But this does not mean men must sit by idly and wait for God to work. They should prepare themselves through the use of the appointed means to receive God's gift of grace. God is not beholden to men if they engage in preparation, but experience shows he normally meets those who have had their hearts prepared through consideration and humiliation.

Humiliation must not be taken too seriously nor too lightly. Tears are not necessary, but likewise should not be scorned. Only when a man comes face to face with his sin can he fully trust in Christ as his Savior. But God breaks men's hearts in different ways. He remains free to work in men as he sees fit. He alone is Lord. He gives faith only to the elect, but those who speculate about election are misguided. Man's responsibility is not to wonder if he is or is not one of the elect, but to use the means God has provided for salvation.

Faith is more than intellectual belief; it involves trust and commitment as well. The baptismal covenant sums up man's relation to God in all his offices. Assurance of salvation can be given with faith, but normally is not. Most Christians will never attain full assurance. Men therefore should not preoccupy themselves with quests for assurance, but should instead focus on duty.

Most Christians do not know the exact moment of their conversion. Those churches which require a conversion narrative as a basis of membership are misguided. The testimony of Scripture and the history of the church shows that church membership has always been conferred upon men who give a mere profession of faith. Those who require a conversion narrative are guilty of 'undoing by overdoing'.

Conversion is but the starting point of a life of holiness. Holiness is the very essence of Christianity. Antinomianism, or any teaching that leans in that direction, must be opposed. Many who claim the name 'Christian' live in self-deceit. Only those who experience genuine conversion are 'true Christians'. Even though God gives effectual grace to his elect to cause them to turn, they must do the actual work themselves. Faith is not merely believing yourself to be justified, but accepting Christ according to his threefold offices of Prophet, Priest, and King.

This summarizes in brief fashion Baxter's teaching on conversion. How do these observations relate to those of other scholars who have treated the subject of Puritan conversion? We noted in the Introduction that most scholars writing in the field on Puritan conversion have not considered Baxter's views when formulating their conclusions. Yet in light of Baxter's significance the picture cannot be complete until his teaching is considered. Other Puritans certainly wrote on conversion, but Baxter wrote more than any other, and apparently was read more than any other on this topic.[37] Men and women eagerly applied what he taught concerning conversion.[38] Baxter himself gives some indication of the influence of his *Call to the Unconverted*:

> God hath blessed [it] with unexpected success beyond all the rest that I have written (except *The Saints Rest*). In a little more than a year there were about twenty thousand of them printed by my own consent, and about ten thousand since, besides many thousands by stolen impressions.... Through God's mercy I have had information of almost whole households converted by this small book ... God ... hath sent it over on his message to many beyond the seas.[39]

Orme suggests that the overall effects of this book in the conversion of people 'have been greater probably than have arisen from any other mere human performance', and that its influence is 'beyond all calculation'.[40]

How does Baxter's teaching fit into the research others have done in the field of Puritan conversion? Baxter emphasized the absolute necessity of conversion. Simpson and Cohen's assertion that conversion is the 'essence' of Puritanism describes Baxter's thought well.[41] Rooy correctly says that, 'The soteriological consideration that men must be brought to personal conversion dominates the Puritan message.'[42] It certainly dominated Baxter's message.

This research raises serious questions about a 'morphology of conversion' among the Puritans. We noted in the Introduction that Edmund Morgan argues for such, claiming that, 'The pattern is so plain as to give the [conversion] experiences the appearance of a stereotype.'[43] Baxter's teaching does not fit this pattern. He recognized that God does not break all men's hearts alike.[44] Hambrick-Stowe correctly relates this truth to the general Puritan view, saying, 'Conversion could be gradual, sudden, violent, mild, or scarcely perceptible.'[45] Tipson's research on William Perkins bears this out as well: he concluded that Perkins did not reduce conversion to well-defined stages in a morphology.[46]

Cohen has added a new dimension to this issue with his study of the Puritan usage of Lydia and David as stereotypes of spiritual experience. He says, 'Among the ministry's favorite figures, whose lives played variations on the theme of helplessness transmitted by submission into faith, were one from Acts and one from Psalms. The spiritual biography of Lydia, the dye seller of Acts, related one style of effectual vocation, the passage from death to grace.'[47] Cohen carefully guards against over-emphasizing these prescriptions, acknowledging that the Puritans always recognized that the Spirit moves in different ways in different people.[48] In spite of this, however, he argues that the Puritan preachers set forth Lydia as a model for a typical conversion experience.

Baxter used Lydia to emphasize the importance of using the means God had provided: 'There is a heavenly light, and power, and majesty in the word of God, which in the serious reading or hearing of it, may pierce the heart, and prick it, and open it that corruption may go out, and grace come in.... The heart of Lydia was opened to attend to the preaching of Paul, Acts xvi. 14.'[49] Lydia also served as an example of being a faithful witness to one's household: 'For as it is your duty to endeavour it, so God useth to bless his believing servants, with the conversion of their household with them; as the case of the jailer, and Lydia, (Acts xvi) Zaccheus; Stephanus, and others, show us. You shall therefore delay our open profession of your resolved conversion till you do it in the presence of them all.'[50]

Baxter also used other biblical examples. The apostle Paul was a favorite of his to demonstrate God's variety in dealing with men in conversion. He says, 'God worketh not alike on all: sometime (as on Paul) he so suddenly changeth the mind and will, as that at once he both produceth the Act of mans consent, and also taketh away even the moral (though not the natural) power to the contrary in the antecedent instant.'[51] Paul also served as an example of the change that issued from genuine conversion:

How eagerly was Saul going on in his persecution, till the light from heaven did stop his course, and the voice and grace of Christ did change his mind! Acts 9. But do you read ever Paul did persecute any more? or doth he deal and take time to consider of the matter before he would leave his former sin? No; but he presently forbears, and betakes himself to another course.... Now you see that conversion makes an effectual change of the life.... By this one mark you may know whether the sins of your lives, be they great or small, are certain proofs of an unconverted, graceless heart or not. In every true converted man, the main bent of his heart and life is against sin, and his chief desire and endeavour is to destroy it; but in others it is not so.[52]

The point is obvious. If this were not the experience of his hearers, they had reason to doubt the genuineness of their experience.

The encounter between Peter and Cornelius provided Baxter with a model for evangelism. 'God worketh by instruments,' he claimed. 'When he will convert a Cornelius, a Peter must be sent for, and willingly heard. When he will recall and save a sinner, he hath usually some public minister or private friend, that shall be a messenger of that searching and convincing truth, which is fit to awaken them, enlighten them and recover them.'[53] Christians were to live in a state of readiness to share the gospel; non-Christians were to seek out those who could give them spiritual guidance.

Another key issue in Puritan conversion is that of the role of preparation. Pettit called attention to this issue through his work *The Heart Prepared*, but misinterpreted the Puritan position. He argued that preparation put a claim on God. God takes away all resistance, but is helpless to do so without man's consent.[54] Tipson's critique of this view is on target: 'What Pettit has termed "preparation" would not have been recognized as legitimate by the [Puritan] tradition.'[55] But Pettit is not alone in misinterpreting the Puritans at this point. We have noted that this erroneous view has been set forth by Laurence, Perry Miller, and Lovelace as well.[56]

Baxter emphasized that there was no merit in the activity of preparation. A man cannot force God's hand, cannot make him give special grace if the man humbles himself properly. Preparation is the normal way to faith, not a warrant for faith. Baxter says that the teaching that men must find special marks antecedent to faith to give them a warrant to believe is, 'false Doctrine, I think, in the judgment of all.'[57] Cohen and other scholars have correctly interpreted the Puritan tradition at this point.[58] God's working in man is from beginning to end a testimony of divine grace.

ENDNOTES

Introduction

[1] Richard Baxter, *A Treatise of Conversion* (1657), in *The Practical Works of Richard Baxter*, vol. II. (London: George Virtue, 1838), 435, 447, 448, 399.

[2] Alan Simpson, *Puritanism in Old and New England* (Chicago: University of Chicago Press, 1955, 1964 reprint), 3. See also Charles L. Cohen, *God's Caress: The Psychology of Puritan Religious Experience* (New York: Oxford University Press, 1986), 4, and Jerald C. Brauer, 'Conversion: From Puritanism to Revivalism,' *The Journal of Religion* 58 (1978): 229-35.

[3] Various scholars have placed the heart of the movement in matters of polity, theological dogma, the doctrine of soteriology, principles of authority, fellowship of holiness, or class orientation. For a brief overview of these positions, see Richard Greaves, 'The Nature of the Puritan Tradition,' in R. Buick Knox, ed., *Reformation, Conformity and Dissent: Essays in Honour of Geoffrey Nuttall* (London: Epworth Press, 1977), 255-73.

[4] The works by Shields and Rooy are notable exceptions. However Shields treats Baxter as one of seven theologians considered; Rooy includes him as one of five. See James L. Shields, 'The Doctrine of Regeneration in English Puritan Theology, 1604–1689,' Unpublished Ph.D. dissertation, Southwestern Baptist Theological Seminary, Fort Worth, Texas, 1965, and Sidney Rooy, *The Theology of Missions in the Puritan Tradition* (Grand Rapids: Eerdmans, 1965). Rooy's study was done for the Th.D. degree at the Free University of Amsterdam, and was subsequently published by Eerdmans.

[5] The Bibliography lists studies which examine Baxter's views of ecclesiology, pastoral ministry, Scripture, ethics, government, etc. At the risk of stating the obvious, let me emphasize that my purpose here is not to criticize others' work (much of which is excellent), but to demonstrate the need for and importance of the present study for our understanding of Puritan conversion and for furthering the cause of Baxter studies.

The best overall examination of Baxter's thought is the study by J. I. Packer, 'The Redemption and Restoration of Man in the Thought of Richard Baxter,' unpublished D. Phil. dissertation, Oxford University, 1954. Packer discusses conversion in Chapter XIII, 'The Work of the Holy Spirit.' It was published by Paternoster Press in 2003.

[6] *Treatise of Conversion* (1657), *Call to the Unconverted* (1657), *Now or Never* (1663), and *Directions and Persuasions to a Sound Conversion* (1658). These four treatises serve as the foundation for this study. In his chapter surveying Baxter's writings on conversion, Orme claims: 'In this department of writing, I am not aware that he had properly any predecessor in the English language.... Conversion in all its

important aspects, and unutterably important claims, had not before been discussed, at least in our language; nor had any man previously employed so boundless a range of topics, in conjunction with such an energetic and awakening style of addressing sinners.' See William Orme, *The Life and Times of Richard Baxter* (Boston: Crocker & Brewster, 1831), Vol. II, 72.

[7] Orme, *Life and Times*, Vol. II, 72.

[8] N. H. Keeble notes: 'The influence of his books is incalculable: from the early 1650s they enjoyed greater sales than those of any other English writer.' See Keeble, 'Introduction' to *The Autobiography of Richard Baxter* (London: J. M. Dent & Sons Ltd, 1974), xiv. Sommerville's research demonstrates the enormous popularity of Baxter's *Call to the Unconverted*. See C. John Sommerville, *Popular Religion in Restoration England* (Gainesville, Fla.: University of Florida Press, 1977), 47ff.

Phillips suggests that a profitable topic for research would be 'Richard Baxter's influence on Continental Pietism,' noting that 'quite a number of Baxter's publications were quickly translated into German, and seem to have been quite popular among the groups which fostered the Pietist movement'. See James M. Phillips, 'Between Conscience and the Law: The Ethics of Richard Baxter,' unpublished Ph.D. dissertation, Princeton University, 1958, 345-46.

[9] A. B. Grosart, the great nineteenth century Puritan scholar, once said in a lecture of Baxter that he 'drew more hearts to the great Broken Heart than any single Englishman of his age'. Cited in Peter Lewis, *The Genius of Puritanism* (Haywards Heath, Sussex: Carey Publications, 1977), 25.

[10] *Reliquiae Baxterianae*, I, 114-5. Hereafter this work will be cited as R.B., with the appropriate section and page citations following. Baxter goes on to note that the Indian missionary John Elliot translated the *Call to the Unconverted* as soon as he had finished translating the Bible. Baxter also refers to its translation into French, German, and Dutch.

William Bates remarks that six brothers were at one time converted by this book, and that 'every week he received letters of some converted by his books'. See Bates, *A Funeral Sermon for ... Mr. Richard Baxter* (1692), 113.

[11] Orme, *Life and Times*, Vol. II, 79.

[12] E.g. Hugh Martin, *Puritanism and Richard Baxter* (London: SCM Press, 1954), 122-23, and John Stephen Flynn, *The Influence of Puritanism on the Political and Religious Thought of the English* (Port Washington, N.Y.: Kennikat Press, 1920, 1970 reprint), 138.

[13] Baxter's *The Reformed Pastor* remains a classic on the subject of pastoral ministry. For its influence on subsequent ministers, see the 'Introductory Essay' in *The Reformed Pastor*, edited with an Introduction by John T. Wilkinson (London: Epworth Press, 1939, 1950 rev. ed.), 15-47.

[14]R. B., I, 84-85. Perhaps even more telling for the quality of his ministry is the following statement, written after his Ejection: 'though I have been now absent from them about six years, and they have been assaulted with pulpit-calumnies, and slanders, with threatenings and imprisonments, with enticing words, and seducing reasonings, they yet stand fast and keep their integrity ... not one, that I hear of, that are fallen off, or forsake their uprightness.' Ibid., 86.

[15]The debate over a definition for Puritanism can be traced in Jerald C. Brauer, 'Reflections on the Nature of English Puritanism,' *Church History* 23 (1954): 99-108; Basil Hall, 'Puritanism: the Problem of Definition,' in G. J. Cuming, ed., *Studies in Church History*, II (Camden, N.J.: Thomas Nelson and Sons, 1965), 283-96; Charles H. George, 'Puritanism as History and Historiography,' *Past and Present* 41 (1968): 77-104; William Lamont, 'Puritanism as History and Historiography: Some Further Thoughts,' *Past and Present* 44 (1969): 133-46; David D. Hall, 'Understanding the Puritans,' in Stanley N. Katz, ed., *Colonial America: Essays in Politics and Social Development* (Boston: Little, Brown, 1971), 1-50; Ian Breward, 'The Abolition of Puritanism,' *Journal of Religious History* 7 (1972): 20-34; Richard Greaves, 'The Nature of the Puritan Tradition,' in R. Buick Knox, ed., *Reformation, Conformity and Dissent: Essays in Honour of Geoffrey Nuttall* (London: Epworth Press, 1977), 255-73; Paul Christianson, 'Reformers and the Church of England under Elizabeth I and the Early Stuarts,' *Journal of Ecclesiastical History* 31 (1980): 463-82; and Patrick Collinson, 'A Comment: Concerning the Name Puritan,' *Journal of Ecclesiastical History* 31 (1980): 483-88.

[16]This study makes no attempt to give a comprehensive bibliography on these other facets of Puritanism. The reader is urged to consult the bibliographies of the numerous survey works available, e.g. John Adair, *Founding Fathers: The Puritans in England and America* (Grand Rapids: Baker, 1982), 286-97, and Leland Ryken, *Worldly Saints: The Puritans as They Really Were* (Grand Rapids: Zondervan, 1986), 268-75.

[17]The reader should note that this analysis treats only the field of Puritan conversion. For those desiring further information on studies of Christian conversion in general, consult Bernhard Citron, *New Birth: A Study of the Evangelical Doctrine of Conversion in the Protestant Fathers* (Edinburgh: Edinburgh University Press, 1951), and David F. Wells, *Turning to God: Biblical Conversion in the Modern World* (Grand Rapids: Baker, 1989).

For information on religious conversion in general, consult the excellent bibliographical article by Lewis R. Rambo, 'Current Research on Religious Conversion,' *Religious Studies Review* 8 (1982): 146-59. Rambo examines the research on conversion from the following perspectives: anthropological, sociological, historical, psychological, psychoanalytic (including a special section on Augustine), and theological (including a special section on the Apostle Paul). Rambo's article would serve as a good starting point for anyone beginning research in the field of conversion.

[18]Simpson, *Puritanism in Old and New England*, 6.

[19]Edmund S. Morgan, *Visible Saints: The History of a Puritan Idea* (Ithaca, N.Y.: Cornell University Press, 1963, 1975 edition), 90-91. He asserts: 'The pattern is so plain as to give the [conversion] experiences the appearance of a stereotype.'

[20]Patricia Caldwell, *The Puritan Conversion Narrative: The Beginning of American Expression* (Cambridge: Cambridge University Press, 1983), 39. Caldwell says she 'regrets' that she formerly propounded the view of a 'more or less formulaic conversion' in her article, 'The Antinomian Language Controversy,' *Harvard Theological Review* 69 (1976): 366.

[21]New Haven: Yale University Press, 1966. See also the 2nd edition, which contains a helpful Introduction by David D. Hall (Middletown, Conn.: Wesleyan University Press, 1989).

[22]Chapel Hill, N.C.: University of North Carolina Press, 1982.

[23]Hambrick-Stowe, *The Practice of Piety*, 136-241.

[24]Unpublished Ph.D. dissertation, Yale University, 1972.

[25]Tipson, 'The Development of a Puritan Understanding of Conversion,' 261.

[26]Shields, 'The Doctrine of Regeneration in English Puritan Theology, 1604-1689,' vii.

[27]Rooy, *The Theology of Missions in the Puritan Tradition*.

[28]Ibid., 310.

[29]Cohen, *God's Caress*. This book won the Allan Nevins Prize of the Society of American Historians.

[30]Among many are: C. John Sommerville, 'Conversion versus the early Puritan Covenant of Grace,' *Journal of Presbyterian History* 44 (1966): 178-97; John C. English, 'The Puritan Doctrine of Christian Initiation,' *Studia Liturgica* 6 (1969): 158-70; Howard M. Feinstein, 'The Prepared Heart: A Comparative Study of Puritan Theology and Psychoanalysis,' *American Quarterly* 22 (1970): 166-76; J. Sears McGee, 'Conversion and the Imitation of Christ in Anglican and Puritan Writing,' *The Journal of British Studies* 15 (1976): 21-39; Murray G. Murphey, 'The Psychodynamics of Puritan Conversion,' *American Quarterly* 31 (1979): 135-47; Mary Cochran Grimes, 'Saving Grace Among Puritans and Quakers: A Study of 17th and 18th Century Conversion Experiences,' *Quaker History* 72 (1983): 3-26; Mark R. Shaw, 'Drama in the Meeting House: The Concept of Conversion in the Theology of William Perkins,' *Westminster Theological Journal* 45 (1983): 41-72.

[31]In his autobiography Baxter discusses forty changes of emphasis in his person and views (R.B., I, 124-38). Many of these point to inward character changes (e.g. moderation of temper, less desire for controversy,

etc.), while other changes are more directly related to churches, to other Christians, and to the Scriptures.

[32]See A. G. Matthews, *The Works of Richard Baxter: an Annotated List*, 1932, revised from Congregational Historical Society *Transactions*, XI (1932).

[33]Robert Paul questions the accuracy of Matthews' count as he owns a volume written by Baxter which is not on the list: *Monthly Preparations for Holy Communion*, Third Edition Corrected (Boston: Printed for D. Henchman, 1728). See Robert S. Paul, 'Ecclesiology in Richard Baxter's Autobiography,' in *From Faith to Faith*, ed. by Dikran Y. Hadidian (Pittsburgh: Pickwick Press, 1979), 391, note 4. William Orme lists a total of 168 works for Baxter, but he arrives at this higher number by repeatedly listing component parts of a treatise as independent works. See Orme, *Life and Times*, vol. II, 345-50.

[34]Foremost attention is given to Baxter's *Practical Works*, 4 Vol. (1838), as it is here that his writings which specifically deal with conversion have been collected. Citations from the *Practical Works* will include only the volume number (I-IV), the page number, an abbreviation of the book title (see the Bibliography for a list of abbreviations), and the original date of publication. I am indebted to Sidney Rooy for this arrangement which helps the reader to identify the precise book being cited from the *Practical Works*. A listing of primary source materials not in the *Practical Works* but consulted for this study may be found in the Bibliography. Baxter is the author of works listed by title only unless otherwise indicated. I have silently modernized spelling, capitalization and italics in quoted material whenever such changes seemed necessary for the sake of clarity.

The focus of this study is on Baxter's published works. J. I. Packer, after examining the Baxter MS treatises preserved at Dr. William's library in London, concurs with Baxter scholar William Orme that 'among the printed works of Baxter sufficient is to be found already on all the subjects of which they [the manuscripts] treat'. See Orme's edition of the *Practical Works*, 23 vols. (London: James Duncan, 1830), vol. I, 765, cited in Packer, 'Redemption and Restoration,' xv.

[35]One such work is Ryken's *Worldly Saints: The Puritans as They Really Were*. Packer notes in the Foreword (ix), that 'most people's image of Puritanism still has on it much disfiguring dirt that needs to be scraped off.'

[36]Secondary material on Baxter is evaluated at appropriate places in the study.

[37]John Stoughton, *History of Religion in England*, rev. ed. (London: Hodder and Stoughton, 1881), vol. IV, 381.

[38]C. F. Allison, *The Rise of Moralism: The Proclamation of the Gospel from Hooker to Baxter* (New York: The Seabury Press, 1966), 192. While not making this charge against Baxter directly, Allison appears to do

so indirectly when he asserts: 'The divines who introduced this trend toward moralism postulated a freedom of will that was of Pelagian proportions' and that they began 'from assumptions that can be characterized only as Pelagian'.

[39]John Hunt, *Religious Thought in England* (London: Strahan & Co., 1870), Vol. I, 265.

[40]Frederick J. Powicke, *The Reverend Richard Baxter Under the Cross, 1662-1691* (London: Jonathan Cape, Ltd., 1927), 233-38.

[41]Packer, 'Redemption and Restoration,' x.

[42]Alexander Gordon, *Heads of English Unitarian History* (London: Philip Green, 1895), 98. Gordon asserts that 'Baxter's Calvinism differed from that of the Westminster divines, simply by the purity of its adhesion to the original type, unaffected by the anti-Arminian reaction'.

[43]See Geoffrey Nuttall, *Richard Baxter* (London: Thomas Nelson and Sons, 1965), 121. Baxter vigorously denied all these charges. He tells us the only label he desires: 'If you know not [what to call me], I will tell you, I am a CHRISTIAN, a MEER CHRISTIAN.... If the Name CHRISTIAN be not enough, call me a CATHOLICK CHRISTIAN.' See Baxter, Preface to *Church-History of the Government of Bishops and their Councils Abbreviated* (1680).

1. The Life and Ministry of Richard Baxter

[1]The starting point for any consideration of Baxter's life must be his own autobiography, *Reliquiae Baxterianae* (1696), published by his friend and colleague Matthew Sylvester. This was issued in abridged form in 1925 by J. M. Lloyd Thomas, and reissued in 1974 by N. H. Keeble under the title *The Autobiography of Richard Baxter* (London: J. M. Dent & Sons). Citations in this chapter are from Keeble's edition (hereafter cited simply as *Autobiography*) except where the account only appears in the *Reliquiae Baxterianae* (cited as R.B.).

The best biography is Nuttall's *Richard Baxter*, surpassing F. J. Powicke's two works, *A Life of the Reverend Richard Baxter, 1615-1691* (London: Jonathan Cape, Ltd, 1924), and *The Reverend Richard Baxter Under the Cross, 1662-1691* (London: Jonathan Cape, Ltd, 1927). Nuttall has filled in numerous gaps in our knowledge of Baxter's life by utilizing historical references scattered through Baxter's other published works and especially in his manuscript correspondence, which Nuttall was the first to calendar and read in chronological order.

[2]*Autobiography*, 3. Ladell speculates that 'the boy's mother was not strong enough to attend to her child, and his father was too busy with pressing financial difficulties to care to have him under his roof.' See A. R. Ladell, *Richard Baxter: Puritan and Mystic* (London: S.P.C.K., 1925), 36.

Powicke, *A Life*, 15, places young Richard's mother with him in Rowton for these ten years, both then being apart from his father.

Unfortunately Powicke gives no justification for this departure from Baxter's straightforward declaration: 'And there I lived *from my parents* with my grandfather... [emphasis added].'

[3]*Autobiography*, 3.

[4]Baxter's father was converted 'by the bare reading of the Scriptures in private, without either preaching, or godly company, or any other books but the Bible.' Ibid., 4. Eayrs notes that copies of the Scriptures were rapidly multiplied after the new translation of 1611. See George Eayrs, *Richard Baxter and the Revival of Preaching and Pastoral Service* (London: National Council of Evangelical Free Churches, 1912), 8.

[5]*Autobiography*, 4-5. These men 'read Common Prayer on Sundays and Holy-Days' and 'taught school and tippled on the weekdays.'

[6]Baxter says, 'Only three or four constant competent preachers lived near us, and those (though conformable all save one) were the common marks of the people's obloquy and reproach, and any that had but gone to hear them, when he had no preaching at home, was made the derision of the vulgar rabble under the odious name of a Puritan.' Ibid., 4. Nuttall notes that it later became one of Baxter's primary aims to 'assist in the effective remedying of such a state of affairs.' Nuttall, *Richard Baxter*, 8.

[7]IV:316, CR (1658).

[8]*Autobiography*, 4.

[9]Ibid., 5.

[10]Ibid., 6.

[11]This was a 'corrected' abridgment made by the Protestant Edmund Bunny in 1584 of the Jesuit Robert Persons' *Book of Resolution* (1582).

[12]*Autobiography*, 7. Baxter's account of his conversion, taken from the *Autobiography*, has appeared recently in *Conversions: The Christian Experience*, edited by Hugh T. Kerr and John M. Mulder (Grand Rapids: Eerdmans, 1983), 29-33.

[13]R.B., I, 3. Unfortunately for our purposes, the abridged *Autobiography* omits this and other portions of Baxter's account of his conversion.

[14]Ibid. The significance of this statement becomes even greater when placed in the context of the debate over a 'morphology of conversion' within Puritanism. If there was such a pre-determined pattern, Baxter's conversion certainly did not follow it.

[15]Ibid., 4. It is interesting to speculate that this may have been why he placed so much emphasis on writing books on conversion and encouraging others to read them.

[16]Baxter's greatest regret was the neglect of languages in his education: 'Besides the Latin Tongue, and but a mediocrity in Greek (with an inconsiderable trial at the Hebrew long after) I had no great skill in Languages.' R.B., I, 6.

Stephen says Baxter was 'ignorant of Hebrew – a mere smatterer in Greek – and possessed of as much Latin as enabled him in after-life to use it with reckless facility.' See *An Excerpt from Reliquiae Baxterianae, with an Essay by Sir James Stephen on Richard Baxter*, ed. by Francis John (New York: Longmans, Green, and Co., 1910), 68-69.

[17]Baxter gives some account of his reading: '[I] read a multitude of our English Practical Treatises, before I had ever read any other Bodies of Divinity.... Next [to] Practical Divinity, no Books so suited with my Disposition as Aquinas, Scotus, Durandus, Ockam, and their Disciples; because I thought they narrowly searched after Truth, and brought Things out of the darkness of Confusion: For I could never from my first Studies endure Confusion!' R.B., I, 6. Eayrs mentions that Dr. Stalker believes that Baxter probably read more books than any human being has ever done! See Eayrs, *Richard Baxter*, 131.

[18]*Autobiography*, 8.

[19]Ibid., 12.

[20]Baxter laments that he saw 'a stage-play instead of a sermon on the Lord's-days in the afternoon,' and that he heard 'little preaching but what was as to one part against the Puritans.' His succinct statement says it all: 'I was glad to be gone.' See Ibid., 12.

[21]Baxter nearly lost his life in an accident while traveling home, falling from his horse into the path of an oncoming wagon. The horses miraculously stopped, and Baxter was dragged away from destruction. Davies argues that this incident was the turning point of Baxter's life: 'From that hour the needle of his heart pointed towards heaven.' See John Hamilton Davies, *The Life of Richard Baxter of Kidderminster: Preacher and Prisoner* (London: W. Kent and Co., 1887), 17.

[22]Baxter's life was a continual struggle against death. He was harassed by a constant cough, frequent bleedings from the nose, severe headaches, dropsy, renal pains, etc. One has called him a 'museum of diseases.'

John Brown asserts: 'If Richard Baxter had done nothing but take care of himself as an invalid, no one would have had the heart to blame a man to whom life was thus one long and weary battle with disease.' See Brown, *Puritan Preaching in England* (New York: Charles Scribner's Sons, 1900), 168.

[23]*Autobiography*, 15 [emphasis added].

[24]Baxter's account of his subscription is characteristically frank: 'so precipitant and rash was I that I had never once read over the Book of Ordination, which was one to which I was to subscribe; nor half read over the Book of Homilies, nor exactly weighed the Book of Common Prayer, nor was I of sufficient understanding to determine confidently in some controverted points in the Thirty-nine Articles.' Ibid., 16.

[25]Ibid., 17.

[26]Baxter says this oath was a 'chief means to alienate me and many others from it [Conformity]. For now our drowsy mindlessness of that subject was shaken off by their violence.' Ibid., 19.

[27]Ibid., 18.

[28]Ibid., 25.

[29]Barbara Stewart provides an excellent discussion on the town of Kidderminster in her work, 'Richard Baxter: The Beloved Pastor of Kidderminster,' unpublished Masters thesis, Regent College, Vancouver, British Columbia, April 1985, 18-32. See also Powicke's treatment in *A Life*, 35-46.

[30]Powicke records that the vicar's preaching was so terrible that his own wife would leave the services in shame. See Powicke, *A Life*, 84.

[31]That the vicar took the people seriously can be seen in the financial arrangements he offered. The new lecturer would be paid a sum of £60 per annum out of the £200 which the vicar's living provided. The vicar secured the agreement by posting a bond of £500.

[32]Nuttall, *Richard Baxter*, 24.

[33]At the time of his ordination, while professing that 'a fervent desire of winning Souls to God was my motive,' Baxter acknowledges that he 'had no inclination' to 'a Pastoral Charge.' See the Preface in *Plain Scripture Proof of Infants Church-Membership and Baptism* (1653).

[34]Baxter tells what outraged many of them: 'And once all the ignorant rout were raging mad against me for preaching the doctrine of original sin to them, and telling them that infants before regeneration had so much guilt and corruption as made them loathsome in the eyes of God; whereupon they vented it abroad in the country that I preached that God hated or loathed infants, so that they railed at me as I passed through the streets.' *Autobiography*, 28. Nuttall argues, however, that he 'offended them even more by his insistence on holiness of life and his desire for discipline.' Nuttall, *Richard Baxter*, 29.

[35]Davies mentions that in one year he expended £100 in purchasing Bibles for poor families. Davies, *Life*, 46. Baxter contracted with his publishers to receive back every fifteenth book (for the purpose of giving away), along with a small royalty (eighteen-pence) for every ream of the other fourteen, which he designated to the poor.

[36]*Autobiography*, 27. Baxter indicates that his doubts arose because 'I had so long neglected the well settling of my foundations, while I had bestowed so much time in the superstructures and the applicatory part.'

[37]Ibid.

[38]Davies argues that 'from the beginning to the end of the civil troubles Baxter was a Royalist at heart.' Davies, *Life*, 98. Nuttall claims that 'Baxter's political hopes were to be disappointed, and he never ceased to condemn the execution of the King; but at the beginning of the war so convinced a Puritan could not do otherwise than side with the Parliament.' Nuttall, *Richard Baxter*, 31-32. Baxter himself says that 'both parties were to blame' and that he 'will not be he that shall justify either of them.' *Autobiography*, 36-37.

[39]Boyle notes that the soldiers at Coventry were 'reformers, not revolutionists. They were still aiming after such changes only as would restore the balance between King and Parliament.' G. D. Boyle, *Richard Baxter* (New York: A. C. Armstrong & Son, 1884), 16. Baxter's own words bear this out. He mentions how the different sides would respond to the question, 'Who are you for?' Those on the king's side said, 'For the king,' and the others said, 'For king and parliament.' *Autobiography*, 36.

[40]*Autobiography*, 50. Ladell asserts that Baxter 'fancied that his teaching then [in the early days of the war] would have checked the rapid growth of Sectarianism and Independency which now had reached beyond control.' Ladell disputes Baxter's statement as optimistic thinking. Ladell, *Richard Baxter: Puritan and Mystic*, 56.

[41]His first published book, *Aphorisms of Justification* (1649), was written to counter the errors of Antinomianism.

[42]*Autobiography*, 52.

[43]His own account of the origin and progress of the work is interesting: 'The second book which I wrote (and the first which I began) was that called *The Saints' Everlasting Rest*. Whilst I was in health I had not the least thought of writing books, or of serving God in any more public way than preaching. But when I was weakened with great bleeding, and left solitary in my chamber at Sir John Cook's in Derbyshire, without any acquaintance but my servant about me, and was sentenced to death by the physicians, I began to contemplate more seriously on the everlasting rest which I apprehended myself to be just on the borders of. And that my thoughts might not too much scatter in my meditation, I began to write something on that subject...' Ibid., 94.

Baxter apologizes for the lack of marginal citations, noting that he wrote most of the book when he had no resources but a Bible and a Concordance. Yet he says, 'I found that the transcript of the heart hath the greatest force on the hearts of others.' Ibid., 95.

[44]From a letter to Anthony à Wood, cited in J. M. Lloyd Thomas' 'Introduction' to Baxter's *Autobiography*, xxv. Baxter notes in the dedication that he wrote the book with 'one foot in the grave'.

[45]*Autobiography*, 26. Throughout the remainder of his life he was 'seldom an hour free from pain'. Ibid., 76.

[46]See R.B., I, 21 for Baxter's complete list.

[47]*Autobiography*, 26 [emphasis added]. Eayrs notes that Baxter was 'at death's door twenty times.' Eayrs, *Richard Baxter*, 49.

[48]He returned to his previous position as lecturer (curate), refusing to accept the vicarage, but Eayrs notes (p. 23), that 'Baxter was vicar in all but name and emoluments.' Powicke relates the story of how the townspeople, without Baxter's knowledge or approval, had petitioned the Westminster Assembly to appoint Baxter to the position of vicar. Baxter served three years as Lecturer before he found out what the

people had done. He did not regard it as making any difference to his position. 'In his own eyes,' Powicke says, 'he was, and remained to the last, simply Minister, or Preacher of the Gospel, at Kidderminster.' See Powicke, *A Life*, 83.

[49]Baxter and his assistant set aside two days a week for private catechizing and instruction, enabling them to speak personally to every family in the parish each year. Baxter explains this practice more fully in *The Reformed Pastor*.

[50]Before the war, Baxter preached twice each Sunday in the parish church, St. Mary's, Kidderminster. After the war, he preached once each Sunday and once every Thursday. The Thursday evening discourse was followed by a meeting of the most earnest hearers at Baxter's house. Baxter's pastoral practice is examined more closely in the second part of this dissertation. See also Charles F. Kemp, *A Pastoral Triumph: The Story of Richard Baxter and His Ministry at Kidderminster* (New York: Macmillan, 1948).

[51]Ladell, *Puritan and Mystic*, 60.

[52]The *Treatise on Conversion* and *Call to the Unconverted* were originally preached. Baxter wrote his pulpit notes in shorthand. Thomas Baldwin, who lived with him and took over the ministry at Kidderminster when Baxter was ejected, learned to decipher Baxter's shorthand notes, and transcribed many of his sermons for the printer.

[53]*Autobiography*, 84. There were 'three or four moderate Conformists that were for the old Episcopacy.'

[54]R.B, I, 84: 'Before I ever entered into the ministry, God blessed my private conference to the conversion of some, who remain firm and eminent in holiness to this day ... in the beginning of my ministry, I was wont to number them as jewels; but since then I could not keep any number of them.'

[55]R.B., I, 85.

[56]Ibid.

[57]*Autobiography*, 79. Cf. Brown's statement: 'If I were asked what, in the year 1646, was one of the most unpromising towns in England to which a young man could be sent, who was starting his career as a preacher and pastor, I should feel inclined to point at once to the town of Kidderminster in Worcestershire. With a population at that time of between three and four thousand, mainly carpet-weavers, it had been, morally and spiritually, so grossly neglected as almost to have sunk into practical heathenism.' See Brown, *Puritan Preaching in England*, 165-66.

[58]Baxter says that they, 'thirsted after the salvation of their neighbours and were in private my assistants, and being dispersed through the town, were ready in almost all companies to repress seducing words, and to justify godliness, and convince, reprove, exhort men according

to their needs; as also to teach them how to pray, and to help them to sanctify the Lord's day.' R.B., I, 87.

[59]*Autobiography*, 79-84.

[60]Ibid., 80.

[61]Ibid., 83-84. He says, 'And it much furthered my success, that I stayed still in this one place (near two years before the wars and above fourteen years after).... It was a great advantage to me to have almost all the religious people of the place of my own instructing and informing, and that they were not formed into erroneous and factious principles before, and that I stayed to see them grown up to some confirmedness and maturity.'

[62]Ibid., 140.

[63]Ibid., 80.

[64]The House of Commons ordered the next day that the sermon be printed. See *A Sermon of Repentance* (1660).

[65]Baxter says the response was mixed: 'The moderate were pleased with it, the fanatics were offended with me for keeping such a thanksgiving, the diocesan party thought I did suppress their joy.' *Autobiography*, 143. Stephen argues that the sermon 'could not have been recited by the most rapid voice in less than two hours.' See *An Excerpt from Reliquiae Baxterianae, with an Essay by Sir James Stephen on Richard Baxter*, ed. by Francis John (New York: Longmans, Green, and Co., 1910), 93.

[66]The sermon was published by a special command. See *The Life of Faith* (1660).

[67]*Autobiography*, 156.

[68]*The Reformed Liturgy* (1661).

[69]It is customary to blame Baxter for the dismal outcome of the conference due to his bluntness. Nuttall defends Baxter against such charges by noting that Baxter realized that from the very beginning of the proceedings that hope of agreement was doomed. 'In these circumstances,' Nuttall says, 'clear statement was called for rather than bringing into play what little diplomacy he possessed. See Nuttall, *Richard Baxter*, 89. Baxter's own statement too often is ignored in this regard: 'the reason why I spake so much was because it was the desire of my brethren, and I was loth to expose them to the hatred of the bishops.... And I thought it a cause that I could comfortably suffer for, and should as willingly be a martyr for charity as for faith.' See *Autobiography*, 170.

[70]Nuttall asserts that Baxter's immediate action had considerable influence on other ministers. Nuttall, *Richard Baxter*, 92.

[71]Margaret had been converted under Baxter's preaching at Kidderminster. Baxter tells the story of their marriage in his tribute to her titled *A Breviate of the Life of Margaret, the Daughter of Francis Charlton,*

of Apply in Shropshire, Esq; and Wife of Richard Baxter. For the use of all, but especially of their Kindred (London: B. Simmons, 1681). It was reprinted in 1928 as *Richard Baxter and Margaret Charlton: A Puritan Love Story,* ed. by John T. Wilkinson (London: George Allen & Unwin Ltd.).

[72]E.g., in his *Christian Directory,* Baxter claims that while it is not 'unlawful' for ministers to marry, 'so great a hinderance [sic] ordinarily is this troublesome state of life to the sacred ministration which they undertake, that a very clear call should be expected for their satisfaction.' *Works,* I:400. Though this was not published until after his marriage (1673), it may be taken to be representative of his thought throughout his life. See also my article, 'The Puritan View of Marriage: The Nature of the Husband/Wife Relationship in Puritan England as Taught and Experienced by a Representative Puritan Pastor, Richard Baxter,' *Trinity Journal* 10 n.s. (Fall 1989): 131-58.

[73]*Breviate,* 46.

[74]*Autobiography,* 174.

[75]After his marriage he not only recorded his belief that for himself at Kidderminster 'my single Life afforded me much advantage' but he continued to commend celibacy for ministers in general. He says that even Margaret 'lived and died in the same mind.' *Breviate,* 101.

[76]Before he would agree to marriage, however, Baxter insisted that Margaret agree to three conditions: '1) That I would have nothing that before our Marriage was hers; that I (who wanted no outward supplies) might not seem to marry her for covetousness; 2) That she would so alter her affairs, that I might be intangled in no Law-suits; 3) That she would expect none of my time which my Ministerial work should require.' See *Breviate,* 47.

[77]Ibid, 70. Baxter claimed that 'These near nineteen years I know not that ever we had any breach in point of love, or point of interest, save only that she somewhat grudged that I had persuaded her for my quietness to surrender so much of her Estate, to a disabling her from helping others so much as she earnestly desired.' Ibid., 47.

[78]The Conventicle Act of 1664 forbade the assembly of more than five persons who were above sixteen years of age (except they comprised the same household) for purposes of worship, otherwise than by the forms of the Church of England. Baxter felt he could continue to hold meetings in his home despite this Act, because his activities (preaching, praying and singing Psalms) were in agreement with the forms of the Church of England. See Powicke, *The Rev. Richard Baxter,* 23.

[79]R.B., III, 2.

[80]Ibid.

[81]*Autobiography,* 199. His observations in the aftermath of the fire are worth noting: 'It was a sight that might have given any man a lively sense of the vanity of this world, and all the wealth and glory of it, and

of the future conflagration of all the world. To see the flames mount up towards heaven, and proceed so furiously without restraint; to see the streets filled with people astonished, that had scarce sense left them to lament their own calamity; to see the fields filled with heaps of goods, and sumptuous buildings, curious rooms, costly furniture and household stuff, yea, warehouses, and furnished shops and libraries, etc., all on a flame, and none durst come near to receive anything ...'

[82]Ibid., 207-10. His imprisonment, Baxter says, was 'no great suffering to me.' He had a good jailer, a large room, and Margaret had the freedom of visitation. He notes that except for the interruption of his sleep, the accommodations there were better than the lodgings he stayed in during his frequent trips to London! Yet he regretted his imprisonment for the interruption it caused his work, removing him from the 'poor people in such hopeful beginnings of a common reformation'.

[83]R.B., III, 59.

[84]His book *The Cure of Church Divisions* (1670) sparked the rumor that Baxter had conformed. See R.B., III, 149. Powicke traces the progression of this rumor in *A Life*, 211.

[85]*Autobiography*, 221. Eayrs notes that this was the first license granted in such general terms. Eayrs, *Richard Baxter*, 109.

[86]Baxter constantly asserted that he was not violating the law by his preaching, as he still had 'a license to preach publicly in London diocese, under the Archbishop's own hand and seal'. See Baxter's Letter to the Earl of Lauderdale, cited in *Life of the Rev. Richard Baxter* (London: The Religious Tract Society, n.d.), 90-91.

[87]On one occasion, the authorities even took Baxter's bed from underneath him, despite the fact that he lay there sick! *Autobiography*, 251. But Baxter keeps it all in perspective: 'Naked came I into the world, and naked must I go out. But I never wanted less (what man can give) than when man had taken all away.... God was pleased quickly to put me past all fear of men, and all desire of avoiding suffering from them by concealment, by laying on me more Himself than man can do. Then imprisonment with tolerable health would have seemed a palace to me. And had they put me to death for such a duty as they persecute me for, it would have been a joyful end of my calamity. But day and night I groan and languish under God's just-afflicting hand ... scarce any part or hour is free [from pain]. As waves follow waves in the tempestuous seas, so one pain and danger followeth another in this sinful, miserable flesh. I die daily, and yet remain alive. God, in his great mercy, knowing my dullness in health and ease, doth make it much easier to repent and hate my sin and loathe myself, and contemn [sic] the world, and submit to the sentence of death with willingness, than otherwise it was ever like to have been. O how little is it that wrathful enemies can do against us, in comparison of what our sin and the justice of God can do!' Ibid., 252.

[88]Some of his books, saved from capture by the adroitness of his wife, were sent to Harvard University in America. See Davies, *Life*, 368.

[89]Baxter did not continue his autobiography beyond the year 1685. Biographers therefore must rely on other sources to fill in information about this time period.

[90]The charge specifically brought against Baxter was that he reflected on the bishops of the Anglican Church in a manner which legally was seditious. The passages objected to were: Matthew 5:19; Mark 3:6; Mark 9:39; Mark 11:31; Mark 12:38-40; Luke 10:2; John 11:57; and Acts 15:2.

[91]See Lord Macaulay, *The History of England*, Vol. I (London: Macmillan, 1913), 484-88 and Orme, *Life of Baxter*, 364-70. The following abbreviated account is from Orme, 368-69:

Lord Chief Justice Jeffries said: 'Richard, Richard, dost thou think we'll hear thee poison the court? Richard, thou art an old fellow, an old knave; thou hast written books enough to load a cart, every one as full of sedition, I might say treason, as an egg is full of meat. Hadst thou been whipped out of thy writing-trade forty years ago, it had been happy. Thou pretendest to be a preacher of the gospel of peace, and thou hast one foot in the grave; it is time for thee to begin to think what account thou intendest to give. But leave thee to thyself, and I see that thou'lt go on as thou hast begun; but, by the grace of God, I'll look after thee.... Come, what do you say for yourself, you old knave? – come, speak up.'

Baxter responded, 'Your lordship need not fear, for I'll not hurt you. But these things will surely be understood one day; what fools one sort of Protestants are made, to persecute the other. I am not concerned to answer such stuff, but I am ready to produce my writings for the confutation of all this, and my life and conversation are known to many in this nation.'

[92]Bates, *A Funeral Sermon*, 123. Bates says, 'It would have been his joy to have been transfigured in the Mount.'

[93]Ibid.

[94]Ibid., 123-24.

[95]Matthew Sylvester, *Elisha's Cry after Elijah's God* (1696), 15. This sermonic tribute to Baxter by Sylvester is bound together with my copy of the *Reliquiae Baxterianae*.

[96]Eayrs, *Richard Baxter*, 126.

[97]Bates, *Funeral Sermon*, 121-22.

2. The Theological Foundation For Conversion

[1]Packer argues that a failure on the part of many of Baxter's interpreters to begin here has led them astray when they examined his theology. Packer, 'Redemption and Restoration,' xiv.

[2]*Of Justification* (1658), 4. Baxter elsewhere warns, 'think not that you well understand divinity, till, 1. You know it as methodized and jointed in a due scheme.' I:730, CD:CEccl (1673).

[3]*An End of Doctrinal Controversies* (1691), 147. Baxter divided the Christian religion into three parts: the essential, the integral, and the accidental. In theology, Baxter said, the 'great, essential, and chief integral parts are few, and easily discerned'. Not so for the rest of the material – all the facts must be taken into account for a true synthesis, and they are not discovered easily. Two things hinder us from a certain knowledge in the rest: 'one is the great number of particles ... the other is the littleness of the thing, which maketh it undiscernible to any but accurate and studious minds.' See IV:569, TKL (1689). See also p. 600: 'So the Scripture is a body of essentials, integrals, and accidentals of religion, and every unstudied fellow cannot anatomize it.'

[4]Perry Miller, *The New England Mind: The Seventeenth Century* (Cambridge: Harvard University Press, 1939, 1963 reprint), 95. Miller cites Baxter as an example of this 'engrossing preoccupation'.

[5]He says, 'And be especially careful that you ... throw not away every truth, which you cannot presently place rightly in the frame ... for a further insight into true method ... may reconcile you to that which now offendeth you. What God hath joined together, be sure that you never put asunder; though yet you cannot find their proper places.... False method rejecteth many a truth.' I:271, CD:CEth (1673).

[6]Keith L. Sprunger, 'Ames, Ramus, and the Method of Puritan Theology.' *Harvard Theological Review* 59 (1966): 134.

[7]See Walter J. Ong, *Ramus: Method and the Decay of Dialogue: From the Art of Discourse to the Art of Reason* (Cambridge, Mass.: Harvard University Press, 1958). Ong gives a biographical sketch of Ramus on pp. 17-35.

[8]Miller, *The New England Mind: The Seventeenth Century*, 499.

[9]Ibid., 138. For a brief overview of the Ramist system, see pages 111-53.

[10]See the example in Ong, *Ramus*, 31.

[11]Sprunger, 'Ames, Ramus, and the Method of Puritan Theology,' 139.

[12]R.B., I, 6. He goes on to refer to those disputes which denied or abused principles of method as 'incoherent Dreams'. Fisher summarizes Baxter's 'skill' in this regard: 'One cannot forbear to sympathize with those who deplored or smiled at Baxter's tedious distinctions. No man could divide a hair with so exquisite nicety.' See George Fisher, 'Theology of Richard Baxter,' *Bibliotheca Sacra* IX (1852): 157.

[13]R.B., III, 69.

[14]Ibid., 70. Baxter thus devotes the first third of his *Methodus Theologiae* to an examination of God, man, and the rest of the created order.

[15]R.B., III, 69. Baxter says he could not find any whose 'Confusion, or great Defects, I could not easily discover, but not so easily amend'.

[16]Ibid. This section of the *Reliquae* was written in 1670, thus placing Baxter's 'conversion' to trichotomizing back to 1644.

[17]IV: 600, TKL (1689).

[18]Baxter, 'To the Reader', in William Allen, *A Discourse of the Nature, Ends, and Difference of the Two Covenants* (1673), A2.

[19]The full title was *Defensio fidei catholicae de satisfactione Christi adversus Faustum Socinum Senensem* (1617). In his *Christian Directory*, Baxter referred to the *De Satisfactione* as 'extraordinary clear and sound', and listed it among the books necessary to be in 'the Poorest Library'. See I:732-733, CD:CEccl (1673). For a complete list of the works of Grotius in Baxter's library, see Geoffrey Nuttall, 'A Transcript of Richard Baxter's Library Catalogue,' *Journal of Ecclesiastical History* 2 (October 1951): 207-221, and 3 (April 1952): 74-100, items 1-4, 467, 479, 496, 513, 522, 531.

[20]Baxter had the following to say about Grotius's influence on him: 'I must in Gratitude Profess that I have learnt more from Grotius, then from almost any Writer ... that ever I read.' *The Grotian Religion Discovered* (1658), 4.

Yet this was not meant to be an unqualified endorsement of all of Grotius's views. Baxter was just as quick to criticize Grotius in areas where Baxter felt he erred (e.g. his design for ecclesiastical unity, which appeared to Baxter to be simply the sounding of a retreat to Rome). For an excellent overview of Baxter's views of Grotius, see Geoffrey Nuttall, 'Richard Baxter and *The Grotian Religion*,' in *Reform and Reformation: England and the Continent, c. 1500-c. 1750*, ed. D. Baker (Oxford, 1979), 245-50.

[21]R.B., I, 107.

[22]R.B., III, 69. The full title is *Theo-Politica: Or, A Body of Divinity, Containing The Rules of the Special Government of God* (1659). Baxter read it earlier in manscript form.

[23]R.B., I, 107-8. Cf. his similar statement about Grotius in footnote 20.

[24]Ibid., 108 [emphasis added].

[25]This work, Baxter says, cost him 'harder studies' than any other. See R.B., III, 70.

[26]Packer, 'Redemption and Restoration,' 87. I will not be examining the *Methodus Theologiae* in this treatment of Baxter, noting Packer's assertion (p. 85) that 'There is nothing in the *Methodus* which was not more or less clearly presented in earlier writings'.

[27]Powicke, *Rev. Richard Baxter*, 63.

[28]Geoffrey Nuttall, *Richard Baxter and Philip Doddridge: A Study in Tradition* (London: Oxford University Press, 1951), 17-18.

[29]See Alexander Gordon, 'Richard Baxter as a founder of Liberal Nonconformity,' in *Heads of English Unitarian History* (London: Philip Green, 1895), 56-101. Cf. Nuttall, who shows there was also an 'orthodox' tradition which flowed from Baxter as well. See *Richard Baxter and Philip Doddridge: A Study in a Tradition*, 29, n. 71.

[30]Jones notes that 'the inconsistencies and defections of Baxterian theology and practice became the weapons in hands less conservative than Baxter's of tearing down Presbyterianism in the 18th century.' Hywel R. Jones, 'The Death of Presbyterianism' (Puritan and Reformed Studies Conference Papers, 1969), 37-38.

See also C. Gordon Bolam, Jeremy Goring, H. L. Short, and Roger Thomas, *The English Presbyterians: From Elizabethan Puritanism to Modern Unitarianism* (Boston: Beacon Press, 1968). As the title suggests, the book claims a line of development between Presbyterians and Unitarians.

[31]Packer, 'The Doctrine of Justification in Development and Decline among the Puritans' (Puritan and Reformed Studies Conference Papers, 1969), 28.

[32]W. C. De Pauley, 'Richard Baxter Surveyed,' *The Church Quarterly Review* 164 (1963): 33. Walter B. T. Douglas asserts that when Baxter gives a high place to reason it is 'regenerate reason'. See Douglas, 'Politics and Theology in the Thought of Richard Baxter.' *Andrews University Sem St* 15 (Autumn 1977): 122.

[33]II:394, UI:AR (1655).

[34]He says, 'It greatly confirmeth my belief of the holy Scriptures, to find by certain experience, the original and universal pravity of man's nature, how great it is, and wherein it doth consist; exactly agreeing with this sacred word; when others have made such a full discovery of it.' See II:129, MR (1671).

[35]II:245, UI (1655).

[36]Baxter renounced those who disparaged reason as being antithetical to faith, saying 'an infant, or a madman, would make the best christian, if reason were at such odds with faith as they imagine'. III:88, note h, SER (1650).

[37]'In my youth,' Baxter says, 'I was ... greatly delighted with metaphisical and scholastick Writings.' R.B. I, 126.

[38]This is not to suggest that Baxter thought argument alone could bring a man to faith. We shall see in the ensuing pages that Baxter constantly asserted that only the enlightening of the Holy Spirit brings faith.

[39]Keeble points out that Baxter 'refused to equate true Christianity with any doctrinal or ecclesiastical system'. Keeble, *Richard Baxter: Puritan Man of Letters*, 26.

[40]'I spend my time, and strength and spirits in almost nothing but studying after Truth.' *Plain Scripture Proof* (1650), 2.

In the Preface to his *Catholick Theologie* (1675), Baxter would say, 'My genius was inquisitive and earnestly desirous to know the truth.'

[41]III:236, SER (1649).

[42]*Aphorismes of Justification*, 'Appendix', 12.

[43]IV:608, TKL (1689). Baxter fails to note that his idea of convincing evidence might have differed from that of his critics!

⁴⁴'Our God is Holy, and Holiness becometh all that draw near him, and is the mark of all that shall see his face.' *Catholick Theologie* (1675), I, i, 132, hereinafter cited as C.T. with the appropriate book, section, and page numbers.

De Pauley claims that Hebrews 12:14 ('holiness, without which no man shall see the Lord') was Baxter's favorite verse, noting that a quick perusal of the 23 volume edition of his works shows Baxter cited this verse approximately 80 times. De Pauley, 'Richard Baxter Surveyed,' 36.

⁴⁵Bates says of Baxter, 'His reverance for the Divine Purity, made him very shy and jealous of any Doctrine that seemed to reflect a blemish and stain upon it.' Bates, *Funeral Sermon*, 110.

⁴⁶For a background to the controversy, see Gertrude Huehns, *Antinomianism in English History* (London: Cresset Press, 1951), and Ernest F. Kevan, *The Grace of Law: A Study in Puritan Theology* (Grand Rapids, Mich.: Baker, 1976), 22-28.

⁴⁷III:689, LF (1669). See also C.T., I, i, 3.

⁴⁸III:767, LF (1669).

⁴⁹III:798, DL:KG (1663).

⁵⁰Ibid. Packer asserts that with his emphasis on God as *Dominus*, Baxter 'safeguards the absolute freedom of God in His dealings with man as forthrightly as any Augustinian could desire'. See Packer, 'Redemption and Restoration,' 128.

⁵¹III:798, DL:KG (1663).

⁵²Ibid., 800. Baxter says, 'He is the Lord or Owner of the world; even of brutes as properly as of man: but he is the sovereign King or Governor only of the reasonable creature; because no other are capable of that proper moral government which now we speak of.'

⁵³II:19, RCR:NR (1666). See also IV:71, CF (1682), where Baxter asks and answers the following question: 'Q.10. Why is man ruled by laws, rather than beasts and other things?'

A. Because man hath reason, and free-will, which maketh them subjects capable of laws, which beasts are not.'

⁵⁴II:22, RCR:NR (1666). Cf. C.T., I, iii, 36, 'God made man such an Intellectual Free Agent, that he might be a fit subject for Sapiential Moral Government: and accordingly he settled a Kingdom in the World: And as he governeth meer Natural Agents, by Natural motion, so he governeth Man as a Moral agent, by Laws and Moral means and motion: For he ruleth all things according to their Natures.'

⁵⁵III:767, DL:KG (1663). Cf. p. 800, where Baxter lists only two parts of God's government, subsuming the act of persuasion under the category of execution.

⁵⁶II:20, RCR:NR (1666). Baxter particularly focused on the execution of the law, maintaining that 'the glory of his governing wisdom, and Punishing and Rewarding Justice, is a great and notable part of that

glory which man must give him now and for ever ... his Judging and Executing according to that moral aptitude commonly called Merit, by Punishments and Rewards: And that to deny God the glory of all this, is no small error in a Philosopher or Divine.' C.T., I, iii, 115.

[57]III:802, DL:KG (1663).

[58]Ibid., 802-3.

[59]Ibid., 803.

[60]II:19, RCR:NR (1666).

[61]Here we note Baxter's appreciation for Lawson's integration of politics and theology. Lawson asserted the following in his *Theo-Politica* (1659), 16: 'The Common-wealth is administered by Laws and Judgments: Laws determine the Duties and Dues of men: Judgment renders the Dues of Rewards, or Punishments, according to the observation or violation of the Laws.'

[62]C.T., I, iii, 115.

[63]IV:71, CF (1682).

[64]C.T., I, iii, 115.

[65]Ibid.

[66]C.T., I, i, 27. See also C.T., I, iii, 86: 'Whoever says that God is not able to make a creature with power to determine one volition of its own without His efficient physical predetermination aforesaid, sayeth more against God's *omnipotency* (though on pretence of a contradiction) than I dare say or think.'

[67]C.T., I, ii, 27.

[68]Baxter preferred to use the term *Nature* instead of the more widely used term *Works*, because as we shall see, Baxter believed that the Covenant of Grace was also in some sense a Covenant of Works.

[69]Baxter asserts, 'The Law said (in sense) (*Obey perfectly and live; Sin and die*).' See C.T., I, ii, 14.

[70]III:837, DL:WG (1663).

[71]C.T., II, 113-14.

[72]C.T., I, i, 91.

[73]Ibid.

[74]II:902, RMeth (1653).

[75]I:93, CD:CEth (1673).

[76]Ibid.

[77]Ibid.

[78]Ibid.

[79]C.T., I, iii, 60. Baxter goes on to say: 'Even when Adams appetite was to the forbidden fruit, and some think that this was the first part of the sin, it seemeth that it was rather in the wills *not* restraining that appetite when it could have done it: And then positive sins do follow thereupon.'

[80]*Two Disputations of Original Sin* (1675), 69.

[81]Ibid., 158.

[82]Ibid., 159. Baxter believed that the grounds which justify penalizing mankind for Adam's sin must be found in Adam's natural relation to the rest of mankind. To deny this was to make it appear but an arbitrary and unjust arrangement on God's part. See C.T., II, 111.

[83]*Two Disputations of Original Sin*, 157.

[84]Ibid., 218.

[85]C.T., I, ii, 29. Cf. II:403, TCon (1657): 'So that we are all born with corrupted natures, inclined to earth and earthly things, and strange and averse to heaven and heavenly things; prone to evil and backward to good; estranged from God, and making our carnal selves our god: pride, self-love, covetousness, voluptuousness, unbelief, ignorance, error, hypocrisy, ungodliness, strife, contention, cruelty, and all wickedness, have their roots at once in us, and if temptation serve, we shall bring forth the fruit.'

[86]IV:264, PM (1672). Baxter, following the common Reformed usage, covers both 'guilt and pravity' by the phrase 'original sin'. Packer, 'Redemption and Restoration,' 151, n. 2.

[87]He dealt with this issue forthrightly – on the title page of *Two Disputations of Original Sin* he cites from Exodus 20:5,6 and 34:7: 'Visiting the iniquity of the Fathers upon the children (and upon the childrens children) unto the third and fourth Generation of them that hate me.'

[88]*Two Disputations of Original Sin*, 113. See also *An End of Doctrinal Controversies*, 95: 'We receive our Original Guilt and Pravity immediately from our next Parents, and but remotely from Adam: It could never have come to us but through them from whom we receive our Nature; from them we receive the guilt and pravity of our Nature.'

[89]*Two Disputations of Original Sin*, 224. He said: 'I think I have done more to free the Christian Religion from difficulties, by asserting such an imputation of all Parents sins, as aforesaid, than you have done by denying all.'

[90]*An End of Doctrinal Controversies*, 95.

[91]*Two Disputations of Original Sin*, 238.

[92]Ibid., 230.

[93]Ibid., 240. Baxter also saw in this doctrine a partial answer to the issue of the heathen: 'May we not hence see some ground to justify God's severity against those infidel parts of the World, whose Ancestors have refused the Gospel, and the Lord Jesus? And are not those infidels guilty of their fore-fathers sin, in the sense before-mentioned? If Christ died for them, and offered them himself, his grace and benefits, and they reject him, it is a just punishment to posterity, if for this sin of their Fathers, he leave their Country in darkness, and seek out a people that shall give him better welcome. And if he do not so by us, who have so abused him, it is not because in justness he may

not, but because in mercy he will not: and the greater and freer is that mercy.' Ibid., 241.

[94]C.T., II, 240. Baxter avows, 'no man in the world doth perish for Adam's sin alone, without his own.' II:143, RCR:Chr (1666).

[95]*An End of Doctrinal Controversies*, 173.

[96]III:507, CU (1658).

[97]*An End of Doctrinal Controversies*, 177.

[98]II:690, SB (1662): 'God giveth you your choice, though your own wickedness do hinder you from choosing aright.... For if you are willing, Christ is willing; and if Christ be willing, and you be willing, what can hinder your salvation?'

[99]C.T., II, 97. See also II:689-90, LF (1669): 'When I say it is in your choice, I do not say that you have the wit or the heart to make a right choice. No, if you had but so much wit and grace, I need not use all these words to you to persuade you to chose the better part. Your wills are free from any force that God puts upon them to determine them to sin; or from any force that Satan or any enemy you have can use to determine them to sin. All they can do is morally to entice you. God doth not make you sin. If you choose your death, and forsake your own mercy, it is not God that determineth your wills to make this choice. Yes, he commandeth, and persuadeth, and urgeth you to make a better choice. And though Satan tempt you, he can do no more. You have so much power, that you may have Christ if you will. You cannot say, I am truly willing to have Christ, and cannot. This much free-will undoubtedly you have.'

[100]II:497, TCon (1657). Baxter claimed, 'if you can but prove that a man offended willingly, you have proved him culpable: for nature hath taught all the world to bring the fault to the will, and there to leave it, and look no further for the cause.'

[101]Ibid.

[102]Baxter asks, 'In a word, shall we not believe that there is a Hell, and know much of the nature of it; when we see a Hell already begun on earth, and the whole world walloweth in folly, filth, impiety, and woe?' C.T., I, iii, 65.

[103]*Two Disputations of Original Sin*, 76.

[104]Packer, 'Redemption and Restoration,' argues that Baxter's account of man is the 'fullest and most characteristic that Puritanism produced' (p. 111) and that in his doctrine of anthropology, 'He parts company with his contemporaries only to surpass them' (p. 167).

[105]*Universal Redemption* (1694), 53: 'Seeing no Man can fulfill the First Law, or Covenant, and no Man can be saved by a Covenant not kept, and Christ Redeemed not Man into Absolute liberty, (to be from under Law and Rule, which were Misery to him and not liberty). Therefore it hath pleased the Father and Mediator to make to Man a New Law and Covenant suited to his present State of Misery.'

[106]C.T., I, ii, 42.

[107]For an extensive treatment of the Covenant of Grace among the Puritans, see John von Rohr, *The Covenant of Grace in Puritan Thought* (Atlanta: Scholars Press, 1986).

[108]The supralapsarian position held that the election of some to eternal life was made before the decree to permit the Fall. Benjamin B. Warfield, *The Plan of Salvation* (Grand Rapids: Eerdmans, 1970 rev. ed.), 31, has placed the differing schools of thought on the Order of Decrees into chart form.

[109]He says: 'If any say too much in making our Holiness Gods only End, it ill beseemeth those to be their censurers, who have tempted them to it, by erring more on the contrary extream. And it is not to be denied or hid, that more than downright Antinomians, have so ill expounded the points of Christs Suretiship, and of the Imputation of our sin to him, and of the Imputation of his Righteousness to us, as hath proved the great occasion of some mens running into the contrary error.... And it is not an easie or a common thing, for men that write against any dangerous errour and extream, to keep up large impartial thoughts, and see the danger on the contrary side; For mans mind is limited and narrow, and cannot think with equal seriousness and clearness of many things at once. And the wisest man alive, when he is earnestly pleading against any errour, is in great danger of forgetting what is on the other side the way, and of thinking so eagerly what to say against the opinion he opposeth, as to forget both what may be said for it, and what worse his own arguings may infer.' *How Far Holinesse is the Design of Christianity* (1671), 14.

[110]Baxter was convinced he knew why Antinomianism had surfaced. 'I have seldom observed any Extreme in Hereticks or Schismaticks,' he contended, 'which was not notably caused by the Clergies contrary extream. Antinomianism rose among us from our obscure Preaching of Evangelical Grace, and insisting too much on Tears and terrors.' *Apology for the Nonconformists Ministry* (1681), 226.

Even more startling were his comments in *An End of Doctrinal Controversies*, 315: 'Yet it must be confessed, that of late times many have laid more upon the sorrowing, weeping, and fearing part of Repentance, than was meet, and said too little of the turning of the Soul from worldly and fleshly sinful Pleasures, to the delightful Love and Praises of God, and willing Obedience and Conformity to his Will, which is the principal part of true Repentance. And I think God permitted the Antinomians to rise up, and cry up Free-Grace, and call the Ministers Legallists, to rebuke our Error in this point, and to call us to preach up his Grace more plentifully, and to consider better that Gospel-obedience doth chiefly consist in Thankfulness, Love and Joy, and in the words of Praise, and Works of Love. I am sure this use we should make of their Abuses.'

[111]*Autobiography*, 284.

[112]R.B., I, 111.

[113]*A Treatise of Justifying Righteousness* (1676), 22.

[114]Ibid., 22. Powicke contends that Baxter's experience in the army was 'decisive,' convincing him that 'Antinomianism was another name for Anti-Christ, which called for nothing but the sternest censure'. Powicke, *A Life*, 237.

[115]Baxter laments the fact that he 'remained long in the borders of Antinomianism' and 'very narrowly escaped'. *Aphorismes of Justification*, 'Appendix', 163.

[116]For a discussion of Grotius' viewpoint on the atonement, see Robert S. Franks, *A History of the Doctrine of the Work of Christ*, vol. 2 (London: Hodder and Stoughton, n.d.), 48-73, and H. D. McDonald, *The Atonement of the Death of Christ: In Faith, Revelation, and History* (Grand Rapids: Baker, 1985), 203-7.

[117]II:894, RMeth (1653): 'And therefore Christ's sufferings could not be more eminently for us, than by enabling the offended Majesty to forgive us; and so taking the greatest impediment out of the way. For when impediments are once removed, God's nature is so gracious and prone to mercy, that he would soon pardon us when once it is fit to be done, and so morally possible in the fullest sense.'

Packer perceptively shows the ramifications of this for one's view of God: 'This assumes that the demand for retribution in the original law was not grounded in the nature of God, but only in the exigencies of government. What is at issue here is the divine holiness. Reformed theology sees both the precept and the penalty of the law of God as a permanent expression of God's eternal and unchangeable holiness and justice, and argues that God does not save sinners at His law's expense; rather, He saves them by satisfying His law on their behalf, so that He continues to be just when He becomes their justifier. Baxter's scheme makes the wrath of God against sin something less than a revelation of His abiding character, and so opens the door to the idea that benevolence is really the whole essence of his moral being: an idea made explicit by the Liberalism of a later age.' Packer, 'The Doctrine of Justification in Development and Decline among the Puritans,' 27-28.

[118]Kevan brings this out succinctly: 'Richard Baxter rejects the idea that the Law is eternal, and it is this which constitutes the fundamental difference between his teaching and that of most of his Puritan contemporaries. The general view was that the Law is the permanent expression of the eternal and unalterable requirements of God's holiness and justice, but Richard Baxter, proceeding on the hypothesis of the rectoral liberties of God, asserts that the Law is but a means to an end, and that God may change His Law providing the same end is attained.' Kevan, *Grace of Law*, 67.

[119]C.T., I, ii, 69: 'It is not properly the Law which is satisfied, but the Law-giver as above Law as is said: But yet improperly the Law may be said to be satisfied in that the ends of the Law-giver in it are obtained.' Cf. *Universal Redemption*, 379: 'It was not the Law it self that Christ satisfied (if we speak properly) but the Law-giver.... The Law knows no proper satisfaction.'

[120]C.T., II, i, 41. See also III:633, LF (1669): 'God desired not Christ's suffering for itself; but as it was a convenient means to demonstrate his justice and his holiness, and to vindicate the honour of his government and law.'

[121]*Imputative Righteousness* (1679), 76: 'For the truth is; The Law that condemned us was not fulfilled by Christs suffering for us, but the Lawgiver satisfied instead of the fulfilling of it: And that Satisfaction lyeth, in the substitution of that which as fully (or more) attaineth the ends of the Law as our own suffering would have done.'

[122]Kevan, *Grace of Law*, 67.

[123]*Universal Redemption*, 10.

[124]Ibid., 10-11.

[125]For a summary of Anselm's views, see McDonald, *Atonement*, 163-73.

[126]C.T., I, ii, 69. Though acknowledging his indebtedness to Grotius, Baxter says that on this point he judges Grotius to 'come short of accurateness and soundness'.

[127]Lamont defends Baxter from the charge of Arminianism at this point, saying, 'he [Baxter] introduced certain Arminian elements into the [Calvinistic] superstructure – the rationale for instance of God's laws and punishments being found, not in His nature, but in His rectorial relation to man – but he parted from Grotius in his emphasis on God as *dominus*.' Lamont, *Richard Baxter and the Millennium* (London: Croom Helm, 1979), 137.

Cf. Lamont's seemingly contradictory statement in an earlier article: 'Baxter did not *become an Arminian* merely because of the antics of Major Wilkie.' See William M. Lamont, 'Richard Baxter, The Apocalypse and the Mad Major,' *Past and Present* 55 (1972): 88 [emphasis added].

[128]For a classic defense of limited atonement, see John Owen, *The Death of Death in the Death of Christ*, with an Introductory Essay by J. I. Packer. (Edinburgh: The Banner of Truth Trust, 1985 reprint). See also Jack N. Macleod, 'John Owen and *the Death of Death*,' (Puritan and Reformed Studies Conference Papers, 1983), 70-87.

[129]*Universal Redemption of Mankind* (1694), 286. The publication date of this work is deceiving. Baxter wrote much of this book before 1650 but it was not published until after his death in 1694.

[130]See Warfield, *The Plan of Salvation*, 31. Warfield classifies the Amyraldian position as 'inconsistently Particularistic'.

[131]Brian G. Armstrong, *Calvinism and the Amyraut Heresy: Protestant Scholasticism and Humanism in Seventeenth-Century France* (Madison: University of Wisconsin Press, 1969), 59. Armstrong's basic thesis is that Amyraut was the true heir of Calvin's thought and that Amyraut's opponents were the ones who deviated from Calvin's original teaching because of their scholastic method.

[132]Did John Calvin hold to a limited or unlimited atonement? A Provocative work by R. T. Kendall, *Calvin and English Calvinism to 1649* (Oxford: Oxford University Press, 1979) argues for the latter. Kendall's argument that Calvin taught an unlimited atonement runs counter to the overwhelming consensus of traditional scholarship which maintains that Calvin limited the atonement to only the elect. Paul Helm has responded to Kendall in *Calvin and the Calvinists* (Edinburgh: The Banner of Truth Trust, 1982). The issue continues to be debated, with the reader directed to the following articles for surveys of the arguments and literature: Roger Nicole, 'John Calvin's view of the extent of the atonement [bibliog essay].' *Westminster Theological Journal* 47 (1985): 197-225; and M. Charles Bell, 'Calvin and the Extent of the Atonement,' *Evangelical Quarterly* 55 (1983): 115-23.

Nicole, who maintains that Calvin held to a limited atonement, nevertheless realizes there are strong arguments for the other position. He notes the following point made in a study done by Curt D. Daniel (Hyper-Calvinism and John Gill,' unpublished dissertation, University of Edinburgh, 1983): 'Daniel makes a comment to the effect that most of the contenders in this area tend to ascribe to Calvin the view which they hold themselves, that is to say, they appear to have yielded to the temptation to annex Calvin in support of their own position! Unfortunately this remark seems to apply also to Daniel's treatment and to the present article.' Nicole, 'John Calvin's View,' 208, citing Daniel, 781, 782, 827.

While it is outside the scope of this study to attempt an assessment of this issue, one recent article must be noted. Alan Clifford, in his 'Geneva Revisited or Calvinism Revisited: The Case for Theological Reassessment,' *Churchman* 100 (1986): 323-34, uses Baxter as an example of one who believed that Calvin held to an unlimited atonement. Clifford concludes his article with the assertion that, 'Baxter [unlimited atonement] rather than Owen [limited atonement] is the true heir of Calvin's Scriptural theology,' 330.

[133]*Universal Redemption*, 446-47 [emphasis added]. Therefore, 'Christ by his Law of Grace, hath made it every Mans duty that hears it, to believe in him, and accept him, as our Saviour that hath made satisfaction for their Sins, and so dyed for them, and is their Redeemer.' *Universal Redemption*, 44.

Note Baxter's emphasis on those who *hear*. This was due to his uncertainty about the condition of the heathen who had no chance to hear. On this issue, Baxter said the following: 'I cannot find in Scripture where it is clearly revealed to us, on what terms God will Judge those that heard not of Christ ... how God will proceed with them, or whether any Heathen be ever saved? I cannot find that he hath revealed. For indeed it doth not concern us to know it. I dare not say that any of them ... are saved: Nor dare I say that I am certain they are not: They that are certain let them be thankful for their knowledge, and not be angry with me for confessing my Ignorance.' *Universal Redemption*, 475.

[134]Ibid., 448.

[135]Ibid., 396: 'If an hundred Traytors be condemned, and the Prince Ransom them all at a Price, agreeing in the payment of it, that they shall now be all his own, and none of them be delivered for all that, who will not thankfully own him and acknowledge his favour: Here it is just that all the Refusers of Pardon yet perish: And their Death is directly for the refusing of the Remedy, and secondarily from their old crime because they would not have it remedied.'

[136]C.T., I, ii, 51. Watson judiciously sums up Baxter's view: 'If Baxter really meant that any steps these non-elect persons could take, would actually put them into possession of saving faith, he would have said so in so many plain words, and then between him and the Arminians there would have been no difference, so far as they who perish are concerned. But coming nearer to Christ, and nearer to saving faith are with him quite distinct. His concern was not to show how the non-elect might be saved, but how they might with some plausibility be damned.' See Richard Watson, *Theological Institutes*, Vol. II (New York: Carlton & Lanahan, 1850), 419.

[137]*Universal Redemption*, 117. Cf. Ibid., 436: 'No Arminianism at all. I say not that God giveth all men sufficient Grace to Salvation, or to Believe.... That there is such a thing as sufficient Grace, not effectual.'

[138]Ibid., 437.

[139]C.T., II, 140. Note the key term 'naturally impossible'. This reflects back on Baxter's distinction between 'cannot' and 'will not'. Baxter says: 'Hereafter speak plainly in your contendings, and instead of (Cannot) say, An unconverted man will not believe, and his will is viciously undisposed to it, yea ill-disposed against it.' C.T., I, iii, 44.

Baxter seems to be arguing that it would be naturally impossible to come to Christ if he indeed had not died for you; but if he truly did die for you, then your not coming to him is not *naturally* impossible, but *morally* impossible – and therefore the fault lies in your will, not in God.

[140]*Universal Redemption*, 44.

[141]Powicke, *Rev. Richard Baxter*, 238.

[142]Richards is one example among many who attribute the source of Baxter's views on universal redemption to the Amyraldians: 'It was

under their influence that Baxter rejected the strict Calvinistic doctrines of double predestination and a limited atonement, which he had found in the works of strict Calvinists like William Twisse, and adopted their theory of "hypothetical universalism".' See David J. Richards, 'Richard Baxter's Theory of the Atonement,' unpublished M. A. Thesis, Wheaton College, 1982, 15.

Some go back even further to Cameron, Amyraut's teacher. Macleod places the blame for Baxter's 'corruption' on Cameron and his 'mongrel compromising teaching'. See John Macleod, *Scottish Theology* (Edinburgh: Free Church of Scotland, 1943), 62.

[143]Also known as Louis du Moulin (1606-1680). Molinaeus had made the charge in the Preface to his *Paraenesis ad aedificatores Imperii in Imperio* (1656).

[144]Baxter, *Certain Disputations of Right to Sacraments, and the true nature of Visible Christianity*. Second Edition, corrected and amended (1658), B1v. The reader should note that Baxter usually referred to Amyraut by the Latinized form of his name, Amyraldus.

[145]Ibid., B2.

[146]*Universal Redemption of Mankind, By the Lord Jesus Christ: Stated and Cleared by the late Learned Mr. Richard Baxter. Whereunto is added a short Account of Special Redemption, by the same Author* (1694).

As we have previously noted, though not published until 1694, this work was written substantially by 1650. Baxter appears to have refrained from publishing it primarily because he felt other works treated the subject better. Note his quotation on page 376, where he says, 'Here Amyraldus and Dallaeus coming forth stopt me.'

See also Baxter's *Aphorismes*, where he says: 'But these things which you draw out of me here unseasonably, I am handling in a fitter place, (in a small Tract of Universall Redemption:). But the last week I have received Amiraldus ... who hath opened my very heart, almost in my owne words; and hath so fully said the very same things which I intended, for the greater part, that I am now unresolved whether to hold my hand, or to proceed.' See *Aphorismes of Justification*, 'Appendix', 164.

[147]In his *Catholick Theologie* (1675), a2-a3, Baxter recorded the progression of events as he studied afresh how to counter Antinomianism: 'I remembered two or three things in Dr. Twisse (whom I most esteemed) which inclined me to moderation in the five Articles: 1. That he every where professeth, that Christ so far dyed for all, as to purchase them Justification and Salvation conditionally to be given them, if they believe.' In his *Universal Redemption*, 287-88, Baxter noted that Twisse had asserted that Christ had died for all men in such a sense that salvation could be offered to all. He quotes Twisse's explanation of John 3:16 in support of his assertion.

Baxter elsewhere seems to give the exact opposite view of Twisse's opinion. In answering the argument, 'All those are certainly saved for whom Christ Satisfied: But all men are not Saved: Therefore Christ Satisfied not for all men,' Baxter says: 'This is the main Argument urged by Dr. Twiss and most others against Universal Satisfaction.' See *Universal Redemption*, 377.

How can we reconcile these statements? Two possible explanations are that Twisse's statements lending support to a universal redemption were never integrated into his overall theology, or that Baxter read these statements out of context. Either way, regardless of what Twisse meant to say, Baxter found in him support for his abandoning the doctrine of limited atonement in favor of universal redemption.

[148]*Certain Disputations of Right to Sacraments*, B3.

[149]Ibid. See also R.B., I, 110, where he acknowledged his accord with 'Amiraldus's way about universal Redemption and Grace'.

[150]Packer, 'Redemption and Restoration,' x.

[151]*Certain Disputations of Right to Sacraments*, C2/C2v. Baxter says the following in *Universal Redemption*, 56: 'Christs dying for Men, is Antecedent to their believing in him: Their believing presupposeth his dying for them; His Death saveth them because they believe; but he did not die for them because they believe, but they must believe because he dyed for them. The Act both as performed and commanded here presupposeth the Object. The Command therefore of believing presupposeth that Christ dyed for Men.'

[152]II:892, RMeth (1653).

[153]II:980, GGV (1671).

[154]C.T., I, ii, 53. Baxter then draws a further conclusion from this observation: 'From whence we certainly infer, that Christ never absolutely intended or decreed that his death should eventually put all men in possession of these Benefits ... Christ therefore died for all, but not for all equally, or with the same intent, design or purpose.'

[155]C.T., I, i, 66.

[156]Ibid. 'It is not possible that any Creature can have any good which is not a pure gift of God, however he may require of man Conditions of Reception, in the order of Creation. Therefore the Decree must be free.'

[157]*Universal Redemption*, 483.

[158]Ibid., 483.

[159]E. g. De Pauley (mis)quotes from Hugh Martin's, *Puritanism and Richard Baxter*, 135: 'Baxter asserts that those who are saved are indeed saved by God's purpose and election, but the salvation offered in Christ is sufficient for all, and all men, if *they* choose, can avail themselves of it.' De Pauley's emphasis on the word 'they,' not found in Martin's book, is misleading, giving the impression that Baxter felt that some among the

non-elect would so choose. Baxter emphatically denied any such thing. De Pauley, 'Richard Baxter Surveyed,' 35.

[160]*Works*, I:xliv. The author of the Preface notes that 'I never found [this] in his writings, nor met with any one who had'. Stoughton likewise notes this tendency to ascribe to Baxter this view that others beside the elect would be saved. He then likewise discounts it: 'I do not pretend to have read all Baxter's works: but in those with which I am acquainted, I find no trace of such an opinion, neither does it appear in Orme's careful summary of Baxter's theological writings.' Stoughton, *History of Religion in England*, Vol. IV, 383-84.

[161]Irvonwy Morgan, *The Nonconformity of Richard Baxter* (London: Epworth Press, 1946), 79 [emphasis added].

[162]C.T., I, i, 123.

[163]Ibid., 81.

[164]IV:868, SJ (1654).

[165]C.T., I, i, 82.

[166]Ibid., 67.

[167]Ibid., 67-68.

[168]Ibid., 67.

[169]*Universal Redemption*, 435. He remarks, 'I say it again confidently, all men that perish (who have the use of reason) do perish directly for rejecting sufficient Recovering Grace.... By sufficient I mean, not sufficient directly to save them; (for such none of the Elect have till they are saved) nor yet sufficient to give them Faith, or cause them savingly to Believe: But it is sufficient to bring them nearer to Christ than they are, though not to put them into immediate possession of Christ by Union with him, as Faith would do.'

[170]Ibid., 483: 'And in the word (Infallible) ... It is the same thing which our Divines mean by the word (Irresistible) or Insuperable.'

[171]*Universal Redemption*, 20.

[172]III:794, DL:KG (1663). He also says, 'And that which Augustine so much insisteth on, I think is also plain in Scripture, that the salvation of the elect is better secured in the hands of Christ, than his own or any of his posterity's was in the hands of Adam.' Ibid., 793.

[173]C.T., I, ii, 116. 'I am not he that would be separated from the Communion of all the ancient Churches, and Doctors,' Baxter asserted.

[174]C.T., II, 258.

[175]C.T., I, ii, 116.

3. Controversy Regarding Justification

[1]Baxter, *A Treatise of Justifying Righteousness*, 22. For further information about Saltmarsh and the other 'Antinomian' chaplains, see Leo F. Solt, *Saints in Arms: Puritanism and Democracy in Cromwell's Army* (Stanford: Stanford University Press, 1959), 6-42.

[2]"In its [Calvinism's] most extreme form, spoken of as Antinomianism, any participation of a man in his own salvation was denied.' Bolam, Goring, Short, and Thomas, *The English Presbyterians: From Elizabethan Puritanism to Modern Unitarianism*, 103, n. 1.

[3]Allison cites the way one critic of antinomianism, Thomas Gataker, handled this issue: 'Gataker refers to a certain divine who told a woman to reason thus: God will save sinners, I am a sinner: therefore God will save me. Gataker suggests that the woman might equally well reason thus: God will damn sinners; I am a sinner: therefore God will damn me.' Thomas Gataker, *Antinomianism Discovered* (1653), 35, cited in Allison, *The Rise of Moralism*, 157.

[4]*A Defence of Christ and Free Grace* (2nd pagination of *The Scripture Gospel Defended*, 1690), 28.

[5]Ibid., 29. Baxter summarizes the Antinomians' teachings in the *Christian Directory*, I:58, 'The antinomians tell you, that The moral law is abrogated, and that the gospel is no law; (and if there be no law, there is no governor nor government, no duty, no sin, no judgment, no punishment, no reward); that the elect are justified before they are born, or repent, or believe; that their sin is pardoned before it is committed; that God took them as suffering and fulfilling all the law in Christ, as if it had been they that did it in him: that we are justified by faith only in our consciences: that justifying faith is but the believing that we are justified: that every man must believe that he is pardoned, that he may be pardoned in his conscience; and this he is to do by a divine faith, and that this is the sense of the article, 'I believe the forgiveness of sins,' that is, that my sins are forgiven; and that all are forgiven that believe it.'

[6]C.T., a2-a3.

[7]Ibid. He says, 'I laid by prejudice and I went to the Scripture, where its whole current, but especially Matth. 25, did quickly satisfie me in the Doctrine of Justification.'

[8]R.B., I, 107. Other works include: *Four Disputations of Justification* (1658); *A Treatise of Justifying Righteousness* (1676); *Imputative Righteousness* (1679); a portion of *The Christian Directory* (1673); *The Life of Faith* (1660); *An End of Doctrinal Controversies* (1691); *An Appeal to the Light* (1674); *How far Holiness is the Design of Christianity* (1671); *The Scripture Gospel Defended* (1690); and his *Confession of Faith* (1655, unfortunately unavailable to me for this book).

[9]C.T., a3.

[10]Ibid., a4.

[11]*Two Disputations of Original Sin*, 4. Packer has compiled a list of 'corrections' to the *Aphorismes* in his 'Redemption and Restoration,' Appendix II, 485-87.

[12]*A Treatise of Justifying Righteousness*, 22.

[13]*The Scripture Gospel Defended*, A2.

[14]Baxter claims, 'I had no book but my Bible, I set to study the truth from thence ... by the blessing of God, [I] discovered more in one weeke, then I had done before in seventeen years reading, hearing, and wrangling.' *Aphorismes*, 'Appendix,' 110-11.

[15]Baxter returned to this passage time after time in his teaching on justification. 'When I have oft studyed how to forsake my present Judgement,' Baxter admitted, 'the bare reading of the 25 of Matthew hath still utterly silenced me, if there were no more.' *Of Justification*, 171.

[16]*Universal Redemption*, 53 [emphasis added].

[17]This anticipates our discussion in Chapter Four concerning faith as a channel for conversion. We examine it here because of its vital link to Baxter's view of Justification.

[18]John C. English, 'The Puritan Doctrine of Christian Initiation,' *Studia Liturgica* 6 (1969): 162-63. See also Richard A. Muller, *Dictionary of Latin and Greek Theological Terms* (Grand Rapids: Baker Book House, 1985). Muller, 115-16, concludes his discussion of these three components of *fides salvifica* by asserting, 'Saving faith, therefore, cannot be merely intellectual, it must also be volitional.'

[19]English, 'The Puritan Doctrine of Christian Initiation,' 170. Note that *fiducia* assumes the other two aspects to be present.

[20]*Universal Redemption*, 111. Baxter admits that there were several opinions among the divines on this issue. He says that 'some think it must be but one Act,' placing it either in the understanding (Camero) or in the will (Amesius). 'Some and most,' Baxter asserts, 'place it in both faculties and so in divers Acts (and that rightly). And inded [sic] it hath divers Acts in each faculty: For as it is more then one particular Truth or exunciation which is the object of Assent, and therefore must have divers Acts of Assent; so it is in more than one shape and profitable respect that the Goodness of the object is presented to the Will, and therefore it must there have several Acts, as consent, affiance, &c.'

[21]II:244, UI (1655).

[22]III:652, DP (1658). In this sense he often uses the synonym *affiance* in place of *fiducia*. Cf. *An End of Doctrinal Controversies* , 226.

[23]III:652, DP (1658). Using the analogy of a ship and pilot carrying an individual safely across the sea, Baxter further clarifies this point: 'affiance as in the understanding, is its assent to the sufficiency and fidelity of the pilot and ship that I trust: affiance in the will is the choosing of this ship ... to venture my life with, and refusing all others; which is called consent, when it followeth the motion and offer of him whom we trust. Affiance in the vital power of the soul, is the fortitude and venturing all upon this chosen Trustee; which is the quieting (in some measure) disturbing fears, and the ... first degrees of the soul toward execution.' See also C.T., I, ii, 55.

Cf. the contemporary fascination among preachers to illustrate this point with waterfalls, tightropes and wheelbarrows!

[24]IV:810, ML, 'Tell any man in this congregation that he shall have a gift of ten thousand pounds, if he will but go to London for it; if he believe you, he will go but if he believe not, he will not; and if he will not go, you may be sure he believeth not, supposing that he is able ... but a true and sound belief is not consistent with so great neglect of the things that are believed.'

[25]No one can do this, Baxter avows, except 'by the Spirit.' *Of Justification*, 300.

[26]III:655, LF (1669).

[27]Ibid., 581.

[28]*An End of Doctrinal Controversies*, 229.

[29]*Aphorismes of Justification*, 'Appendix', 21. Yet having defined what he means by faith, Baxter is quick to mention that no man can perform the condition of faith by his own natural power of free-will, but only with the enabling of God's irresistible and effectual grace.

[30]Ibid., 276.

[31]III:680, LF (1669).

[32]Allison argues that there was a real difference in Baxter's position. See Allison, *The Rise of Moralism*, 157. At the conclusion of this section I will critique Allison and others who argue for a real difference.

[33]I do not propose to defend every assertion made by Baxter, as I think some of them are phrased quite poorly. I do believe, however, that he was substantially closer to the 'orthodox' position than some have interpreted him to be.

[34]II:897, RMeth (1653).

[35]Kevan notes that the terms justification and sanctification have sometimes been confused. He claims, 'In accurate theological definition, however, the terms justification and sanctification are kept apart, as standing for two distinct, though complementary, acts of Divine grace. Justification is understood, forensically, to indicate the act of God in declaring the sinner to be free from all legal charge, on account of the satisfaction made by Christ on his behalf; and sanctification is that act of God by which the believer's life is transformed more and more after a godly pattern.... [The Antinomians] erroneously used the categories of justification when speaking of sanctification, and consequently ascribed qualities of perfection to the latter which belong only to the former.' Kevan, *The Grace of Law*, 95.

He goes on to say, in footnote 132: 'Richard Baxter commits the opposite error, and uses the language of sanctification to expound the doctrine of justification, and, as a result, takes away from justification that perfection which truly belongs to it.'

[36]III:675, LF (1669).

[37]Ibid.

[38]Allison, *The Rise of Moralism*, 160.

[39]III:32, SER (1650).

[40]*Of Justification* , 129. Baxter recognized that there are some who start with a faith that cannot be distinguished from that of the elect, but who will ultimately fail to produce the works that secure their final acceptance in the final judgment. They seem to have genuine faith, but they were never really converted and will eventually fall away. In that sense the second justification is simply a confirmation that the first one was real.

[41]Ibid., 25.

[42]James Buchanan, *The Doctrine of Justification* (Grand Rapids: Baker, 1956 reprint), 237.

[43]George E. Ladd, *A Theology of the New Testament* (Grand Rapids: Eerdmans, 1974), 441. He cites others who recognize this truth: G. Schrenk, *TDNT* II, 217; L. Morris, *The Apostolic Preaching of the Cross*, 258; V. Taylor, *Forgiveness and Reconciliation*, 33, 36; D. E. H. Whitely, *The Theology of St. Paul*, 160; D. Hill, *Greek Words and Hebrew Meanings*, 151; and J. Jeremias, *The Central Message of the NT*, 64. Ladd says, 'While all of these authors recognize the eschatological dimension of justification, they do not all emphasize the significance of this fact.'

[44]Ladd, *A Theology of the New Testament*, 441.

[45]Ibid., 442. Ladd explains: 'The eschatological judgment is no longer alone future; it has become a verdict in history. Justification, which belongs to the Age to Come and issues in the future salvation, has become a present reality inasmuch as the Age to Come has reached back into the present evil age to bring its soteric blessings to men.... The future judgment has thus become essentially a present experience.' Ibid., 442-43.

[46]Baxter asserted that 'we are Justified by Christ's whole Righteousness, Passive, Active, and Habitual...' *A Treatise of Justifying Righteousness*, 24. He also denied that 'Christ meriteth that we shall have Grace to fulfil the Law ourselves and stand before God in a Righteousness of our own...' Ibid., 25.

[47]Watson, *Theological Institutes*, Vol. II, 218. Note Baxter's *An End of Doctrinal Controversies*, 259, where he asks, 'Whether imputing Christ's righteousness to us, be a Scripture-phrase? Ans. Not that I can find.' In his work, *An Appeal to the Light, Or, Richard Baxter's Account of Four accused Passages of a Sermon on Eph. 1:3*, Baxter does say, that 'though it be not a Scripture phrase, we may truly say that thus Christ's righteousness is imputed to us.' He then qualifies what he means: 'Christ's righteousness is ours as to the effects, uses and ends, and in the time, measure and order determined by himself: but it is not ours in the same sense as it is his; for his person and ours being not the same...' *An Appeal to the Light*, 1-2.

[48]III:668, LF (1669). Baxter expands his comments in *A Treatise of Justifying Righteousness*, A4v: 'divers great Volumes and other sad Evidence tells me that by their invented sence of Imputation, they have tempted many Learned men to deny Imputation of Christ's Righteousness absolutely, and bitterly revile it as a most Libertine Irreligious Doctrine.'

[49]III:668, LF (1669).

[50]Ibid.

[51]*An End of Doctrinal Controversies*, 260.

[52]Ibid., 125. Baxter elsewhere says, 'The disputes whether it be Christ's Divine, his habitual, his active or his passive righteousness, that is made ours to our justification, seemeth to be but the offspring of the error of the undue sense of Christ's personating or representing us in His righteousness; and the parcelling out of the uses and effects (that one is imputed to us instead of habitual righteousness, another instead of actual, and the third pardoneth our sins), is from the same false supposition. It is well that they suppose not that his Divine righteousness is imputed to our Deification.' C.T., I, ii, 41.

[53]*Of Justification*, 249.

[54]He alludes to this by saying, 'They [all non-Antinomian Protestants] agree that we are Justified by none but a Practical or working Faith.' See Baxter, 'To the Reader', in Allen, *A Discourse*, A6.

Baxter also makes this clear in his *Directions and Persuasions to a Sound Conversion*, saying 'If the work be thoroughly done at first, you will persevere, when others fall away.' II:585, DP (1658).

[55]*Of Justification* , 226. Paul Helm dislikes regarding faith as the 'condition' of salvation because it can make it appear that faith, not Christ, is the source of man's salvation. Baxter used the term 'condition,' but he used it in such a manner as to protect the truth which Helm wants to protect. Helm prefers to call faith an 'instrument', thus protecting the truth that 'without a personal appropriation of the work of Christ to the individual, that individual does not become a beneficiary of the work of Christ.' See Paul Helm, 'A Bad Habit: Regarding Faith as the Condition of Salvation,' *The Banner of Truth* 128 (May 1974): 16-17.

I would argue that this was precisely what Baxter was trying to protect when he used the term 'condition' against the Antinomians. He always maintained that Christ was the meritorious cause of justification.

[56]*Of Justification*, 276.

[57]II:899, RMeth (1653).

[58]*Of Justification*, 277-78.

[59]II:901, RMeth (1653).

[60]Ibid., 965.

[61]James Buchanan, *The Doctrine of Justification*, 238. Buchanan quotes Dr. Chalmers in this context: 'I would have every preacher insist

strenuously on these two doctrines – a present Justification by grace, through faith alone – and a future Judgment according to works.' Buchanan notes that all faithful ministers have 'made use of both, that they might guard equally against the peril of self-righteous legalism, on the one hand, and of practical Antinomianism, on the other.' (238-39).

[62]To those who interpret these passages to mean Christ's righteousness instead of faith, Baxter asks: 'Is it Christs Righteousness, or our Faith which is said to be imputed to us for Righteousness? Rom. 4. Ans. I. The text speaketh of imputing Faith, and by Faith is meant Faith, and not Christs Righteousness in the word.' *Imputative Righteousness*, 88.

[63]*Of Justification*, 268-69. Baxter criticizes the Westminster Assembly for expressly denying that faith is imputed for righteousness: 'How well soever they may mean, Gods oft repeated Word should rather have been expounded, than denied.' See C.T., II, 254.

[64]C.T., II, 252.

[65]Ibid.

[66]*Of Justification*, 226.

[67]*An End of Doctrinal Controversies*, 251.

[68]III:684, LF (1669).

[69]*Of Justification*, 135.

[70]Baxter refers to Augustine's opinion that, 'Election is the ascertaining Cause of Perseverance, giving the Special Grace of Perseverance.... And I think it past doubt, That God doth elect some to Perseverance, and all persevere whom he so electeth, and because he electeth them and no other.' But in face of Augustine's assertion that many also are truly sanctified and justified that are not elect, and so do not persevere, Baxter confesses, 'I do not know.' *An End of Doctrinal Controversies*, 309-10.

[71]E.g. Romans 11:22; I Corinthians 9:27; 15:1-2; 2 Corinthians 5:10-11; Colossians 1:21-23; 2 Peter 1:10-11.

[72]II:957, RMeth (1653). Even more powerful is the following passage: 'God by commanding faith and repentance, and making them necessary conditions of Justification, and by commanding perseverance, and threatening the Justified and Sanctified with damnation if they fell away; and making perseverance a condition of Salvation, doth thereby provide a convenient means for the performance of his own Decree, of giving Faith and Repentance and perseverance to his Elect; For he effecteth his ends by suitable moral means; and such is this Law and Covenant, to provoke man to due fear, and care and obedience, that he may be wrought on as a man.' C.T., I, ii, 54.

[73]*An Appeal to the Light*, 3.

[74]II:882-83, RMeth (1653): 'I shall never be so confident of any man's fidelity to Christ, as not withal to suspect that he many possibly forsake him...'

[75]Ibid., 913.

[76]Ibid., 920.

[77]Ibid., 947.

[78]Ibid.

[79]Hence Lamont's astute observation: 'The assurance of the Elect comes, not from the fact that there are no conditions, *but from the certainty that he shall fulfil them.*' Lamont, *Richard Baxter and the Millennium*, 150.

[80]von Rohr summarizes Baxter's teaching at this point: 'Even though faith itself, in the last analysis, is the free gift of God, the means should be used for the obtaining of it.' von Rohr, *The Covenant of Grace in Puritan Thought*, 57.

[81]III:666, LF (1669). Note how this is phrased in 'political terminology' on page 665: 'Though love must be the principle or chief spring of our obedience; yet he that knoweth not that fear must drive, as love must draw, and is necessary in its place to join with love, or to do that which the weaknesses of love leave undone, doth neither know what a man is, nor what God's work is, nor what his government is, nor what either magistracy or any civil or domestical government is; and therefore should spend many years at school before he turneth a disputer.'

[82]III:802, DL:KG (1663).

[83]Ibid., 801: 'It is not calling Christ our King, but obeying him before all, that will prove us subjects.'

[84]Traill's observation is perfect here: 'Some think, that if Good Works, and Holiness, and Repentance, be allowed no room in Justification, that there is no room left for them in the World, and in the practice of Believers. So hard seems it to be to some, to keep in their Eye the certain fixed bounds betwixt Justification and Sanctification.' Robert Traill, *A Vindication of the Protestant Doctrine Concerning Justification, And of its Preachers and Professors, From the unjust charge of Antinomianism* (London: Dorman Newman, 1692), 4.

[85]'The Confession,' asserts Packer, 'represents Puritan orthodoxy in its mature form, and is the best starting-point for the study of their treatment of any doctrine.' See Packer, 'The Puritan Treatment of Justification by Faith,' *Evangelical Quarterly* 24 (1952): 139.

[86]Westminster Confession of Faith, Chapter XIII, Article 5.

[87]III:802ff, DL:KG (1663).

[88]McIntyre says, 'Baxter was the hammer of the Antinomians; he unsparingly opposed every view which even appeared to approximate to their manner of teaching.' D. M. McIntyre, 'First Strictures on *The Marrow of Modern Divinity*,' *Evangelical Quarterly* X (1938): 68.

[89]Observe the startling difference in perspective between Traill and Baxter. Traill says, 'There is not a Minister that dealeth seriously with the Souls of Men, but he finds an *Arminian Scheme* of Justification in every unrenewed Heart.' Traill, *A Vindication of the Protestant Doctrine Concerning Justification*, 32.

Baxter found the exact opposite to be true: 'I seriously profess, to my best observation it appears to me, that the Antinomian Doctrine is the very same in almost every point, which I find naturally fastened in the hearts of the common profane multitudes, and that in all my discourses with them I find, that though the ignorant cannot mouth it so plausibly, nor talk so much of free Grace, yet have they the same tenets, and all men are naturally of the Antinomian Religion.' Baxter, *Richard Baxter's Confutation of a Dissertation for the Justification of Infidels* (1654), 288, cited in Lamont, *Richard Baxter and the Millennium*, 128. See also II:897, RMeth (1653).

[90]Here Traill's observation is precisely on target: '...usually such Men that are for middle ways in points of Doctrine, have a greater kindness for that Extream they go half way to, than for that which they go half way from.' Traill, *A Vindication of the Protestant Doctrine Concerning Justification*, 2. Baxter himself recognized that 'if you discover an error to an injudicious man, he reeleth into the contrary error and it is hard to stop him in the middle way.' R.B., I, 118.

Interestingly enough, this same 'charge' has been levelled against the Antinomian, Tobias Crisp, by Benjamin Brook: 'Persons who have embraced sentiments which afterwards appear to them erroneous, often think they can never remove too far from them; and the more remote they go from their former opinions, the nearer they come to the truth. This was unhappily the case with Dr. Crisp. His ideas of the grace of Christ had been exceedingly low, and he had imbibed sentiments which produced in him a legal and self-righteous spirit. Shocked at the recollection of his former views and conduct, he seems to have imagined that he could never go far enough from them.' Benjamin Brook, *Lives*, II.473, cited in Kevan, *The Grace of Law*, 27.

[91]Baxter claims, 'If any say too much in making our Holiness Gods only End, it ill beseemeth those to be their censurers, who have tempted them to it, by erring more on the contrary extream. And it is not to be denied or hid, that more than downright Antinomians, have so ill expounded the points of Christs Suretiship, and of the Imputation of our sin to him, and of the Imputation of his Righteousness to us, as hath proved the great occasion of some mens running into the contrary error.' *How Far Holinesse is the Design of Christianity*, 14.

[92]Powicke summarizes the situation: 'As in many another instance of theological discussion, a change of emphasis was construed to imply a denial of truth.' *Rev. Richard Baxter*, 59.

[93]*Of Justification*, 75.

[94]Ibid., 263.

[95]*Universal Redemption*, 484.

[96]II:10, RCR:NR (1666). Cf. III:11, SER (1650): 'When they are called according to his purpose, then it is certain to them by a certainty of

promise also, as sure as if they were named in that promise; for the promise is, to believers, which they may, though but imperfectly, know themselves to be; and though it be yet upon condition of overcoming, and abiding in Christ, and enduring to the end, yet that condition being absolutely promised, it still remaineth absolutely certain upon promise: and, indeed, if glory be ours only upon a condition, which condition depends chiefly on our own wills, it were cold comfort to those that know what man's will is, and how certainly we should play the prodigals with this, as we did with our first stock. But I have hitherto understood, that in the behalf of the elect, Christ is resolved, and hath undertaken, for the working and finishing of their faith, and the full effecting his people's salvation; and not only given us a (feigned) sufficient grace, not effectual, leaving it to our wills to make it effectual, as some think; so that, though still the promise of justification and salvation be conditional, yet God, having manifested his purpose of enabling us to fulfil those conditions he doth thereby show us a certainty of our salvation, both in his promise and his purpose. Though God's eternal purpose gives us no right to the benefit whatsoever, (some lately say to the contrary,) it being the proper work of God's law or covenant to confer right or due; yet the event or futurition of it is made certain by God's unchangeable decree, his eternal willing it being the first and infallible cause, that, in time, it is accomplished or produced.'

[97]*Universal Redemption*, 486.

[98]Ibid., 481.

[99]Ibid., 483.

[100]C.T., I, ii, 71.

[101]*Of Justification*, 288. In III:568, CW (1657), Baxter cautions believers against taking Christ's love and grace for granted: 'Now you have a little grace, you cannot keep it of yourselves. Now you are made alive, you cannot keep yourselves alive. If you be not preserved by him that did revive you and kept by his mighty power to salvation, and if he be not the finisher of your faith, who was the author of it; how speedily, how certainly would you prove apostate, and undo all that hath been so long a doing! If then you stand not on your own legs, but are carried in his arms, you may see in whom it is you should glory.

Nay more, if you were left to yourselves but to resist one temptation, it would bear you down. You now think of many sins with a holy scorn; but the filthiest of those sins would become your pleasure, if you were forsaken by Christ. You now look on whoredom, and gluttony, and drunkenness, and ambition, as dirt and dung; but if Christ should forsake you, this dung would you feed upon, and as dogs you would eat up the filthiest vomit that ever you did disgorge yourselves of, and as swine you would choose that mire for your bed, and rest in it till hell awakened you. By this then you may perceive in whom you should glory.

Use. See then that you abhor all self-advancing thoughts. And receive no doctrine that gives the glory of Christ unto yourselves.'

[102]Note Traill's conclusion about the position held by Baxter and others: 'If they mean only, that these things are Justifications and Fruits of true Faith and of the sincerity of the Grace of God in us; We do agree to the meaning, but highly dislike the expressions, as Unscriptural and Dangerous, tending to the dishonouring of the Righteousness of Christ, and to run men on the Rocks of Pride and Self-Righteousness, that natural corruption drives all men upon.' Traill, *A Vindication of the Protestant Doctrine Concerning Justification*, 41.

[103]Fisher, 'The Theology of Richard Baxter,' 167. He argues elsewhere that Baxter met with opposition primarily because of his 'well-meant, though fruitless efforts, to strip theology of its technical garb, and to present its truths in a new dress.' See Fisher, 'The Writings of Richard Baxter,' *Bibliotheca Sacra* IX (1852): 308.

[104]J. Wayne Baker, '*Sola Fide, Sola Gratia*: The Battle for Luther in Seventeenth-Century England,' *The Sixteenth Century Journal* XVI (1985): 133.

[105]Muller, 'Covenant and Conscience in English Reformed Theology: Three Variations on a 17th Century Theme,' *Westminster Theological Journal* 42 (Spring 1980): 334.

[106]D. M. McIntyre, 'First Strictures on *The Marrow of Modern Divinity*,' 68.

[107]Alan C. Clifford, 'The Gospel and Justification,' *Evangelical Quarterly* 57 (1985): 264, n. 79.

[108]Allison, *The Rise of Moralism*, 157. Allison cites rather bland quotations from Eaton, Saltmarsh, and Crisp in his presentation of the Antinomian position and then concludes: 'On the basis of theological content ... such as was printed, the "antinomians" do not seem to have been especially shocking, and it is difficult to see why they aroused so much concern among so many divines during the century, and later' (p. 172). True, on the basis of the 'theological content' which Allison presents, it *would* be difficult! The fact is that the Antimonians did say outrageous things, and while many were not avowedly libertine, Baxter was correct in seeing that their extreme statements could result in libertinism. One example will suffice. Baxter recalled an Antinomian named Coppe who maintained that since he was one of God's Elect, he was free from moral restraints. Baxter said he could 'swear a full mouth'd oath, and can kiss his Neighbours wife in Majesty and Honour.' Baxter, *Plain Scripture Proof*, 148.

[109]*Of Justification*, 75 [emphasis added]. Note what the 'orthodox' James Buchanan says at this point: 'We are justified by Faith, and Faith is counted, or imputed to us, for righteousness; but Faith is not itself the righteousness on account of which we are justified.' *The Doctrine of Justification*, 366.

He continues: 'A real influence or efficacy is ascribed to Faith in connection with our Justification, but it is such only as belongs to a divinely appointed means of receiving and appropriating a free gift.... In regard to the influence or efficacy which is ascribed to Faith in connection with our Justification, the question, whether it may be best described as a means, – or as an instrument, – or as a condition, is of little importance, so far as it relates merely to the use of these terms, – for every one of them might be applied to it in a sound sense.' *The Doctrine of Justification*, 379. Again, I assert that Baxter would agree wholeheartedly with these statements.

[110]Kevan recognizes this, saying that Baxter 'contends that obedience to Christ's Law must never be misrepresented as 'our own Righteousness' (C.T. I. iii, 100), because its acceptance by God is solely on the ground of 'Christ's Righteousness' as 'the meritorious cause.' (C.T. II, 252).' Kevan, *The Grace of Law*, 206.

[111]Solt, *Saints in Arms*, 37.

[112]III:12, SER (1650).

4. The Process of Conversion

[1]Matthew 18:3, KJV.

[2]II:434, TCon (1657).

[3]I:36, CD:CEth (1673).

[4]II:435, TCon (1657).

[5]Ibid., 438. He says (p. 448): 'You read here that Christ protesteth, 'Verily, that except ye be converted ye shall not enter into the kingdom of heaven,' and when you read it, yet you say, you will not believe it. And yet you will say, that you are christians and believe Christ. What contradictions are these!'

[6]I:19, CD:CEth (1673).

[7]II:449, TCon (1657).

[8]Ibid.

[9]Ibid., 450-53.

[10]Ibid., 454. Thus, 'every time you hear the bell toll, it should frighten you; every time you go among the sick, or see any brought to the grave, it should frighten you; yea, every thing that you look on should be a matter of terror to you till you are out of this condition.'

[11]Ibid., 403.

[12]Ibid.

[13]Ibid.

[14]III:62-63, SER (1650).

[15]Ibid., 71.

[16]IV:94, CF (1682).

[17]*An End of Doctrinal Controversies*, 182-83.

[18]II:497, TCon (1657). See also II:266, UI:SpW (1655).

[19]*An End of Doctrinal Controversies*, 214.

[20]I:23, CD:CEth (1673).

[21]II:496, TCon (1657).

[22]Ibid., 496-97.

[23]Ibid., 497.

[24]Ibid., 476.

[25]Ibid., 416.

[26]Ibid., 476.

[27]Ibid. Baxter's retort to those who chose to remain at home is scathing: 'If you can find something else to do when you should hear the word of God, God will find something else to do when he should give you his saving grace.'

[28]Ibid., 478.

[29]Ibid. Baxter knew firsthand the value of reading. We recall that his conversion was due in large part to the books he read: 'And thus without any means but books, was God pleased to resolve me for himself.' R.B., I, 4.

[30]Ibid., 415. While God uses all these means of propagating His Word, Baxter claimed they all stand in subordination to public preaching: 'It was never God's end in writing the Scripture, nor the end of ministers in writing good books, to keep you from the public hearing of the word. Each duty must know its place. I had rather the books that I have written were all burnt, than that men should by them be kept from the public and greater ordinances.' II:476, TCon (1657).

[31]I:15, CD:CEth (1673).

[32]II:478, TCon (1657).

[33]Ibid., 412.

[34]Ibid., 478.

[35]Ibid.

[36]Ibid.

[37]Brauer notes, 'Though orthodox with regard to the doctrine of justification and eternal election, covenant theology, by its structure, tended to focus attention on the human response evoked by covenant. The centrality of conversion sits well with a covenant theology.' Jerald C. Brauer, 'Conversion: From Puritanism to Revivalism,' *Journal of Religion* 58 (1978): 235.

[38]Baxter says, 'Preparatory Grace and Duty is ordinarily Man's Disposition, as he is the Recipient of God's Grace, and the Agent of believing.' Baxter acknowledges that God is free, and can work on the unprepared if He so chooses, but warns that 'it is not to be taken for his ordinary way.' *An End of Doctrinal Controversies*, 230.

[39]Ibid., 289.

[40]*Universal Redemption*, 437.

[41]II:451, TCon (1657).

[42]II:582, DP (1658).

[43]*Universal Redemption*, 435.

[44]II:597, DP (1658). Baxter asserts, 'And when God calleth men to conversion, or reformation, he useth to call them to consideration as the way to it; Hag. i.5, 'Thus saith the Lord of hosts, 'Consider your ways.'' Ibid., 598.

[45]II:404, TCon (1657).

[46]Ibid.

[47]Ibid., 442.

[48]II:598, DP (1658).

[49]II:404, TCon (1657).

[50]II:586, DP (1658). See also II:481, TCon (1657): You will never hit the way to heaven if you do not know it.... O think not knowledge a needless thing, but make out after it, and rest not till you do obtain it.'

[51]II:586, DP (1658).

[52]Ibid.

[53]Ibid., 587. Baxter recognized that many 'miscarriages' in conversion were caused by a lack of proper understanding of these things. He says, 'Whereas, if you seem to turn and scarce know why, and seem to take up a christian life before you are thoroughly possessed with the nature, grounds, and reasons of it, no marvel if you are quickly lost again in the dark, and if every caviller that you meet with can nonplus you, and make you stagger, and call in question all that you have done, and ravel all your work.' II:587, DP (1658).

[54]Ibid.

[55]Ibid.

[56]Ibid.

[57]II:470, TCon (1657). E.g., 'And here, first, if you be not yet resolved, I shall desire that you will soberly answer me to these few questions following....' Baxter proceeds with a long list of questions for consideration, of which we list a sample: Where would you be right now, if death had cut you off in an unconverted state? If you refuse this offer, how do you know if you will ever have another? Which is better: God or the creature? Do you believe that man is made for this world only or for a better one? Have you ever well considered who they be that are for your conversion, and who they be that are against it? Do you think that man who after all this shall refuse to turn to God, and after all this shall remain unconverted, will have any just excuse before the Lord? See II:470-75, TCon (1657).

[58]Ibid., 471.

[59]Ibid. Cf. I:21, CD:CEth (1673).

[60]II:456, TCon (1657): 'Fear is not the principal affection of a true convert; and therefore terrifying arguments are not the principal means; yet these must be used or else God had never put such an affection into man's heart, nor such terrifying passages into his work; and we all feel

the need and usefulness of it; for in reason he that is in danger should know it. But yet, it is love that must be the predominant affection; and therefore it is the discovery of the amiableness of God, and the wonderful gain that comes by godliness, that must be the principal argument that we must use with you. For we know that men will not be directly affrighted in to love, though they must be affrighted from the contrary that hindereth it: do not think that God hath no better argument to use with you, than to take you by the throat, and say, Love me or I will damn thee.'

[61]II:591, DP (1658).

[62]Ibid.

[63]II:456, TCon (1657).

[64]Ibid., 457. Baxter calls this benefit 'the very root of all the rest.'

[65]Ibid., 458.

[66]Ibid.

[67]Ibid., 459.

[68]Ibid.

[69]Ibid.

[70]Ibid.

[71]Ibid, 460.

[72]Ibid.

[73]Ibid.

[74]Ibid., 461.

[75]Ibid., 462. Baxter here cites Romans 8:28, saying that he has received so much comfort from that verse that he 'would not have been without it for a world.'

[76]Ibid., 463.

[77]Ibid., 464-65.

[78]Ibid., 467.

[79]Ibid., 468.

[80]Ibid., 455.

[81]Ibid., 469.

[82]II:589, DP (1658).

[83]Ibid., 590.

[84]Ibid.

[85]Ibid., 592.

[86]Ibid.

[87]Ibid.

[88]I:21, CD:CEth (1673).

[89]Ibid.

[90]II:471, TCon (1657).

[91]Ibid., 472.

[92]I:28, CD:CEth (1673).

[93]II:593, DP (1658).

[94]I:28, CD:CEth (1673).

[95]II:441, TCon (1657).

[96]I:15, CD:CEth (1673).

[97]Baxter, *The Grand Question Resolved: What We Must Do To Be Saved* (1692), edited by A. B. Grosart (Edinburgh: Crawford & M'Cabe, 1868), 19.

[98]Ibid.

[99]II:593, DP (1658).

[100]Ibid.

[101]Ibid., 597.

[102]Ibid., 599.

[103]Ibid.

[104]Ibid., 603.

[105]Ibid., 599.

[106]Ibid.

[107]C.T. I, iii, 14. Packer summarizes it well: 'The occasionally voiced suggestion that there was something legalistic in their stress on the need for a 'preparatory work' of contrition and humbling for sin before men can close with Christ is quite false: the only point they were making ... was that, because fallen man is naturally in love with sin, it is psychologically impossible for him to embrace Christ whole-heartedly as Saviour, not just from sin's penalty but from sinning itself, until he has come to hate sin and long for deliverance from it. The 'preparatory work' is simply the creating of this state of mind.' Packer, 'Puritanism as a Movement of Revival,' *Evangelical Quarterly* (1980): 8.Baxter makes this point clear. He says the teaching that men must find special marks antecedent to faith to give them a warrant to believe is, 'false Doctrine, I think, in the judgment of all.' *Universal Redemption*, 151.

[108]Baxter says, 'Till humiliation make a sinner feel his sin and misery, it is not possible that Christ as Christ should be heartily welcome to him, or received in that sort as his honour doth expect.... never is Christ valued and sought after as Christ, till sorrow hath taught us how to value him; nor is he entertained in the necessary honour of a Redeemer, till humiliation throw open all the doors: no man can seek him with his whole heart, that seeks him not with a broken heart.' II:602, DP (1658).

[109]Baxter asserts, 'The common cause that men live and die without the grace of repentance, sanctification, and justification which should save them, is because they will not believe but that they have it, when they have it not; and that they are penitent, and justified, and sanctified already.' I:17, CD:CEth (1673).

[110]III:667, LF (1669).

[111]C.T., II, 221.

[112]Ibid. Baxter claims, 'A man on the gallows will be glad of a pardon; but a stander-by, that thinks he is innocent, would not regard it, but take it for an accusation.' II:603, DP (1658).

[113]II:604, DP (1658).

[114]C.T., II, 221-22.

[115]Ibid.

[116]IV:811, ML. See also II:603, DP (1658): 'when the heart is truly broken, it will then stand no longer on such terms with Christ, but yield up all: it will then no longer condition with him, but stand to his conditions, and thankfully accept them. Any thing will then serve with Christ, grace, and the hopes of glory.'

[117]II:604, DP (1658).

[118]Baxter himself experienced this: 'Another of my doubts was because my grief and humiliation was no greater, and because I could weep no more for this.' But he confesses, 'I understood at last that God breaketh not all mens hearts alike.' R.B. I, 7.

[119]II:956, RMeth (1653). He also said, 'I advise all men to take heed of placing religion too much in fears and tears and scruples, or in any other kind of sorrow.' *Autobiography*, 217.

[120]II:605, DP (1658).

[121]Ibid.

[122]Ibid.

[123]II:826, MS-I (1661).

[124]II:605, DP (1658). In II:828, MS-I (1661), Baxter says: 'it is but a very few that are faulty in over-studying themselves, in comparison of the many thousand that err on the other hand, in the careless neglecting of themselves.'

[125]II:828, MS-I (1661).

[126]Ibid., 826.

[127]Ibid., 840.

[128]Ibid., 841.

[129]Ibid., 842.

[130]II:608, DP (1658).

[131]Ibid.

[132]This point has been missed by numerous writers, with many making the exact opposite assertion. For example, Laurence maintains that 'Preparationists ... made a pilgrim's activities in preparation the condition of his acceptance with God at least as much as his believing.' David Laurence, 'Jonathan Edwards, Solomon Stoddard, and the Preparationist Model of Conversion,' *Harvard Theological Review* 72 (1979): 277. Miller asserts that it was a short step from a preparationist theology to 'an open reliance upon human exertions and to a belief that conversion is worked entirely by rational argument and moral persuasion.' Perry Miller, "Preparation for Salvation' in Seventeenth-Century New England,' *Journal of the History of Ideas* IV (1943): 286. Lovelace charges that in the teaching of preparation among the Puritans the 'very un-Reformed notion of congruent merit began to reappear'.

Richard Lovelace, *The American Puritanism of Cotton Mather* (Grand Rapids: Eerdmans, 1979), 106.

I beg to differ with these and other such statements. The Puritans did not teach that preparation could in any way lay a claim on God to provide more grace. Cohen's comment is accurate: 'Puritans denied that preparation could be a 'meritorious cause' of conversion.' Cohen, *God's Caress*, 86-87.

[133]II:608, DP (1658).

[134]At this point Cohen's phraseology is unfortunate. He says, 'Conversion occurs only after a period of preparation has eliminated all confidence in one's own abilities.' *God's Caress*, 109. His lack of any qualification to this statement leaves the impression that the Puritans taught the absolute necessity of preparation. They did not. They always recognized that God had the freedom to work outside of His normal means, e.g. in the conversion of the Apostle Paul.

Owen Watkins's observation is astute: 'The Puritan pastors, with wider knowledge of what was happening to different people, emphasized the variety of dealings with God that they might have.' See Owen C. Watkins, *The Puritan Experience: Studies in Spiritual Autobiography* (New York: Schocken Books, 1972), 46.

[135]II:417, TCon (1657).

[136]II:581, DP (1658).

[137]The reader will note that we have already examined Baxter's concept of faith in our treatment of his view of justification. We treat it again here briefly to provide a context for our ensuing discussion on assurance.

[138]I:30, CD:CEth (1673). Baxter says, 'To think you are rich, will not make you rich: to believe that you are well, or to know the remedy, is not enough to make you well.' Ibid., 33.

[139]Ibid., 33.

[140]II:405, TCon (1657). Baxter says, 'If you tell a man that a bear or a cut-throat thief is following after him, if you see him not stir any faster, nor mend his pace, you will say, sure he doth not believe it; but if you see him run as for his life, it is a sign that he believes it.'

[141]Ibid., 412.

[142]Ibid.

[143]Ibid., 495.

[144]IV:173, PM (1672).

[145]Ibid.

[146]Ibid.

[147]C.T., I, ii, 118.

[148]II:610, DP (1658).

[149]IV:204, PM (1672).

[150]II:622, DP (1658).

[151]Ibid.

[152]Ibid., 623.

[153]Ibid., 630.

[154]I:24, CD:CEth (1672).

[155]II:489, TCon (1657); II:630, DP (1658).

[156]John Calvin, *Institutes of the Christian Religion*, ed. John T. McNeill (Philadelphia: The Westminster Press, 1960 reprint), III, ii, §7. Calvin says, 'Now we shall possess a right definition of faith if we call it a firm and certain knowledge of God's benevolence toward us, founded upon the truth of the freely given promise in Christ, both revealed to our minds and sealed upon our hearts through the Holy Spirit.'

Helm, *Calvin and the Calvinists*, 23-26, argues that Calvin's teaching was synonymous with that of the Puritans, i.e. that there can be true faith without assurance. Helm's claim is disputed by Anthony N. S. Lane, 'John Calvin: The Witness of the Holy Spirit,' (Puritan and Reformed Studies Conference Papers, 1982), 8, who says, 'If there is anything that can be stated with total confidence about Calvin's theology, it is that faith and assurance are not to be divided.'

[157]II:899, RMeth (1653).

[158]Ibid.

[159]Ibid.

[160]C.T., II, 234.

[161]III:671, LF (1669).

[162]Ibid.

[163]I:899, CD:CP (1673).

[164]III:671, LF (1669).

[165]Ibid.

[166]Ibid.

[167]IV:177, PM (1672). Baxter clarifies himself even further: 'Alas! it is not the restraint of a wicked work or two, or the outward civilizing of your lives, that is true conversion. It is such a change as I am not describing to you, that turneth you quite another way. If you are true christians that hear me, you know it or may know it to be thus with yourselves. For certainly you have had experience of this in your souls. It were no impossible thing for you now, if you were but willing, to know certainly whether you be converted, yea or no. One would think that a man's end might be discerned above all things. Cannot you know what you like and love best.... Sirs, deal truly between God and your souls. What hath your hearts? what game do you follow? what do you mind above all? I ask not whether you set not a foot now and then out of the way; but which way are you travelling?' II:410, TCon (1657).

[168]IV:177, PM (1672).

[169]II:947, RMeth (1653). He says, 'You must therefore first be resolved, wherein the truth of saving grace doth consist, and then in all your

failings and weaknesses first know, whether they contradict sincerity in itself, and are such as may give just cause to question your sincerity: if they be not, (as the ordinary infirmities or believers are not,) then you may and must be humbled for them, but you may not doubt of your salvation for them. I told you before by what marks you may discern your sincerity; that is, wherein the nature of saving faith and holiness doth consist; keep that in your eye, and as long as you find that sure and clear, let nothing make you doubt of your right to Christ and glory.' Ibid., 951.

[170]Ibid., 901.

[171]Ibid.

[172]Ibid., 902. Laurence claims that Jonathan Edwards surpasses the earlier Puritan writers with his emphasis not on *how* belief must occur, but on *what* spiritual knowledge is. Certainly Baxter must be accorded a prior place in this line of thought. Laurence, 'Jonathan Edwards, Solomon Stoddard, and the Preparationist Model of Conversion,' 282-83.

[173]II:902, RMeth (1653).

[174]Ibid. Keeble argues that in 'putting sincere desire before achievement or experience Baxter simplifies earlier Puritan advice and shows himself more charitable and realistic.' See Keeble, *Puritan Man of Letters*, 135.

[175]II:903, RMeth (1653).

[176]Ibid., 906.

[177]Ibid., 898.

[178]Ibid. Baxter later changes the third element from 'raising comforts' to leading the believer to 'rejoyce.' *An End of Doctrinal Controversies*, 281. In *Universal Redemption*, 162, Baxter separates the *giving* of the graces from the *working* of the graces, resulting in four elements. In C.T., I, ii, 90, he adds a fifth element: the giving of the love of God.

[179]II:898, RMeth (1653). Baxter notes that the 'sudden looseness' in the lives of many who claimed this 'inner witness' proved to him that 'the Spirit of comfort was not their comforter; for he is also a Spirit of holiness.' Ibid., 912-13.

[180]Ibid., 898.

[181]*A Defence of Christ and Free Grace* (2nd pagination of *The Scripture Gospel Defended*), 26.

[182]C.T. I, ii, 91.

[183]*An End of Doctrinal Controversies*, 281.

[184]II:827, MS-I (1661).

[185]II:923, RMeth (1653).

[186]Ibid., 892. As Baxter notes, 'You must have grace before you can discover it.' Ibid., 896.

[187]Ibid., 895.

[188]III:657, LF (1669). Baxter says 'Too many are confident that they are justified, who ought not only to Fear that they are not, but to know it.' C.T., II, 256.

[189]C.T., I, ii, 91.

[190]II:931, RMeth (1653). Baxter laments, 'Oh how narrow is the path between these two mistaken roads, and how hard a thing, and how rare is it to find it and to keep in it.'

[191]Ibid.

[192]Ibid., 887.

[193]I:503, CD:CEc (1673). Baxter says, 'I have by long experience found it to have so great and common a hand in the fears and troubles of mind, that I meet not with one of many, that live in a great troubles and fears for any long time together, but melancholy is the main seat of them.' II:888, RMeth (1653).

[194]II:889, RMeth (1653).

[195]I:503, CD:CEc (1673).

[196]Ibid.

[197]II:909, RMeth (1653). Baxter recognizes that 'if every true Christian should have certainty of Salvation, when he sinneth as fouly, as frequently, as grosly, and liveth as slothfully as ever will stand with sincerity, it would tempt such to go on in Sin, and be no better.' C.T. I, ii, 113.

[198]II:925, RMeth (1653). Baxter calls for an important distinction: 'in all your troubles you be sure to distinguish between matter of doubting and matter of humiliation.... Learn therefore to be humbled for every sin, but not to doubt of your sincerity and salvation for every sin.' Ibid., 965.

[199]Packer suggests that Baxter probably refers to Robert Bolton, *Instructions for a Right Comforting Afflicted Consciences* (1631); Thomas Hooker, *The Souls Preparation for Christ. Or, a Treatise of Contrition* (1632); John Rogers, *The Doctrine of Faith* (1627). Packer notes, 'In all three, stress is laid on the necessity for a thorough, 'affectionate' repentance by the sinner.' Packer, 'Redemption and Restoration...', 40, n. 3.

[200]R.B., I, 6.

[201]II: 952, RMeth (1653): 'According to that experience which I have had of the state of christians, I am forced to judge that most of the children of the godly that ever are renewed, are renewed in their childhood, or much towards it then done; and that among forty christians there is not one that can certainly name the month in which his soul first began to be sincere; and among a thousand christians, I think not one can name the hour. The sermon which awakened them, they may name, but not the hour when they first arrived at a saving sincerity.'

We must therefore discount Brauer's assertion that, 'Inevitably the Puritan was led to pinpoint the moment of conversion and usually did so.' Jerald C. Brauer, 'Conversion: From Puritanism to Revivalism,' *Journal of Religion* 58 (1978): 241.

[202]II: 910, RMeth (1653).

[203]II:842, MS-I (1661).

[204]II: 952, RMeth (1653). Baxter asserts that if a man is demonstrating his true consent to his baptismal covenant, 'I dare say you are regenerate, though you know not just when you first consented.' II:843, MS-I (1661).

[205]II:911, RMeth (1653). Baxter notes that he came to these conclusions not 'merely by reading books, but mainly by reading my own heart, and consulting my own experience, and the experience of a very great number of godly people of all sorts, who have opened their hearts to me, for almost twenty years' time... And whether the confidentest men for the contrary be not those that study books more than hearts, and spend their days in disputing, and not in winning souls to God from the world.' Ibid., 912.

[206]C.T., I, ii, 112.

[207]II:919, RMeth (1653). Perry Miller's assertion that under the Covenant of Grace Puritans 'enjoyed clear sailing to the haven of assurance' clearly does not square with Baxter's views developed over several years of personal ministry. See Miller, 'The Marrow of Puritan Divinity,' 271. Baxter says, 'in my experience (who have conversed with as many that are careful of their Souls as most have done I think) it is a very small number that I could ever hear say, I am certain of my Justification and Salvation ... the certainty of Salvation is very rare.' C.T., I, ii, 90.

[208]II:909, RMeth (1653).

[209]II:496, TCon (1657). Baxter continues: 'Will you begin at the top of the ladder and not the bottom? Did God ever damn any man that was truly converted and sanctified, because he was not elected? No such matter: prove any such thing if you can: nay, we can fully prove the contrary, for he hath promised salvation to all that are truly converted and sanctified.'

[210]I:504, CD:CEc (1673). Baxter illustrates this by noting that a husband and wife are uncertain every day, whether one might try and kill the other. Yet they can live comfortably together, because it is so unlikely, that it is not to be feared.

[211]Ibid., 503-4. See also II:889-92, RMeth (1653).

[212]Ibid., 504.

[213]II:914, RMeth (1653).

[214]Ibid., 888. Thus one should, 'Converse with men of strongest faith, that have this heavenly mirth, and can speak experimentally of the joy of the Holy Ghost; and these will be a great help to the reviving of your spirit, and changing your melancholy habit.'

[215]Ibid., 916. Baxter encourages them to write these down, and 'oft review them.'

[216]Ibid., 939.

5. Presenting the Gospel: Manner and Methods

[1]To my knowledge, the term 'evangelism' was not used by the Puritans. Their favorite expression seems to have been 'preaching the gospel.' I substitute the term evangelism to protect two truths: laymen as well as clergy were involved in this activity; and the pastor's ministry of persuasion took place not only in the context of the sermon during worship services, but also outside of the church building. These truths are not readily apparent in the phrase 'preaching the gospel.' This also explains the use of the broader term 'presenting' in the title for this chapter.

[2]IV:381, RP (1656). He constantly sought ways to be more effective in reaching men for Christ: 'Oh that any one of you could tell me what I should say more, or what I should do now to save the souls of ignorant, fleshly, worldly sinners from damnation! and to convert the unconverted, and turn the hearts of men to God! Oh that you could but tell me how I might accomplish it!' II:500, TCon (1657).

[3]III:230, SER (1650).

[4]IV:381, RP (1656).

[5]Ibid.

[6]II:496, TCon (1657).

[7]Ibid, 476.

[8]Ibid.

[9]Ibid., 478.

[10]II:618, 621, DP (1658).

[11]II:502, CU (1657).

[12]IV:444, RP (1656).

[13]Ibid.

[14]II:555, NN (1663), citing from Ezekiel 3:18-20.

[15]IV:444, RP (1656).

[16]II:539, CU (1657).

[17]II:571, NN (1663).

[18]Brauer overstates the true situation when he places Puritan conversion under the 'control of a religious elite, the clergy.' Brauer, 'Conversion: From Puritanism to Revivalism,' 239. Cohen recognizes what Baxter emphasizes here: 'Ministers had no monopoly on instructing and counselling; family, friends, and acquaintances of prospective Saints also performed these tasks.' Cohen, God's Caress, 173. Ralph Barton Perry also recognized this truth in his Puritanism and Democracy (New York: Harper & Row, 1944), 321.

Baxter makes clear he is not suggesting that the distinction between minister and parishioner be blurred. While every Christian should share the Gospel with others, public preaching can only be undertaken by the minister. See III:213, SER (1659).

19I:562, CD:CEccl (1673). He says that the man who does not profess God with his tongue is a 'practical atheist.'

20II:431-32, TCon (1657).

21II:552, NN (1663).

22Ibid.

23II:490, TCon (1657).

24Ibid.

25II:553, NN (1663).

26III:214, SER (1650).

27II:507, CU (1657).

28IV:425, RP (1656).

29Ibid.

30See, for example, II:565, NN (1663): 'Why standest thou idle ... when thou art redeemed for work? for evangelical work.'

31II:433, TCon (1657).

32This list does not claim to be exhaustive, nor is it presented in any particular order of priority.

33I have chosen the term 'evangelizer' because it avoids the professional connotations of 'evangelist'. To my knowledge Baxter himself did not use this term.

34IV:369, RP (1656).

35IV:1033, PAA (1656). Baxter says, 'I will make my free confession to you to my shame, That I never grew cold, and dull, and pitiless to the souls of others, till I first grew too cold and careless of my own (unless when weakness or speculative studies cool me, which I must confess they often do.)'

36II:560, NN (1663).

37I:563, CD:CEccl (1673).

38I:813, CD:CP (1673). He says that the Christian who does not profess God with his tongue is a 'practical atheist.'

39III:233, SER (1650).

40IV:371, RP (1656). Baxter chided ministers who would study to *preach* exactly, and study little or not at all to *live* exactly.

41Ibid, 372.

42II:559, NN (1663). Baxter laments his own failings at this point: 'For my own part, though I have long lived in a sense of the preciousness of time, and have not been wholly idle in the world; yet when I have the deepest thoughts of the great, everlasting consequents of my work, and of the uncertainty and shortness of my time, I am even amazed to think that my heart can be so slow and senseless, as to do no more in such a case. The Lord knows, and my accusing, wounded conscience knows, that my slothfulness is so much my shame and admiration, that I am astonished to think that my resolutions are no stronger, my affections no livelier, and my labour and diligence no greater, when God is the commander, and his love the encourager, and his wrath the spur, and heaven or hell must be the issue.' See II:565, NN (1663).

[43]IV:355, RP (1656).

[44]Ibid., 380.

[45]Ibid., 355.

[46]II:553, NN (1663).

[47]Ibid., 555.

[48]IV:385, RP (1656).

[49]II:502, CU (1657).

[50]IV:394, RP (1656).

[51]Ibid, 426.

[52]Ibid.

[53]Ibid., 412. He says, 'we speak so drowsily or gently, that sleepy sinners cannot hear; the blow falls so light, that hard-hearted sinners cannot feel it.'

[54]Ibid.

[55]Ibid., 394: 'I know not what it doth by others, but the most reverend preacher, that speaks as if he saw the face of God, doth more affect my heart, though with common words, than an unreverend man with the most exquisite preparations.'

[56]II:573, NN (1663).

[57]III:217, SER (1650).

[58]IV:393, RP (1656).

[59]II:399, TCon (1657).

[60]III:218, SER (1650).

[61]Ibid.

[62]Ibid.

[63]IV:456, RP (1656).

[64]Ibid., 393.

[65]Ibid.

[66]Ibid., 442.

[67]Baxter told ministers they should study how to do personal work just as seriously as they studied for their sermons. Ibid., 360.

[68]'Prayer must carry on our work as well as preaching: he preacheth not heartily to his people, that will not pray for them.' Ibid., 393.

[69]Ibid., 371. Baxter helps his readers in terms of practice by giving specific directions for 'the right managing of this work.' See Ibid., 454-63.

[70]IV:1034, PAA (1672). Baxter says, 'Poor sinners! I know that I am speaking all this to those that are dead in sin; but it is a death consisting with a natural life, which hath a capacity of spiritual life; or else I would no more speak to you than to a stone. And I know that you are blind in sin; but it is a blindness consisting with a reasonable faculty, which is

capable of spiritual illumination; or else I would no more persuade you than I do a beast.'

[71]III:232, SER (1650).

[72]IV:412, RP (1656) [emphasis added]. Packer asserts, 'The Puritans did not regard evangelistic sermons as a special class of sermons, having their own peculiar style and conventions; the Puritan position was, rather, that, since all Scripture bears witness to Christ, and all sermons should aim to expound and apply what is in the Bible, all proper sermons would of necessity declare Christ and so be to some extent evangelistic.... The only difference was that some sermons aimed more narrowly and exlusively at converting sinners than did others.' Packer, 'The Puritan View of Preaching the Gospel,' (Puritan and Reformed Studies Conference Papers, 1959), 13.

[73]IV:151, CF (1682). 'When a dull hearer and a dull speaker meet together, a dead heart and a dead exhortation, it is far unlike to have a lively effect.' III:217, SER (1650).

[74]III:216, SER (1650). Baxter's teaching here mirrors the findings of Erroll Hulse in his article, 'The Puritan Approach to Persuading Souls,' (Puritan and Reformed Studies Conference Papers, 1973), 7-19. Hulse says concerning the Puritans, (p. 18), 'The whole of their preaching was one protracted and powerful appeal to the whole man, that the sinner being born again might be persuaded once and for all to turn and close with Christ.' Unfortunately the only reference Hulse makes to Baxter in the article is to point out that his Amyraldianism was a minority viewpoint among the Puritans.

[75]IV:426, RP (1656).

[76]Ibid.

[77]This was the method Baxter encouraged others to use; due to his continual poor health, he had his parishioners come and visit him in his home.

[78]IV:443, RP (1656). Baxter says: 'I have found by experience, that an ignorant sot that hath been an unprofitable hearer so long, hath got more knowledge and remorse of conscience in half an hour's close discourse, than they did from ten years' public preaching.' The point comes home even more when we remember that Baxter was perhaps the greatest preacher of his day!

[79]Ibid., 439.

[80]Ibid., 457. Baxter writes out for his fellow ministers the essence of what he says at this point. Much of it involves telling his parishioners it is his solemn duty under God to instruct them about spiritual matters.

[81]Ibid.

[82]Ibid.

[83]Ibid., 457-58. Baxter lists the questions that he proposes to the one who appears to yet be unconverted.

[84]Ibid., 461. It is noteworthy that it appears Baxter made no effort to press for an immediate 'decision'. While stressing the urgent necessity of turning to Christ, the immediate commitment he pressed for was not to turn to Christ, but to involve oneself in the means of grace.

This rings true to the findings from Packer's study of evangelism among the Puritans. He says, 'The immediate duty of the unprepared sinner is not to try and believe on Christ, which he is not able to do, but to read, enquire, pray, use the means of grace and learn what he needs to be saved from.' Packer, 'Puritan Evangelism,' *The Banner of Truth* IV (1957): 11.

[85]Ibid., 442.

[86]Ibid., 449. Baxter makes it clear where his priority lies: 'I would throw by all the libraries in the world, rather than be guilty of the perdition of one soul.' Ibid., 215.

[87]Ibid., 384.

[88]Ibid., 385.

[89]Ibid., 384. Baxter argued that since people had 'grown unacquainted with the office of the ministry,' that the minister should invite the people to knock frequently at his door.

[90]II:431, TCon (1657).

[91]Ibid., 468.

[92]II:507, CU (1657).

[93]A related aspect is how Baxter dealt with objections raised by the unconverted. He deals with them at length in his *Treatise on Conversion*, specifically in 'The Hinderances of Conversion, With Directions Contrary to Them.' II:476-500, TCon (1657).

[94]Consistent with his view of man, Baxter largely made his appeals on the basis of reason. For example, he says: 'I beseech thee, read over and over again the reasons that I have here offered thee, and judge whether a reasonable man should resist them, and delay an hour to come in to God.' See II:660-1, DP (1658).

[95]Ibid., 589.

[96]Ibid., 664. Baxter says: 'If it had been in my power to have showed you heaven and hell itself, that you might better have known the matters that we speak of, I think I should have done it. But God will not have men live by sense in this life, but by faith.' Ibid., 660.

[97]II:446, TCon (1657).

[98]II:575, NN (1663).

[99]Ibid.

[100]II:469, TCon (1657).

[101]II:591, DP (1658).

[102]Ibid., 643. Unfortunately, some Christians who give their testimonies in public glorify their past life of sin so much one wonders why they ever became a Christian in the first place.

[103]Ibid., 582.

[104]This is the key theme throughout Baxter's treatise, 'Now or Never.' II:545-79, NN (1663).

[105]II:583, DP (1658).

[106]R.B, I, 84-85. Perhaps even more telling for the quality of his ministry is the following statement, written after his Ejection: 'though I have been now absent from them about six years, and they have been assaulted with pulpit-calumnies, and slanders, with threatenings and imprisonments, with enticing words, and seducing reasonings, they yet stand fast and keep their integrity ... not one, that I hear of, that are fallen off, or forsake their uprightness.' Ibid., 86.

[107]John T. Wilkinson, 'Richard Baxter's *Reformed Pastor,' Expository Times* 69 (1957): 16.

6. Conversion and the Church

[1]A perusal of Nuttall's bibliography of Baxter's works (*Richard Baxter,* 132-36) reveals that nearly one-half of Baxter's one hundred forty-one writings were devoted to some aspect of ecclesiology. It therefore comes as no surprise that Edward Hindson chose Baxter as the representative for the chapter on the church in his anthology of Puritan theology. See Hindson, *Introduction to Puritan Theology: A Reader* (Grand Rapids: Baker Book House, 1976), 233-46.

[2]Others have treated different aspects of Baxter's ecclesiology: Irvonwy Morgan, *The Nonconformity of Richard Baxter* (London: Epworth Press, 1946); A. Harold Wood, *Church Unity without Uniformity: a Study of Seventeenth-Century English Church Movements and of Richard Baxter's Proposals for a Comprehensive Church* (London: Epworth Press, 1963); and Horton Davies, *Worship and Theology in England: From Andrewes to Baxter and Fox, 1603-1690* (Princeton: Princeton University Press, 1975). The most comprehensive study of which I am aware is the doctoral dissertation by Donald Miller, 'A Critical Appraisal of Richard Baxter's Views of the Church and Their Applicability to Contemporary Church Problems,' unpublished Ph.D. dissertation, New York University, 1935. Other studies include: Earl Kent Brown, 'Richard Baxter's Contribution to the Comprehension Controversy: A Study in Projected Church Union,' unpublished Ph.D. dissertation, Boston University Graduate School, 1956; Alexander Gillon MacAlpine, 'Ecclesiastical and Civil Polity in the Writings of Richard Baxter,' unpublished S. T. M. thesis, Union Theological Seminary, 1934; and R. L. McCan, 'The Conception of the Church in Richard Baxter and John Bunyan: a Comparison and Contrast,' unpublished dissertation, Edinburgh, 1955.

[3]*The Cure of Church Divisions* (1670), 51.

[4]II:458, TCon (1657). Baxter says, 'A man may be a member of the visible church, or rather, be visibly made a member of the church before

conversion: but that is but as a wooden leg to the body... So that till conversion, even the baptized and the most understanding men, are but as the straw and chaff in God's barn, and as the tares in his field, as Christ himself compareth them. But conversion doth effectually ingraft them into the body, and make them living members.'

[5]*The Cure of Church Divisions*, 33. Hindson says, 'Baxter contrasts the Puritan concept of the church with the Catholic and Anabaptist concepts of a 'pure church,' pointing out that the visible and invisible church are never in fact identical, but that this must remain the goal. Thus, one must never assume that all church members are true Christians simply because they are members, or have been baptized, or have responded to an altar call.' See Hindson, *Introduction to Puritan Theology*, 234.

[6]*The Cure of Church Divisions*, 33.

[7]I:627, CD:CEccl (1673).

[8]*The Cure of Church Divisions*, 52.

[9]Baxter lists common reasons as ignorance, lack of water, and lack of a minister. See I:637, CD:CEccl (1673).

[10]Ibid.

[11]Ibid.

[12]III:735, LF (1669).

[13]I:599, CD:CEccl (1673).

[14]IV:203, PM (1672).

[15]R.B., Appendix III, 63, 62. Bolam picks up on this point correctly: 'Whatever else Baxter might be, or not be, he was not a Congregational; a united undivided parish was the solid basis of all his churchmanship.' See Bolam, *The English Presbyterians*, 54.

[16]R.B., Appendix III, 63.

[17]R.B., III, 67. This is an excerpt from a letter to John Owen, dated Feb. 16, 1668. Packer sees Baxter's pastoral heart reflected here: 'He was never at a loss for a word himself; but one of the most endearing sides of his character was his deep sympathy for saints less articulate than himself, and he often rises to their defence against 'church-gatherers' who would not look twice at a person unless he could give an eloquent testimony concerning his spiritual experience.' Packer, 'Redemption and Restoration,' 317-18.

[18]IV:742, TC (1659).

[19]Tidball correctly sees that Baxter's disagreement with the separatists was not over the issue of godliness, but over how best to achieve it. See Derek J. Tidball, *Skillful Shepherds: An Introduction to Pastoral Theology* (Grand Rapids, Mich.: Zondervan, 1986), 301.

[20]*The Cure of Church Divisions*, 36.

[21]Keeble, 'Introduction' to *Autobiography*, xvii. Bolam creatively explains this in terms of trade-union vocabulary, with the Congregationalists 'contracting-in' and Baxter 'contracting-out.' For membership of

an independent church it was necessary to 'contract-in' by giving proofs of high qualifications; in the case of a parish church, all were eligible for membership until they disqualified themselves, i.e. 'contracted-out.' *The English Presbyterians*, 54.

[22]R.B., I, 130.

[23]E.g. R.B., II, 143: 'And I disliked also the lamentable tendency of this their way to Divisions and Sub-divisions, and the nourishing of Heresies and Sects.'

[24]*The Cure of Church Divisions*, A3-A3v.

[25]Robert S. Paul, 'Ecclesiology in Richard Baxter's Autobiography,' in *From Faith to Faith*, ed. by Dikran Y. Hadidian (Pittsburgh: Pickwick Press, 1979), 383.

[26]Paul acknowledges this fact later in footnote 129, but he fails to note its relevance in terms of evangelism. Holifield also misses this point, saying, 'Baxter would have limited Church membership to godly parents and their children. He knew that many hypocrites were baptized, but he thought it only 'accidental' when 'any ungodly' were admitted into the Church.... Baxter thus took his stand in an epic debate among seventeenth-century Puritans about the nature of the Church and its sacraments. Should the Church in England be a comprehensive institution embracing even the unrighteous in hopes of dispensing grace to them? Should it be a more select community of the outwardly holy and their offspring? Or should it consist purely of faithful adults? Baxter defended selectivity, though without abandoning infant membership.' E. Brooks Holifield, *The Covenant Sealed: The Development of Puritan Sacramental Theology in Old and New England, 1570-1720* (New Haven, Conn.: Yale University Press, 1974), 97.

I do not read Baxter this way. Baxter actually argued for the comprehensive institution instead of the selective institution. Holifield has confused the issue of membership with the issue of the nature of the church – two quite different issues. The parish church would always have both wheat and tares in its midst – but only those who claimed to be wheat could be full members. The tares should be allowed to remain, however, as they will then have an opportunity the hear the gospel preached.

[27]Ladell, *Richard Baxter: Puritan and Mystic*, 66.

[28]I:628, CD:CEccl (1673).

[29]*Treatise of Episcopacy*, 33.

[30]I:599, CD:CEccl (1673).

[31]*The Cure of Church Divisions*, 46.

[32]R.B., Appendix IV, 68.

[33]I:639, CD:CEccl (1673).

[34]R.B., I, 114.

[35]Ibid.

[36]I:651, CD:CEccl (1673).

[37]IV:303, CR (1658).

[38]I:937, RL (1661).

[39]IV:328, CR (1658).

[40]Ibid., 312.

[41]Ibid.

[42]I:637, CD:CEccl (1673).

[43]Ibid., 638. Baxter's first disputation in his *Certain Disputations of Right to Sacraments* is, 'Whether Ministers may admit persons into the Church of Christ by Baptism, upon the bare verbal Profession of the true Christian Saving faith, without staying for, or requiring any further Evidences of Sincerity? Aff.' See *Certain Disputations*, 1. This reflects his view that few Christians could name the exact time of their conversion.

[44]I:638, CD:CEccl (1673).

[45]Ibid.

[46]Ibid.

[47]Ibid., 637.

[48]Ibid., 638.

[49]*The Cure of Church Divisions* , 45-46.

[50]Ibid., 46.

[51]Ibid., 46-47.

[52]Ibid., 47.

[53]Ibid., 50-51.

[54]*Of National Churches* (1691), 26.

[55]IV:294, CR (1658).

[56]*The Cure of Church Divisions*, 45.

[57]IV:296, CR (1658).

[58]I:599, CD:CEccl (1673).

[59]*Five Disputations*, 130.

[60]IV:152, CF (1682).

[61]Ibid.

[62]*Autobiography*, 97.

[63]I:689, CD:CEccl (1673).

[64]IV:305, CR (1658).

[65]Ibid.

[66]Morgan, *The Nonconformity of Richard Baxter*, 166.

[67]*Plain Scripture Proof of Infants Church-membership and Baptism* (1651), 223.

[68]IV:308, CR (1658).

[69]I:494, CD:CEc (1673).

[70]I:561, CD:CEccl (1673).

[71]I:922, RL (1661).

[72]I:560, CD:CEccl (1673).

[73]IV:155, CF (1682).

[74]I:662, CD:CEccl (1673).

[75]Ibid. Baxter here distanced himself from the Baptist position, which held that only believer's baptism was valid. For Baxter, the key in the validity of baptism appears to be the outward ceremony being performed correctly. The only allowances he makes for rebaptism are those related to 'problems' in the ceremony. As long as a person made a profession of the Christian faith, whether or not it was genuine, that man's baptism cannot be repeated. But presumably, a person could have had genuine faith and been baptized, but if the ceremony were incorrect (i.e. the failure to use the Trinitarian formula), then that person could be rebaptized.

[76]Ibid.

[77]Ibid.

[78]Ibid., 202.

[79]IV:185, PM (1672).

[80]I:561, CD:CEccl (1673).

[81]Ibid.

[82]Ibid., 650.

[83]Ibid. Holifield claims that Baxter was battling on three fronts. Against the Baptist assertion that the ordinance was a professing sign, Baxter argued that baptism was a divine seal by which God engaged himself to fulfill His promises, thus placing the emphasis on the objectivity of the covenant promise and the seal. Against the Puritan sacramentalists, he stressed the priority of the covenant, allowing him to guard against their exaggerated concepts of sacramental grace. Against Puritans who wanted to relax the standards of admission, Baxter asserted the voluntaristic and subjective character of earlier Puritan sacramental theology. Every adult candidate for baptism, and every parent, must be able to profess adherence to the baptismal covenant. See Holifield, *The Covenant Sealed*, 94.

[84]Packer, 'Redemption and Restoration,' 316.

[85]IV:178, PM (1672).

[86]II:906, RMeth (1653). Cf. *The Grand Question Resolved*, 39, where he gives a slightly different form: 'Believing in God the Father, Son and Holy Spirit, I do perfectly, absolutely and resolutely give up myself to Him, my Creator and reconciled God and Father, my Saviour and Sanctifier: and repenting of my sins I renounce the devil, the world and the sinful desires of the flesh: and denying myself and taking up my cross, I consent to follow Christ the captain of my salvation, in hope of His promised grace and glory.'

[87]II:904, RMeth (1653).

[88]I:560, CD:CEccl (1673).

[89]*Plain Scripture Proof*, b3v.

[90]Ibid.

[91]See Powicke, *A Life*, 224-36.

[92]Baxter called this the 'very heart of the controversie'. See *Plain Scripture Proof*, 23.

[93]He asserted, 'If I prove, That all Church-members must be admitted by Baptism, and then prove that Infants are Church members: Is not this as much as to prove, they must be Baptized?' *Plain Scripture Proof*, 8.

[94]Ibid., 56.

[95]Ibid., 283.

[96]Ibid., 113. In IV:154, CF (1682), he expands his remarks: 'That as children are made sinners and miserable by their parents without any act of their own; so they are delivered out of it by the free grace of Christ, upon a condition performed by their parents; else they that are visibly born in sin and misery should have no visible or certain way of remedy: nature maketh them as it were parts of the parents, or so near as causeth their sin and misery: and this nearness supposed, God, by his free grace, hath put it in the power of the parents to accept for them the blessings of the covenant; and to enter them into the covenant of God, the parents' will being instead of their own, who yet have none to choose for themselves.'

[97]*End of Doctrinal Controversies*, 221-23.

[98]Ibid., 223.

[99]I:654, CD:CEccl (1673). Baxter asserted this was true for the immediate parents and '*probably* any true domestic owner of the child, who hath the power to choose or refuse for him' (656, emphasis added). Note his uncertainty on this last point.

[100]Ibid., 653. He says, 'And as adult hypocrites are not pardoned by God, who knoweth the heart, so neither is there any promise of pardon to their seed. No text of Scripture giveth any pardon but to sincere believers and their seed. And the child is in the covenant as the child of a believer devoted to God. And that faith which qualifieth not the parent for pardon, cannot qualify the child for it. I know no more promise of pardon and life to a hypocrite's than to a heathen's child.' IV:157, CF (1682).

[101]I:561, CD:CEccl (1673).

[102]Ibid., 651.

[103]Holifield misinterpreted Baxter at this point. He says, 'Baxter assumed that the infants of Christian parents were included in such a covenant from birth. *Their covenantal blessings were not sufficient to guarantee their salvation*, but they had a distinct advantage over the children of the ungodly, who received neither the blessings nor the seal of the covenant.' *The Covenant Sealed*, 96-97 [emphasis added].

While it is true that there was no guarantee that these infants would 'own' the covenant when they came of age, and therefore ultimately be saved, Baxter did in fact teach that such infants were 'safe' until they came of age, and that if they died in infancy they would be saved. Holifield's statement appears to deny this important truth. See I:654, CD:CEccl (1673).

Fisher errs in the other direction, ascribing to Baxter a type of baptismal regeneration, saying, 'The Holy Spirit renews their [baptized infants] heart from their infancy, and they are to grow up into the exercise of holy faith.' Fisher, 'The Theology of Richard Baxter,' 145, n. 1.

While Baxter acknowledged that, 'Of those baptized in infancy, some do betimes receive the secret seeds of grace' (IV:305, CR (1658)), he makes it perfectly clear that this is not always the case. Fisher misrepresented Baxter's position.

[104]R.B., II, 328.

[105]II:424, TCon (1657). Baxter says, 'it is the covenant of grace, and the grace of the covenant, that sanctifieth them.'

[106]I:29, CD:CEth (1673).

[107]IV:344, CR (1658): 'His infant-title will cease of itself without any other cutting off, if it be not continued by his personal actual believing, when he comes to capable age. His birth privileges alone, or his parents' dedicating him to God in baptism, will serve no longer of itself.'

[108]IV:155, CF (1682). Baxter recalls the deplorable manner in which his confirmation was handled by the Church: 'When I was a schoolboy, about fifteen years of age, the bishop coming into the country, many went in to him to be confirmed. We that were boys, ran out to see the bishop among the rest, not knowing any thing of the meaning of the business. When we came thither, we met about thirty or forty in all, of our own stature and temper, that had come for to be *bishopped*, as then it was called. The bishop examined us not all in one article of the faith; but in a church-yard in haste, we were set in a rank, and he passed hastily over us, laying his hands on our head, and saying a few words, which neither I nor any that I spoke with understood; so hastily were they uttered and a very short prayer recited, and there was an end. But whether we were christians or infidels, or knew so much as that there was a God, the bishop little knew, or inquired. And yet he was esteemed one of the best bishops in England.' IV:315-16, CR (1658).

[109]I:664-65, CD:CEccl (1673).

[110]IV:331, CR (1658).

[111]I:493, CD:CEc (1673).

[112]Ibid., 494.

[113]Ibid., 495.

[114]I:933-34, RL (1661). Baxter gives an example of a closing exhortation following the observance of the Lord's Supper: 'Dear brethren, we have been here feasted with the Son of God at his table, upon his flesh and blood, in preparation for the feast of endless glory. You have seen here

represented what sin deserveth, what Christ suffered, what wonderful love the God of infinite goodness hath expressed to us. You have had communion with the saints; you have renewed your covenant of faith, and thankful obedience unto Christ; you have received his renewed covenant of pardon, grace and glory unto you. O carry hence the lively sense of these great and excellent things upon your hearts; you came not only to receive the mercy of an hour, but that which may spring up to endless joy: you came not only to do the duty of an hour, but to promise that which you must perform while you live on earth. Remember daily, especially when temptations to unbelief and sinful heaviness assault you, what pledges of love you have received; remember daily, especially when the flesh, the devil, or the world, would draw your hearts again from God, and temptations to sin are laid before you, what bonds God and your own consent have laid upon you. If you are penitent believers, you are now forgiven, and washed in the blood of Christ. O go your way and sin no more: no more through wilfulness; and strive against your sins of weakness. Wallow no more in the mire, and return not to your vomit. Let the exceeding love of Christ constrain you, having such promises, to cleanse yourselves from all filthiness of flesh and spirit, perfecting holiness in the fear of God; and as a chosen generation, a royal priesthood, a holy nation, a peculiar people, to be zealous of good works, and show forth the praises of him that hath called you.'

[115]I:495, CD:CEc (1673).

[116]Ibid., 494.

[117]I:937, RL (1661).

[118]I:665, CD:CEccl (1673).

[119]Ibid., 689. See also IV:161, CF (1682). This again reflects Baxter's belief that assurance is ordinarily not of the essence of faith. Sincere faith is necessary to salvation, but not the certainty that it is sincere.

[120]I:494, CD:CEc (1673).

[121]Ibid., 497.

[122]Ibid.

[123]Ibid., 494.

[124]Ibid., 500.

[125]I:930, RL (1661).

[126]III:657, LF (1669).

[127]Ibid.

[128]IV:323-24, CR (1658). Downham argues that the Puritans held to three purposes for discipline: to glorify God by obeying His Word; to safeguard the purity of the Church's faith and life; and to reform and recover the erring member. See D. Downham, 'Discipline in the Puritan Congregation,' (Puritan and Reformed Studies Conference Papers, 1959), 31. Baxter does not mention here the first of these, but he certainly would have been in full agreement with it.

[129]*Treatise of Episcopacy*, 75.

[130]Ibid., 8. In R.B., II, 150, Baxter explains his own practice of church discipline in great detail. This passage makes it clear that the purpose was to drive the sinner to an awareness of his wrongdoing and to secure his voluntary repentance. It certainly was not to administer punishment.

[131]IV:158, CF (1682).

[132]IV:296, CR (1658).

[133]Ibid., 317.

[134]Ibid., 318.

[135]Ibid., 321-22.

[136]Ibid., 322. Baxter confessed (p. 331) he believed that God had allowed the Anabaptists to rise up so that the English churches might recognize the errors of their ways and return to biblical discipline.

He elsewhere documents the complete lack of discipline in the English Church: 'In all my life I never lived in the parish where one person was publicly admonished, or brought to public penitence, or excommunicated, though there were never so many obstinate drunkards, whoremongers, or vilest offenders. Only I have known now and then one for getting a bastard, that went to the bishop's court and paid their fees; and I heard of two or three in all the country, in all my life, that stood in a white sheet an hour in the church; but the ancient discipline of the church was unknown.' IV:400, RP (1656).

[137]*The Cure of Church Divisions*, 84. Cf. I:941, RL (1661): 'If therefore any member of the church be a scandalous sinner, and the crime be either notorious or fully proved, let the pastor admonish him, and set before him the particular command of God which he transgresseth, the supreme authority of God which he despiseth, the promises and mercies which he treadeth under foot, and the curse and dreadful condemnation which he draweth upon himself. Let this be done with great compassion and tender love to the offenders's soul, and with gravity, reverent and serious importunity, as beseemth men employed on the behalf of God, for the saving of a soul.'

[138]I:941, RL (1661).

[139]Ibid.

[140]Ibid., 942.

[141]Ibid., 941.

[142]Wilkinson, in his edition of *The Reformed Pastor* (1950), has reprinted this letter in Appendix III, 191. The original is preserved in the archives of the Corporation of Kidderminster. Powicke has also reprinted a letter of discipline from Baxter to a parishioner. Baxter's pastoral love is evident in this this letter, which he says he wrote with 'an aching head and heart and weeping eyes.' See Powicke, *A Life*, 110-11.

[143]IV:338, CR (1658). He says, 'Preaching is a very cheap and easy work, in comparison of church government.... And indeed I know it to be true, that for all the countenance of authority, he that will faithfully execute the pastoral oversight and discipline, shall live a persecuted life, which by mere preaching he might avoid.'

[144]Ibid., 301.

[145]R.B., I, 92. Baxter justifies his verdict by an appeal to the following facts: 'We kept the Church from irregular Separations ... We helpt to Cure that dangerous Disease among the people, of imagining that Christianity is but a matter of Opinion and dead Belief, and to convince them how much of it consisteth in Holiness ... We greatly suppressed the practice of Sin, and caused People to walk more watchfully than else they would have done. These and many other great Benefits accrewed by it to the Church.'

[146]Haden correctly emphasizes this fact: 'Discipline was to be the beginning and the end of his system of Church government.' W. H. Haden, 'Baxter's Work,' *Baptist Quarterly* n.s. 3 (1927): 205. See also Morgan, *Nonconformity of Richard Baxter*, 80: 'The criterion Baxter had for every doctrine and form of Church order was whether it helped Christ to promote holiness in Christian life.'

[147]Baxter made this abundantly clear, as the following two quotations demonstrate. He termed prelacy a novelty, which was 'not of God, because it is destructive of Discipline.' *Five Disputations of Church-government* (1659), 21. He avowed, 'The main reason that turneth my heart against the English Prelacy is because it did destroy Church Discipline, and almost destroy the Church through want of it ...' Ibid., 112 (unnumbered page).

[148]A. H. Wood, 'Our Debt to Richard Baxter and the Puritans,' *Reformed Theological Review* 9 (1950): 5.

[149]R.B., II, 396.

[150]Cook recognizes this truth: 'The inability of the Church of England and the obvious unwillingness of its bishops to effect any form of New Testament discipline was the main reason for the Separatists' departure from the Established Church.' Paul E. G. Cook, 'The Church,' (Puritan and Reformed Studies Conference Papers, 1977), 21.

[151]Cited in Powicke, *Rev. Richard Baxter*, 72.

[152]R.B., II, 401.

[153]Ibid., 161.

[154]Wood, *Church Unity without Uniformity*, 21.

[155]Nuttall, 'Richard Baxter's Preaching Ministry: Its History and Texts,' [checklist of published sermons]. *Journal of Ecclesiastical History* 35 (October 1984): 540.

[156]For an analysis of the membership of the Worcestershire Association, see Nuttall, 'The Worcestershire Association: its Membership,' *Journal*

of Ecclesiastical History I (1950): 197-206. Nuttall says that within the first three years of the Association's existence as many as seventy-two ministers joined.

[157]Wood, *Church Unity without Uniformity*, 21.

[158]*Christian Concord, or the Agreement of the Associated Pastors and Churches of Worcestershire, with Rich. Baxter's Explication and Defence of it and his Exhortation to Unity* (1653). Wilkinson, in his edition of *The Reformed Pastor* (1950), has reprinted this work in Appendix I, 175-86. All citations are from this Appendix, with the title *Christian Concord* and the appropriate page number.

[159]*Christian Concord*, 176.

[160]Ibid., 178.

[161]Ibid.

[162]IV:439, RP (1656).

[163]I:714, CD:CEccl (1673).

[164]IV:577, TKL (1689). See J. Lewis Wilson, 'Catechisms, and Their Use Among the Puritans' (Puritan and Reformed Studies Conference Papers, 1966), 31-44. Wilson argues that in Baxter's work Puritan ideals reach 'their fulfilment and their crown' (42).

[165]I:936, RL (1661).

[166]R.B., I, 83.

[167]Powicke, *A Life*, 135-36.

Conclusion

[1]Packer, 'Redemption and Restoration', xiv.

[2]Ibid., x.

[3]Baxter says, 'Christ never absolutely intended or decreed that his death should eventually put all men in possession of these Benefits.... Christ therefore died for all, but not for all equally, or with the same intent, design or purpose.' C.T., I, ii, 53.

[4]Morgan, *The Nonconformity of Richard Baxter*, 79.

[5]Ibid., 186.

[6]Ladell, *Richard Baxter: Puritan and Mystic*, 132-33.

[7]Sommerville, *Popular Religion in Restoration England*, 48.

[8]Bolam, *The English Presbyterians*, 104.

[9]Shields, *Doctrine of Regeneration*, 33.

[10]Powicke, 'Richard Baxter's Ruling Passion,' *The Congregational Quarterly* 4 (1926): 308.

[11]II:456, TCon (1657) [emphasis added].

[12]II:635, DP (1658).

[13]Shields defends Baxter from the implication that he *enjoyed* preaching damnation to his auditors, but fails to emphasize that Baxter in fact went much further than that in emphasizing the positive aspect of love. Shields, 'Doctrine of Regeneration,' 57-58.

[14]Nuttall, *The Holy Spirit in Puritan Faith and Experience* (Oxford: Basil Blackwell, 1946), 10.

[15]*Church-History*, a3.

[16]Rooy, *Theology of Missions*, 149. Bolam concurs with this: '... he wanted to avoid all party names in the interests of church concord.' See *The English Presbyterians*, 47.

[17]Basil Hall, 'Puritanism: the Problem of Definition,' in G. J. Cuming, ed., *Studies in Church History*, II (Camden, N.J.: Thomas Nelson and Sons, 1965), 289.

[18]Ibid., 290.

[19]*Autobiography*, 154.

[20]*Church-History*, a3v.

[21]*A Third Defence of the Cause of Peace*, first pagination, 111.

[22]Haller, *The Rise of Puritanism* (New York: Columbia University Press, 1938), 3.

[23]Stephen says, 'Baxter was opposed to every sect, and belonged to none. He can be properly described only as a Baxterian – at once the founder and the single member of an eclectic school, within the portals of which he invited all men, but persuaded none, to take refuge from their mutual animosities.' See Stephen, *An Excerpt from Reliquiae Baxterianae, with an Essay by Sir James Stephen on Richard Baxter*, 130.

[24]Martin claims, 'He abhorred the name and policy of the Separatists.... At the time of the Indulgence in 1672 he would accept a licence only if it were granted to him as "a meer nonconformist" and not under any denominational label.' Martin, *Puritanism and Richard Baxter*, 159. See also *Autobiography*, p. 221.

[25]*The Cure of Church Divisions* (1670), 33.

[26]IV:189, PM (1672).

[27]*Naked Popery* (1677), 39.

[28]*The Second Part of the Nonconformists Plea for Peace* (1680), 34.

[29]*Naked Popery*, 40.

[30]*Church-History*, a5v.

[31]Nuttall, *Holy Spirit*, 10.

[32]Flynn, *The Influence of Puritanism on the Political and Religious Thought of the English*, 138.

[33]Davies, *Life of Richard Baxter*, 41-42.

[34]Tulloch, *English Puritanism and Its Leaders*, 387.

[35]Grosart, *Representative Nonconformists*, 137.

[36]As I mentioned in the Introduction, I do not propose in this dissertation to enter into the debate over a definition of Puritanism. At this point, however, it must be noted that if one chooses to set precise theological boundaries for the Puritan movement, i.e. identifying it with 'orthodox Calvinism,' then Baxter would not fit the pattern. Greaves, in what I think is the best overall treatment of the issue of definition,

argues against defining the movement in this manner: 'Yet while most Puritans were Calvinists, there were significant exceptions, including the Arminians John Milton and John Goodwin. Simultaneously there were important Calvinists, such as Archbishops John Whitgift and James Ussher, who were not Puritans.' Greaves, 'The Nature of the Puritan Tradition,' 255.

[37]Keeble notes: 'The influence of his books is incalculable: from the early 1650s they enjoyed greater sales than those of any other English writer.' See Keeble, 'Introduction' to *The Autobiography of Richard Baxter*, xiv. Sommerville's research demonstrates the enormous popularity of Baxter's *Call to the Unconverted*. See Sommerville, *Popular Religion in Restoration England*, 47ff.

[38]A. B. Grosart, the great nineteenth century Puritan scholar, once said in a lecture of Baxter that he 'drew more hearts to the great Broken Heart than any single Englishman of his age.' Cited in Peter Lewis, *The Genius of Puritanism*, 25.

[39]R.B., I, 114-15. Baxter goes on to note that the Indian missionary John Elliot translated the *Call to the Unconverted* as soon as he had finished translating the Bible. Baxter also refers to its translation into French, German, and Dutch. William Bates remarks that six brothers were at one time converted by this book, and that 'every week he received letters of some converted by his books'. See Bates, *A Funeral Sermon*, 113.

[40]Orme, *Life and Times*, Vol. II, 79.

[41]Simpson, *Puritanism in Old and New England*, 3; Cohen, *God's Caress*, 4.

[42]Rooy, *Theology of Missions*, 310.

[43]Morgan, *Visible Saints*, 90-91.

[44]R.B., I, 7.

[45]Hambrick-Stowe, *The Practice of Piety*, 85.

[46]Tipson, 'The Development of a Puritan Understanding of Conversion,' 321.

[47]Cohen, 'Two Biblical Models of Conversion: An Example of Puritan Hermeneutics,' *Church History* 58 (1989): 183. Unfortunately he does not deal with Baxter in this article.

[48]Ibid., 195.

[49]I:15, CD:CEth (1673).

[50]IV:205, PM (1672).

[51]C.T., I, iii, 22.

[52]II:430, TCon (1657).

[53]I:16, CD: CEth (1673).

[54]Pettit, *Heart Prepared*, 18.

[55]Tipson, 'The Development of a Puritan Understanding of Conversion,' 329. Tipson argues that Pettit's mistake is his failure to properly distinguish between preparation and repentance.

[56]Laurence maintains that 'Preparationists ... made a pilgrim's activities in preparation the condition of his acceptance with God at least as much as his believing.' Laurence, 'Jonathan Edwards, Solomon Stoddard, and the Preparationist Model of Conversion,' 277. Perry Miller asserts that it was a short step from a preparationist theology to 'an open reliance upon human exertions and to a belief that conversion is worked entirely by rational argument and moral persuasion.' Miller, ''Preparation for Salvation' in Seventeenth-Century New England,' 286. Lovelace charges that in the teaching of preparation among the Puritans the 'very un-Reformed notion of congruent merit began to reappear'. Lovelace, *The American Puritanism of Cotton Mather*, 106.

[57]*Universal Redemption*, 151. Packer notes that Spurgeon included Baxter among a list of Puritans who he felt made preparation the 'warrant' of faith. Spurgeon could not stomach such teaching. The above quote shows that neither could Baxter. See Packer, 'The Puritan View of Preaching the Gospel,' 19.

[58]Cohen's comment is accurate: 'Puritans denied that preparation could be a 'meritorious cause' of conversion.' Cohen, *God's Caress*, 86-87. See also Hambrick-Stowe, *The Practice of Piety*, 80; Rooy, *Theology of Missions*, 315; and Shields, 'Doctrine of Regeneration,' 201.

BIBLIOGRAPHY

Primary Sources

Baxter, Richard. *The Practical Works of Richard Baxter*. 4 Vol. London: George Virtue, 1838.

ASC   A Sermon of the Absolute Sovereignty of Christ; and the Necessity of Man's Subjection, Dependence, and Chiefest Love to Him. Psalm ii.10-12. (1654).

CAM   Cain and Abel Malignity, that is, Enmity to Serious Godliness; that is, to a Holy and Heavenly State of Heart and life .... (1689).

CathU   Catholic Unity: or the only Way to bring us all to be of one Religion. Ephesians iv.3. (1659).

CC   Compassionate counsel to all Young Men: especially, I. London Apprentices; II. Students of Divinity, Physic, and Law; III. The Sons of Magistrates and Rich Men. (1681).

CD   A Christian Directory: or, a Sum of Practical Theology, an[d] Cases of Conscience. (1673).

CD:CEth   Part I. Christian Ethics, (or Private Duties).

CD:CEc   Part II. Christian Economics, (or Family Duties).

CD:CEccl   Part III. Christian Ecclesiastics, (or Church Duties).

CD:CP   Part IV. Christian Politics, (or Duties to our Rulers and Neighbours).

CF   The Catechising of Families. A Teacher of Householders how to Teach their Household: useful also to School-masters, and Tutors of Youth. (1682).

CM   The Cure of Melancholy (1682)

CR   Confirmation and Restauration, the Necessary Means

of a Reformation and Reconciliation, for the Healing of the Corruptions and Divisions of the Churches. (1658).

CSCC   The Character of a Sound, Confirmed Christian; as also of a Weak Christian, and of a Seeming Christian. (1669).

CU   A Call to the Unconverted to Turn and Live, and accept of Mercy while Mercy may be had, as ever they would find Mercy in the Day of their Extremity: From the Living God. Ezekiel xxxiii.11. (1657).

CW   The Crucifying of the World by the Cross of Christ. Galatians vi.14. (1657)

DA   The Divine Appointment of the Lord's Day, Proved; as a Separated Day for Holy Worship, especially in the Church Assemblies: and Consequently the Cessation of the Seventh-Day Sabbath. (1671)

DA:AC   An Appendix for further Confirmation of God's own Separation of the Lord's Day, ... (1671).

DL   The Divine Life: in Three Treatises. (1663).

DL:KG   Part I. Of the Knowledge of God. John xvii.3.

DL:WG   Part II. The Description, Reasons and Reward of the Believer's Walking with God. Gen. v.24.

DL:CG   Part III. The Christian's Converse with God: or, the Insufficiency and Uncertainty of Human Friendship; and the Improvement of Solitude in Converse with God. John xvi.32.

DP   Directions and Persuasions to a Sound Conversion. For Prevention of that Deceit and Damnation of Souls, and those Scandals, Heresies, and Desperate Apostasies that are Consequents of a Counterfeit or Superficial Change. (1658).

DT   Mr. Baxter's Dying Thoughts upon Philippians i.23. Written for his own Use in the later times of his Corporal Pains and Weakness. (1683).

DT:A   An Appendix. A Breviate of the Helps of Faith, Hope, and Love. A Breviate of the Proof of Supernatural Revelation, and the Truth of Christianity. I Timothy iii.16. (1683).

DW   Directions for Weak, Distempered Christians, to grow up to a Confirmed State of Grace. Col. ii.6,7. (1668).

FP   The Fool's Prosperity the Occasion of his Destruction. Prov. i. 32,33. (1660).

FS   The Farewell Sermon of Richard Baxter; Prepared to have been preached to his Hearers at Kidderminster at his Departure, but Forbidden. John xvi.22. (1683).

GGV   God's Goodness Vindicated; for the Help of such (especially in Melancholy) as are tempted to deny it, and think Him cruel, because of the Present and Future Misery of Mankind; with respect to the Doctrine of Reprobation and Damnation. (1671).

HGM   How to Do Good to Many: or, the Public Good is the Christian's Life. Gal. vi.20. (1682).

HS   A Sermon Preached at the Funeral of that Holy, Painful, and Fruitful Minister of Christ, Mr. Henry Stubbs .... Acts xx. 24. (1678).

JC   A Sermon preached at the Funeral of that Faithful Minister of Christ, Mr. John Corbet. II Cor. xii.1-9. (1682).

LB   Mr. Baxter's Letter to Mr. Bromiley, 1680, Containing his Judgment about Free-Will, in as Few Words as Possible, for the Satisfaction of Some Persons, who Misunderstood Some of his Books.

LF   The Life of Faith. In Three Parts. Hebrews xi.1. (1669).

LM   Mr. Baxter's Letter in answer to the case of Marrying with a Papist. (1665).

LW   The Last Work of a Believer; His Passing Prayer, Recommending his Departing Spirit to Christ, to be Received by Him. Acts. vii. 59. (1661).

MC   The Mother's Catechism; or, a Familiar Way of Catechising of Children in the Knowledge of God, Themselves, and the Holy Scriptures. (1701).

ML   Making Light of Christ and Salvation (1655)

MP   A Moral Prognostication, first, What shall befall the Churches on Earth, till their Concord, by the Restitution of their Primitive Purity, Simplicity, and Charity; secondly, How that Restitution is Likely to be Made, (if ever) and what shall befall them thenceforth unto the End, in that Golden Age of Love. (1661).

MR   More Reasons for the Christian Religion and No Reason against it .... (1671).

MS-I   The Mischiefs of Self-Ignorance, and the Benefits of Self-Acquaintance .... 2 Cor. xiii.5. (1661).

NN   Now or Never. The Holy, Serious, Diligent Believer justified, encouraged, excited, and directed. And the

	Opposers and Neglecters convinced by the Light of Scripture and Reason. Ecclesiastes lx.10. (1663).
OP	Obedient Patience: Its Nature in General; and its Exercise in Twenty Particular Cases. (1683).
OTN	The One Thing Necessary (1684)
PAA	Mr. Baxter's Preface to Mr. Alleine's *Alarm*. (1672).
PM	The Poor Man's Family Book .... With a Form of Exhortation to the Sick; Two Catechisms; A Profession of Christianity; Forms of Prayer for Various Uses, and some Psalms and Hymns for the Lord's Day. (1672).
RCR	The Reasons of the Christian Religion (1666).
RCR:NR	Part I. Of Natural Religion, or Godliness.
RCR:Chr	Part II. Of Christianity, and Supernatural Revelation.
RL	The Reformed Liturgy. The Ordinary Public Worship on the Lord's Day. (1661).
RM	Reasons For Ministers using the Greatest Plainness and Serious-ness Possible, in all their Applications to their People. (1676).
RMeth	The Right Method for a Settled Peace of Conscience and Spiritual Comfort. In Thirty-two Directions. Matt. xi.28-30. (1653).
RP	Gildas Salvianus. The Reformed Pastor; showing the Nature of the Pastoral Work: Especially in Private Instruction and Catechising: with an Open Confession of our too Open Sins. Acts xx.28. (1656).
RR	Right Rejoicing (1660)
RT	Of Redemption of Time. (1667).
SA	Mr. Baxter's Sense of the Articles of the Church of England; In answer to the Scruples Proposed to him by Some that were Called upon to Subscribe Them. (1689).
SB	A Saint or a Brute. The certain Necessity and Excellency of Holiness ... to be Communicated by the Charitable, that Desire other Conversion and Salvation of Souls, while the Patience of God, and the Day of Grace and Hope Continue. (1662).
SER	The Saint's Everlasting Rest; Or, A Treatise of the Blessed State of the Saints in their Enjoyment of God in Glory. (1649).
SJ	A Sermon of Judgment. 2 Corinthians v.10,11. (1654).

SM	Short Mediations on Romans v.1-5. Of the Shedding Abroad God's Love on the Heart by the Holy Ghost.
SR	A Sermon of Repentance. Ezekiel xxxvi.31. (1660).
TC	The True Catholic, and Catholic Church Described; and the Vanity of the Papists, and all other Schismatics, that confine the Catholic Church to their Sect, Discovered and Shamed. (1659).
TChr	True Christianity; or, Christ's absolute Dominion, and Man's Necessary Self-resignation and Subjection. I Corinthians vi.19,20. Psalm ii.10-12. (1654).
TCon	A Treatise of Conversion, preached and now Published for the Use of those that are Strangers to a True Conversion, especially grossly Ignorant and Ungodly, Matthew xviii.3. (1657).
TD	A Treatise of Death, the last Enemy to be Destroyed. Showing wherein its Enmity Consisteth, and how it is Destroyed. I Corinthians xv.26. (1659).
TKL	A Treatise of Knowledge and Love Compared. In Two Parts: I. Of Falsely Pretended Knowledge. II. Of True Saving Knowledge. I Corinthians viii.2, 3. (1689).
TOW	The True and only Way of Concord of all the Christian Churches. Ephesians iv.3. (1679).
TS-D	A Treatise of Self-Denial. Luke ix. 23, 24. (1659).
UI	The Unreasonableness of Infidelity, manifested in Four Discourses. (1655).
UI:SpW	Part I. The Spirit's Witness to the Truth of Christianity. Gal. iii.1,2. John xx.29.
UI:ChW	Part II. Christ's Witness Within Us, the Believer's special Advantage against Temptations to Infidelity. John xv. 26,27.
UI:US	Part III. For the Prevention of the Unpardonable Sin against the Holy Ghost; A Demonstration that the Spirit and Works of Christ were the Finger of God. Matthew xii.22-32.
UI:AR	Part IV. The Arrogancy of Reason against Divine Revelations, Repressed; or, Proud Ignorance the Cause of Infidelity, and of Men's Quarreling with the Word of God. John iii.9.
VR	The Vain Religion of the Formal Hypocrite, and the Mischief of an Unbridled Tongue, as against Religion, Rulers, or Dissenters. James i.26. (1660).
WL	What Light Must Shine in our Works. Matthew v.16.

_____. *An Appeal to the Light*, 1674.

_____. *An End of Doctrinal Controversies*, 1691.

_____. *Aphorisms of Justification*, 1649.

_____. *Apology for the Nonconformists Ministry*, 1681.

_____. *The Autobiography of Richard Baxter*, abridged J. M. Lloyd Thomas, ed. N. H. Keeble. London: J. M. Dent & Sons, 1974.

_____. *A Breviate of the Life of Margaret, the Daughter of Francis Charlton ... and Wife of Richard Baxter*. London, 1685.

_____. *Catholick Theologie*, 1675.

_____. *Certain Disputations of Rights to Sacraments*. 2nd edition, 1658.

_____. *Christian Concord; or, the Agreement of the Associated Pastors and Churches of Worcestershire*, 1653.

_____. *Church-History of the Government of Bishops and their Councils*, 1680.

_____. *The Cure of Church-Divisions*, 1670.

_____. *A Defence of Christ and Free Grace*, 1690.

_____. *Five Disputations of Church-government and Worship*, 1659.

_____. *Four Disputations of Justification*, 1658.

_____. *The Grand Question resolved, What we Must do to be Saved*, 1692, edited by A. B. Grosart. Edinburgh: Crawford & M'Cabe, 1868.

_____. *The Grotian Religion Discovered*, 1658.

_____. *How Far Holinesse is the Design of Christianity*, 1671.

_____. *Imputative Righteousness*, 1679.

_____. *Methodus Theologiae Christianae*, 1681.

_____. *Naked Popery*, 1677.

_____. *Of National Churches*, 1691.

_____. *A Paraphrase on the New Testament*, 1685.

_____. *Plain Scripture Proof of Infant Church-membership and Baptism*, 1651.

_____. *Poetical Fragments*, 1681.

_____. *Reliquiae Baxterianae: or, Narrative of his Life and Times*, 1696.

_____. *The Scripture Gospel Defended*, 1690.

_____. *The Second Part of the Nonconformists Plea for Peace*, 1680.

_____. *Third Defence of the Cause of Peace*, 1681.

_____. *Treatise of Episcopacy*, 1681.

_____. *Treatise of Justifying Righteousness*, 1675.

_____. 'To the Reader.' In William Allen, *A Discourse of the Nature, Ends, and Difference of the Two Covenants*, 1673.

_____. *Two Disputations of Original Sin*, 1675.

_____. *Universal Redemption of Mankind by the Lord Jesus Christ*, 1694.

Secondary Sources

Adair, John Eric. *Founding Fathers: The Puritans in England and America*. Grand Rapids, Mich.: Baker, 1982.

Allison, C. F. *The Rise of Moralism: The Proclamation of the Gospel from Hooker to Baxter*. New York: The Seabury Press, 1966.

Armstrong, Brian G. *Calvinism and the Amyraut Heresy: Protestant Scholasticism and Humanism in Seventeenth-Century France*. Madison: University of Wisconson Press, 1969.

Atkinson, B. F. C. *Valiant in Fight: A Review of Christian Conflict*. London: Inter-Varsity Fellowship, 1937, 1947 rev. ed.

Baker, J. Wayne. '*Sola Fide, Sola Gratia*: The Battle for Luther in Seventeenth-Century England.' *The Sixteenth Century Journal* XVI (1985): 115-33.

Bates, William. *A Funeral Sermon for the Reverend Holy and Excellent Divine, Mr. Richard Baxter ... With Some Account of His Life*, 1692.

Batson, E. Beatrice. 'Bunyan and Baxter: Readers and Writers.' *The Christian Librarian* 27 (May 1984): 81-84.

van Beek, Marinus. *An Inquiry into Puritan Vocabulary*. Groningen, The Netherlands: Wolters-Noordhoff, 1969.

Bell, M. Charles. 'Calvin and the Extent of the Atonement.' *Evangelical Quarterly* 55 (1983): 115-23.

Beougher, Timothy K. 'The Puritan View of Marriage: The Nature of the Husband/Wife Relationship in Puritan England as Taught and Experienced by a Representative Puritan Pastor, Richard Baxter.' *Trinity Journal* n.s. 10 (Fall 1989): 131-58.

Bolam, C. Gordon; Goring, Jeremy; Short, H. L.; and Thomas, Roger. *The English Presbyterians: From Elizabethan Puritanism to Modern Unitarianism*. Boston: Beacon Press, 1968.

Boyle, George David. *Richard Baxter*. New York: A. C. Armstrong & Son, 1884.

Brauer, Jerald C. 'Conversion: From Puritanism to Revivalism.' *Journal of Religion* 58 (1978): 227-43.

_____. 'Puritan Mysticism and the Development of Liberalism.' *Church History* 19 (1950): 151-70.

————. 'Reflections on the Nature of English Puritanism.' *Church History* 23 (1954): 99-108.

————. 'Types of Puritan Piety.' *Church History* 56 (1987): 39-58.

Breward, Ian. 'The Abolition of Puritanism.' *Journal of Religious History* 7 (1972): 20-34.

————. 'The Significance of William Perkins.' *Journal of Religious History* 4 (1966-67): 113-28.

————. 'William Perkins and the Origins of Reformed Casuistry.' *Evangelical Quarterly* 40 (1968): 3-20.

Bronkema, Ralph. *The Essence of Puritanism.* Goes, Holland: Oosterbaan and Le Cointre, 1929.

Brown, Earl Kent. 'Richard Baxter's Contribution to the Comprehension Controversy: A Study in Projected Church Union.' Unpublished Ph.D. dissertation, Boston University Graduate School, 1956.

Brown, John. 'Richard Baxter, the Kidderminster Pastor,' In *Puritan Preaching in England: A Study of Past and Present.* New York: Charles Scribner's Sons, 1900.

Buchanan, James. *The Doctrine of Justification.* Grand Rapids, Mich.: Baker, 1956 reprint.

Bunn, Leslie H. 'Richard Baxter Speaks to Our Time.' *Hymn* 9 (1958): 79-82.

Caldwell, Patricia. 'The Antinomian Language Controversy.' *Harvard Theological Review* 69 (1976): 345-67.

————. *The Puritan Conversion Narrative: The Beginnings of American Expression.* Cambridge: Cambridge University Press, 1983.

Calvin, John. *Institutes of the Christian Religion.* Edited by John T. McNeill. Philadelphia: The Westminster Press, 1960 reprint.

Carter, Charles Sydney. *Richard Baxter, 1615–1691.* London: Church Book Room Press, 1948.

Christianson, Paul. 'Reformers and the Church of England under Elizabeth I and the Early Stuarts.' *Journal of Ecclesiastical History* 31 (1980): 463-82.

Citron, Bernhard. *New Birth: A Study of the Evangelical Doctrine of Conversion in the Protestant Fathers.* Edinburgh: Edinburgh University Press, 1951.

Clifford, Alan. 'Geneva Revisited or Calvinism Revisited: The Case for Theological Reassessment.' *Churchman* 100 (1986): 323-34.

————. 'The Gospel and Justification.' *Evangelical Quarterly* 57 (1985): 247-67.

Cohen, Charles L. *God's Caress: The Psychology of Puritan Religious Experience*. New York: Oxford University Press, 1986.

_____. 'The Saints zealous in love and labor: the Puritan psychology of work.' *Harvard Theological Review* 76 (1983): 455-80.

_____. 'Two Biblical Models of Conversion: An Example of Puritan Hermeneutics.' *Church History* 58 (1989): 182-96.

Colligan, J. Hay. 'The Antinomian Controversy.' *Congregational Historical Society Transactions* 6 (1915): 389-96.

Collinson, Patrick. 'A Comment: Concerning the Name Puritan.' *Journal of Ecclesiastical History* 31 (October 1980): 483-88.

Cook, Paul E. G. 'The Church.' Puritan and Reformed Studies Conference Papers, 1977, 15-42.

Cragg, C. R. *From Puritanism to the Age of Reason*. London: Cambridge University Press, 1950.

_____. *Puritanism in the Period of the Great Persecution, 1660–1668*. London: Cambridge University Press, 1957.

Davies, Horton. *Worship and Theology in England: From Andrewes to Baxter and Fox, 1603–1690*. Princeton: Princeton University Press, 1975.

Davies, John Hamilton. *Life of Richard Baxter, of Kidderminster: Preacher and Prisoner*. London: W. Kent, 1887.

De Pauley, W. C. 'Richard Baxter Surveyed.' *The Church Quarterly Review* 164 (1963): 32-43.

Derham, A. Morgan. 'Richard Baxter and the Oecumenical Movement.' *The Evangelical Quarterly* 23 (1951): 96-115.

The Dictionary of National Biography. Edited by Leslie Stephen and Sidney Lee. 63 vols. London: Smith, Elder, 1885–1901.

Douglas, Walter B. T. 'Politics and Theology in the Thought of Richard Baxter.' *Andrews University Sem St* 15 (1977): 115-26, and 16 (1978): 305-12.

Downham, D. 'Discipline in the Puritan Congregation.' Puritan and Reformed Studies Conference Papers, 1959, 30-37.

Eayrs, George. *Richard Baxter and the Revival of Preaching and Pastoral Service*. London: National Council of Evangelical Free Churches, 1912.

English, John C. 'The Puritan Doctrine of Christian Initiation.' *Studia Liturgica* 6 (1969): 158-70.

Feinstein, Howard M. 'The Prepared Heart: A Comparative Study of Puritan Theology and Psychoanalysis.' *American Quarterly* 22 (1970): 166-76.

Fisher, George P. 'The Theology of Richard Baxter.' *Bibliotheca Sacra* IX (1852): 135-69.

_____. 'The Writings of Richard Baxter.' *Bibliotheca Sacra* IX (1852): 300-29.

Flynn, John Stephen. *The Influence of Puritanism on the Political and Religious Thought of the English.* Port Washington, N.Y.: Kennikat Press, 1920, 1970 reprint.

Franks, Robert S. *A History of the Doctrine of the Work of Christ.* 2 vols. London: Hodder and Stoughton, n.d.

Freiday, Dean. 'How to Read the Bible: RICHARD BAXTER.' In *The Bible: Its Criticism, Interpretation and Use in 16th and 17th Century England,* 77-87. Catholic and Quaker Studies No. 4. Pittsburgh, 1979.

Gentile, Drew W. 'Richard Baxter's Concept of the Centrality of the Home in Religious Education.' Th.M. Thesis, Dallas Theological Seminary, 1984.

George, Charles H. 'Puritanism as History and Historiography.' *Past and Present* 41 (1968): 77-104.

_____. 'A Social Interpretation of English Puritanism.' *The Journal of Modern History* 25 (December 1953): 327-42.

Gordon, Alexander. 'Richard Baxter as a founder of Liberal Nonconformity.' In *Heads of English Unitarian History.* London: Philip Green, 1895.

Greaves, Richard L. 'The Nature of the Puritan Tradition.' In *Reformation, Conformity and Dissent: Essays in Honour of Geoffrey Nuttall.* Edited by R. Buick Knox. London: Epworth Press, 1977, 255-73.

Grimes, Mary C. 'Saving Grace Among Puritans and Quakers: A Study of 17th and 18th Century Conversion Experiences.' *Quaker History* 72 (1983): 3-26.

Haden, W. H. 'Baxter's Work.' *The Baptist Quarterly* n.s. 3 (1927): 205-10.

Hall, Basil. 'Puritanism: the Problem of Definition.' In *Studies in Church History.* Vol. II. Edited by G. J. Cuming. Camden, N.J.: Thomas Nelson and Sons, 1965.

Hall, David D. 'Understanding the Puritans.' In *Colonial America: Essays in Politics and Social Development.* Edited by Stanley N. Katz. Boston: Little, Brown, 1971, 31-50.

Haller, William. *The Rise of Puritanism: Or, the Way to the New Jerusalem as Set Forth in Pulpit and Press from Thomas Cartwright to John Lilburne and John Milton, 1570–1643.* New York: Harper Torchbooks, 1957.

Hambrick-Stowe, Charles. *The Practice of Piety: Puritan Devotional Disciplines in Seventeenth-Century New England.* Chapel Hill: University of North Carolina Press, 1982.

Helm, Paul. *Calvin and the Calvinists.* Edinburgh: Banner of Truth Trust, 1982.

_____. 'A Bad Habit [regarding faith as the condition of salvation].' *The Banner of Truth* 128 (1974): 14-19.

Hexter, J. H. 'The Problem of the Presbyterian Independents.' *American Historical Review* 44 (1938): 29-40.

Hill, Christopher. *Puritanism and Revolution. The English Revolution of the 17th Century.* New York: Schocken, 1958.

_____. *Society and Puritanism in Pre-Revolutionary England.* 2nd. edition. New York: Schocken Books, 1964, 1967.

Hindson, Edward, editor. *Introduction to Puritan Theology: A Reader.* Grand Rapids: Baker Book House, 1976.

Holifield, E. Brooks. *The Covenant Sealed: The Development of Puritan Sacramental Theology in Old and New England, 1570–1720.* New Haven, Conn.: Yale University Press, 1974.

Huehns, Gertrude. *Antinomianism in English History.* London: Cresset Press, 1951.

Hulse, Erroll. 'The Puritan Approach to Persuading Souls.' Puritan and Reformed Studies Conference Papers, 1973, 7-19.

Hunt, John. *Religious Thought in England.* 4 vols. London: Strahan & Co., 1870–73.

Jones, Hywel R. 'The Death of Presbyterianism.' Puritan and Reformed Studies Conference Papers, 1969, 31-42.

Keeble, N. H. 'C. S. Lewis, Richard Baxter, and 'Mere Christianity.'' *Christianity and Literature* 30 (1981): 27-44.

_____. 'Introduction.' In *The Autobiography of Richard Baxter.* London: J. M. Dent and Sons Ltd., 1974.

_____. *Richard Baxter: Puritan Man of Letters.* Oxford: Clarendon Press, 1982.

_____. 'Richard Baxter's Preaching Ministry: Its History and Texts [checklist of published sermons]. *Journal of Ecclesiastical History* 35 (1984): 539-59.

Kemp, Charles F. *A Pastoral Triumph: The Story of Richard Baxter and his Ministry at Kidderminster.* New York: Macmillan, 1948.

Kendall, R. T. *Calvin and English Calvinism to 1649.* Oxford: Oxford University Press, 1979.

Kerr, Hugh T., and John M. Mulder. *Conversions: The Christian Experience.* Grand Rapids, Mich.: Eerdmans, 1983.

Kerr, William N. 'Baxter and Baxterianism,' *The Encyclopaedia of Christianity*, Vol. I., Wilmington, Delaware, 1964, 599-606.

Kevan, Ernest F. *The Grace of Law: A Study in Puritan Theology*. Grand Rapids, Mich.: Baker, 1976.

Knappen, M. M. *Tudor Puritanism*. Chicago: Univ. of Chicago Press, 1939.

Knott, John Ray. 'Richard Baxter and *The Saint's Rest*.' In *The Sword of the Spirit: Puritan Responses to the Bible*. University of Chicago Press, 1980, 62-84.

Ladd, George E. *A Theology of the New Testament*. Grand Rapids, Mich.: Eerdmans, 1974.

Ladell, Arthur R. *Richard Baxter: Puritan and Mystic*. London: S.P.C.K., 1925.

Lamont, William M. 'Puritanism as History and Historiography: Some Further Thoughts.' *Past and Present* 44 (1969): 133-46.

_____. *Richard Baxter and the Millennium*. London: Croom Helm, 1979.

_____. 'Richard Baxter, The Apocalypse and the Mad Major.' *Past and Present* 55 (1972): 68-90.

Lane, Anthony N. S. 'John Calvin: the Witness of the Holy Spirit.' Puritan and Reformed Studies Conference Papers, 1982, 1-17.

Laurence, David. 'Jonathan Edwards, Solomon Stoddard, and the Preparationist Model of Conversion.' *Harvard Theological Review* 72 (1979): 267-83.

Lawson, George. *Theo-Politica: Or, A Body of Divinity, Containing The Rules of the Special Government of God*, 1659.

Lewis, Peter. *The Genius of Puritanism*. Haywards Health, Sussex: Carey Publications, 1977.

Life of the Rev. Richard Baxter. London: The Religious Tract Society, n.d.

Lloyd-Jones, D. M. *The Puritans: Their Origins and Successors*. Carlisle, Penn.: Banner of Truth Trust, 1987.

Loane, Marcus L. *Makers of Puritan History*. Grand Rapids: Baker, 1980 reprint. Originally *Makers of Religious Freedom in the 17th century*, 1961 Eerdmans.

Lovelace, Richard. *The American Pietism of Cotton Mather*. Grand Rapids, Mich.: Eerdmans, 1979.

MacAlpine, Alexander Gillon. 'Ecclesiastical and Civil Polity in the Writings of Richard Baxter.' Unpublished S. T. M. thesis, Union Theological Seminary, 1934.

Macleod, Jack N. 'John Owen and *the Death of Death.*' Puritan and Reformed Studies Conference Papers, 1983, 70-87.

Macleod, John. *Scottish Theology.* Edinburgh: Free Church of Scotland, 1943.

Mair, Nathaniel Harrington. 'Christian Sanctification and Individual Pastoral Care in Richard Baxter.' Unpublished Th.D. dissertation, Union Theological Seminary, New York, 1966.

Marsden, George M. 'Perry Miller's Rehabilitation of the Puritans: A Critique.' *Church History* 39 (1970): 91-105.

Martin, Hugh. *Puritanism and Richard Baxter.* London: SCM Press, 1954.

Matthews, A. G. *The Works of Richard Baxter: an Annotated List*, 1932.

McCan, R. L. 'The Conception of the Church in Richard Baxter and John Bunyan: a Comparison and Contrast.' Edinburgh Ph.D. 1955.

McDonald, H. D. *The Atonement of the Death of Christ: In Faith, Revelation, and History.* Grand Rapids: Baker, 1985.

McGee, J. Sears. 'Conversion and the Imitation of Christ in Anglican and Puritan Writing.' *The Journal of British Studies* 15 (1976): 21-39.

McGiffert, Michael. 'Grace and Works: The Rise and Division of Covenant Divinity in Elizabethan Puritanism.' *Harvard Theological Review* 75 (October 1982): 463-502.

McIntyre, D. M. 'First Strictures on *The Marrow of Modern Divinity.*' *Evangelical Quarterly* X (1938): 61-70.

Miller, Donald. 'A Critical Appraisal of Richard Baxter's Views of the Church and Their Applicability to Contemporary Church Problems.' Unpublished Ph.D. dissertation, New York University, 1935.

Miller, Glenn. 'Puritanism: A Survey [review article]'. *Union Seminary Quarterly Review* 27 (1972): 169-75.

Miller, Perry. 'The Marrow of Puritan Divinity.' *Publications of the Colonial Society of Massachusetts* XXXII (1937): 247-300.

_____. *The New England Mind: The Seventeenth Century.* Cambridge: Harvard University Press, 1939, 1963.

_____. "Preparation for Salvation' in Seventeenth-Century New England.' *Journal of the History of Ideas* IV (1943): 253-86.

Möller, Jens G. 'The Beginnings of Puritan Covenant Theology.' *The Journal of Ecclesiastical History* xiv (1963): 46-67.

Morgan, Edmund S. *Visible Saints: The History of a Puritan Idea.* Ithaca, N.Y.: Cornell University Press, 1963, 1975.

Morgan, Irvonwy. *The Nonconformity of Richard Baxter*. London: Epworth Press, 1946.

Muller, Richard A. 'Covenant and Conscience in English Reformed Theology: Three Variations on a 17th Century Theme.' *Westminster Theological Journal* 42 (1980): 308-34.

_____. 'The Federal Motif in Seventeenth Century Arminian Theology.' *Nederlands Archief Voor Kerkgeschiedenis* 62 (1982): 101-22.

Murphey, Murray G. 'The Psychodynamics of Puritan Conversion.' *American Quarterly* 31 (1979): 135-47.

Nicole, Roger. 'John Calvin's view of the extent of the atonement [bibliog essay].' *Westminster Theological Journal* 47 (1985): 197-225.

Nuttall, Geoffrey. *The Holy Spirit in Puritan Faith and Experience*. Oxford, Basil Blackwell, 1946.

_____. *Richard Baxter*. London: Thomas Nelson and Sons, 1965.

_____. *Richard Baxter and Philip Doddridge: A Study in a Tradition*. London: Oxford University Press, 1951.

_____. 'Richard Baxter and the Puritan Movement.' In *Heroes of the Faith*, ed. by F. H. Ballard. London: Livingstone Press, 1949, pp. 20-29.

_____. 'Richard Baxter and *The Grotian Religion*.' In *Reform and Reformation: England and the Continent, c. 1500-c. 1750*, 245-50. Edited by D. Baker. Oxford, 1979.

_____. 'Richard Baxter's *Apology* (1654): its Occasion and Composition.' *The Journal of Ecclesiastical History* 4 (1953): 69-76.

_____. 'A Transcript of Richard Baxter's Library Catalogue.' *Journal of Ecclesiastical History* 2 (1951): 207-21, and 3 (1952): 74-100.

_____. *Visible Saints, The Congregational Way, 1640–1660*. Oxford: Basil Blackwell, 1957.

_____. 'The Worcestershire Association: its Membership.' *The Journal of Ecclesiastical History* I (1950): 197-206.

Nuttall, Geoffrey and Chadwick, Owen, eds. *From Uniformity to Unity 1662–1962*. London: S.P.C.K., 1962.

Ong, Walter. *Ramus: Method and the Decay of Dialogue: From the Art of Discourse to the Art of Reason*. Cambridge, Mass.: Harvard University Press, 1958.

Orme, William. *The Life and Times of the Rev. Richard Baxter With a Critical Examination of His Writings*. 2 Vol. Boston: Crocker & Brewster, 1831.

_____. *The Practical Works of the Rev. Richard Baxter: with a Life of the Author, and a Critical Examination of his Writings*, 23 vols. London: James Duncan, 1830.

Packer, J. I. 'The Doctrine of Justification in Development and Decline among the Puritans.' Puritan and Reformed Studies Conference Papers, 1969, 18-30.

_____. 'Foreward.' In *Introduction to Puritan Theology: A Reader*, edited by Edward Hindson. Grand Rapids: Baker Book House, 1976, pp. 9-13.

_____. 'Introductory Essay.' In *The Death of Death in the Death of Christ*, by John Owen. Edinburgh: The Banner of Truth Trust, 1985 reprint.

_____. 'Puritan Evangelism.' *The Banner of Truth* 4 (1957): 4-13.

_____. 'The Puritan Treatment of Justification by Faith.' *Evangelical Quarterly* 24 (1952): 131-43.

_____. 'The Puritan View of Preaching the Gospel.' Puritan and Reformed Studies Conference Papers, 1959, 11-21.

_____. 'Puritanism as a Movement of Revival.' *Evangelical Quarterly* (1980): 2-16.

_____. 'Richard Baxter (1615–1691)', *Theology* LVI (May 1953): 174-78.

_____. 'The Redemption and Restoration of Man in the Thought of Richard Baxter.' Unpublished D. Phil. dissertation, Oxford University, 1954.

Paul, Robert S. 'Ecclesiology in Richard Baxter's Autobiography.' In *From Faith to Faith*, ed. by Dikran Y. Hadidian. Pittsburgh: Pickwick Press, 1979, 357-402.

Perry, Ralph Barton. *Puritanism and Democracy*. New York: Harper & Row, 1944.

Pettit, Norman. *The Heart Prepared: Grace and Conversion in Puritan Spiritual Life*. New Haven: Yale University Press, 1966.

Phillips, James McJunkin. 'Between Conscience and the Law: The Ethics of Richard Baxter.' Unpublished Ph.D. dissertation, Princeton University, 1958.

Powicke, Frederick J. *A Life of the Reverend Richard Baxter, 1615–1691*. London: Jonathan Cape, Ltd., 1924.

_____. *The Reverend Richard Baxter under the Cross, 1662–1691*. London: Jonathan Cape, Ltd., 1927.

_____. 'Richard Baxter's Ruling Passion.' *The Congregational Quarterly* 4 (1926): 300-309.

Rambo, Lewis R. 'Current Research on Religious Conversion.' *Religious Studies Review* 8 (1982): 146-59.

Richards, David J. 'Richard Baxter's Theory of the Atonement.' Unpublished M. A. Thesis, Wheaton College, 1982.

Rooy, Sidney H. *The Theology of Missions in the Puritan Tradition.* Grand Rapids, Mich.: Eerdmans, 1965.

Ryken, Leland. *Worldly Saints: The Puritans as They Really Were.* Grand Rapids, Mich.: Zondervan, 1986.

Shaw, Mark R. 'Drama in the Meeting House: The Concept of Conversion in the Theology of William Perkins.' *Westminster Theological Journal* 45 (1983): 41-72.

Schlatter, Richard, ed. *Richard Baxter and Puritan Politics.* New Brunswick, N.J.: Rutgers University Press, 1957.

Schneider, Herbert W. *The Puritan Mind.* New York: H. Holt & Co., 1930.

Shields, James L. 'The Doctrine of Regeneration in English Puritan Theology, 1604–1689.' Unpublished Ph.D. dissertation, Southwestern Baptist Theological Seminary, Fort Worth, Texas. 1965.

Simpson, Alan. *Puritanism in Old and New England.* Chicago: University of Chicago Press, 1955, 1964.

Solt, Leo F. *Saints in Arms: Puritanism and Democracy in Cromwell's Army.* Stanford: Stanford University Press, 1959.

Sommerville, C. John. 'Conversion Versus the Early Puritan Covenant of Grace.' *Journal of Presbyterian History* 44 (1966): 178-97.

_____. *Popular Religion in Restoration England.* Gainesville, Fla.: University of Florida Press, 1977.

Sprunger, Keith L. 'Ames, Ramus, and the Method of Puritan Theology.' *Harvard Theological Review* 59 (1966): 133-51.

Stephen, James. 'An Essay on Richard Baxter.' In *An Excerpt from Reliquiae Baxterianae.* Edited by Francis John. New York: Longmans, Green, and Co., 1910.

Stewart, Barbara Ann. 'Richard Baxter: The Beloved Pastor of Kidderminster.' Unpublished Masters thesis, Regent College, Vancouver, British Columbia, 1985.

Stoughton, John. *History of Religion in England: From the Opening of the Long Parliament to the End of the Eighteenth Century.* Rev. ed. 8 vols. London: Hodder and Stoughton, 1881.

Sylvester, Matthew. *Elisha's Cry after Elijah's God.* London, 1696.

Tidball, Derek J. *Skillful Shepherds: An Introduction to Pastoral Theology.* Grand Rapids, Mich.: Zondervan, 1986.

Tipson, Lynn Baird. 'The Development of a Puritan Understanding of Conversion.' Unpublished Ph.D. dissertation, Yale University, 1972.

_____. 'How Can the Religion Experience of the Past Be Recovered? The Examples of Puritanism and Pietism.' *Journal of the American Academy of Religion* 43 (1975): 695-707.

Toon, Peter. *Puritans and Calvinism*. Swengel, Penn.: Reiner Publications, 1973.

Traill, Robert. *A Vindication of the Protestant Doctrine Concerning Justification, And of its Preachers and Professors, From the unjust charge of Antinomianism*. London: Dorman Newman, 1692.

Trinterud, Leonard J. 'The Origins of Puritanism.' *Church History* 20 (1951): 37-57.

Tulloch, John. *English Puritanism and Its Leaders*. London: William Blackwood and Sons, 1861.

von Rohr, John. *The Covenant of Grace in Puritan Thought*. Atlanta: Scholars Press, 1986.

_____. 'Covenant and Assurance in Early English Puritanism.' *Church History* 34 (1965): 195-203.

Wakefield, Gordon S. *Puritan Devotion: Its Place in the Development of Christian Piety*. London, Epworth Press, 1957.

Wallace, Dewey D., Jr. *Puritans and Predestination: Grace in English Protestant Theology, 1525–1695*. Chapel Hill: University of North Carolina Press, 1982.

Warfield, Benjamin B. *The Plan of Salvation*. Grand Rapids, Mich.: Eerdmans, 1970 rev. ed.

Watkins, Owen C. *The Puritan Experience: Studies in Spiritual Autobiography*. New York: Schocken Books, 1972.

Watson, Richard. *Theological Institutes*. 2 vol. New York: Carlton & Lanahan, 1850.

Wells, David F. *Turning to God: Biblical Conversion in the Modern World*. Grand Rapids: Baker, 1989.

White, Barrington R, ed. 'Introduction: The English Puritan Tradition.' In *The English Puritan Tradition*. Nashville: Broadman Press, 1980, pp. 9-28.

Wilkinson, John T. *Richard Baxter and Margaret Charlton: A Puritan Love Story*. London: George Allen & Unwin Ltd., 1928.

_____. 'Richard Baxter's *Reformed Pastor*.' *Expository Times* 69 (1957): 16-19.

_____, ed. 'Introduction.' In *The Reformed Pastor*. London, 1939, 1950.

Wilson, J. Lewis. 'Catechisms, and Their Use Among the Puritans.' Puritan and Reformed Studies Conference Papers, 1966, 31-44.

Wood, A. Harold. *Church Unity without Uniformity: a Study of Seventeenth-Century English Church Movements and of Richard Baxter's Proposals for a Comprehensive Church*. London: Epworth Press, 1963.

_____. 'Our Debt to Richard Baxter and the Puritans.' *Reformed Theological Review* 9 (1950): 1-17.

Woodhouse, A. S. P., ed. *Puritanism and Liberty*. Chicago: Chicago University Press, 1951.

Christian Focus Publications

publishes books for all ages

Our mission statement –

STAYING FAITHFUL

In dependence upon God we seek to help make His infallible Word, the Bible, relevant. Our aim is to ensure that the Lord Jesus Christ is presented as the only hope to obtain forgiveness of sin, live a useful life and look forward to heaven with Him.

REACHING OUT

Christ's last command requires us to reach out to our world with His gospel. We seek to help fulfill that by publishing books that point people towards Jesus and help them develop a Christ-like maturity. We aim to equip all levels of readers for life, work, ministry and mission.

Books in our adult range are published in three imprints.

Christian Focus contains popular works including biographies, commentaries, basic doctrine and Christian living. Our children's books are also published in this imprint.

Mentor focuses on books written at a level suitable for Bible College and seminary students, pastors, and other serious readers. The imprint includes commentaries, doctrinal studies, examination of current issues and church history.

Christian Heritage contains classic writings from the past.

Christian Focus Publications, Ltd
Geanies House, Fearn, Ross-shire,
IV20 1TW, Scotland, United Kingdom
info@christianfocus.com

www.christianfocus.com